Celebrating Women's Stories

Faith Through Life's Seasons

Celebrating Women's Stories

Faith Through Life's Seasons

Edited By

Rebecca L. Ebersole
Dorcas I. Steckbeck
E. Morris Sider

Sponsored by
The Brethren in Christ Historical Society

Celebrating Women's Stories: Faith Through Life's Seasons

Toll-Free Order Line: (800) 253 9315 Extension 239
Internet Website: www.evangelpublishing.com

Cover design by Christina Weber

ISBN 1-928915-29-9
Library of Congress Catalog Card Number 2001099479

Printed in the United States of America

02 03 04 05 06 / 10 9 8 7 6 5 4 3 2 1

TABLE OF CONTENTS

DEDICATION

Rebecca L. Ebersole dedicates this book to her mother, Mary Walters Ebersole, and her grandmothers, Alma Lauver Ebersole and Cora Stover Walters, for stirring her imagination and for rooting her life in love.

Dorcas I. Steckbeck dedicates this book to her parents, Mick and Fern (Lehman) Steckbeck, for encouraging her, through their love and influence, to be a woman after God's own heart.

E. Morris Sider dedicates this book to his grandmothers, Lydia Swalm Sheffer and Anna Dick Sider, and his step-grandmother, Mary Ann Gingrich Sider, women of great faith who instilled in him an appreciation for his Christian and family heritage.

INTRODUCTION

This book celebrates women of faith. As you read their stories, we hope you will find inspiration in their perseverance, faithfulness, creativity, sense of vocation, and commitment to the church. Many of them faced trials. Many of them overcame obstacles. Many experienced seasons of joy and pain, success and failure, clarity and confusion, new life and death. But in unique ways, each found the endurance and strength to follow God through the complexity of their circumstances. Their lives teach theology in an anecdotal way.

We began work on this book two years ago with the desire to share stories about women of faith and to illustrate the variety of vocations to which God calls them. Some of these women exercise influence as leaders in the public sphere, some lead lives of quiet influence within their homes and churches, some venture into far-flung countries, and others have lived in the same town their whole lives. With vision and creativity, they model faithfulness for men and women in the church. In this way, each story speaks for itself with a unique voice.

Although the women in this book are members of the Brethren in Christ denomination, any Christian may gain insight and encouragement from their stories. To narrow the scope of the book, we focus on North American women. In the future, we hope that editors may explore compiling a book of Brethren in Christ women worldwide, written by women from a variety of nations.

Even with this narrowing criterion, the selection process proved difficult, as many women's stories merit telling. We solicited suggestions for whom to include through denominational publications and a network of women. From a pool of more than two hundred nominees, we selected 21. For a complete list of women nominees, see the Brethren in Christ Historical Library and Archives. We chose women who have not been significantly profiled before and who represent a variety of geographical locations, vocations, generations, marital states, and backgrounds. Even though our selection process was not perfect, we hope that readers will benefit from the variety of perspectives expressed.

The trees on the book cover represent the endurance of these women who exhibit strength and stamina during years of spiritual drought and refreshment. Through life's seasons, these women illustrate that God's favor does not ensure an easy life uncluttered with ambiguity, but a life in which God's presence provides strong roots for us in all circumstances.

Acknowledgments

The editors wish to thank many people who contributed to the formation of this book. Throughout the book project, the Brethren in Christ Historical Society provided administrative and financial support. We extend our gratitude to people who believed in the importance of these women's stories and provided encouragement, support, and funds for the book. The 21 writers who gave breath to the stories deserve special thanks. We also thank the women and their families who honor us with the privilege of reading a portion of their life stories.

In addition, we appreciate the fine efforts of Christina Weber, who designed the book cover; Greg Ash, who photographed the editors; Gregg Dubbs, who provided thorough proofreading; archive workers Heather Ross, Esther Ebersole, and Lela Hostetler, who assisted with research and administrative tasks; and Joseph Allison, of Evangel Publishing House, who patiently worked with the editors to help their idea become reality. Through the journey to bring this book from concept to completed manuscript, the editors wish to express gratitude to each other for their vision, friendship, and sense of humor through this long and ultimately fulfilling process.

Rebecca L. Ebersole Dorcas I. Steckbeck E. Morris Sider

Reaching for the Ideal, Embracing the Real

Harriet Alice Sider Bicksler

by Mary Walters Ebersole*

Harriet Alice Sider began life surrounded by the familiar tastes and smells of passion fruit, papaya, frangipani, bougainvillea, and gum trees, and by the guardian presence of an African nanny she called *Gogo* (the Ndebele word for Grandma).[1]

Born April 26, 1948, Harriet joined the family of Lewis and Gladys Sider and their seven-year-old son, John, on the Matopo Mission compound nestled among the rocky hills of Southern Rhodesia (now Zimbabwe). Matopo was just one in a string of assignments the Siders accepted as they pursued God's call to mission work in Africa.

Childhood Measured by Change

The many transitions and adjustments of missionary life shaped Harriet's early life. Familiarity quickly became an elusive quality during her childhood. Until age three, her memories consist of outings and care provided by her nanny, whose presence and household help freed Harriet's parents to pursue mission and educational activities at Matopo. Then, by order of the Brethren in Christ Foreign Mission Board, the young Sider fam-

*Mary Walters Ebersole is an educator and school librarian at Lititz Elementary in Lancaster County, Pennsylvania. She lives in nearby Akron with her family, and is active in the Speedwell Heights Brethren in Christ congregation. Mary and Harriet first met at Mechanicsburg High School, and have managed to sustain their friendship, despite geographical distances and divergent career paths, for more than 30 years.

ily moved to Wanezi Mission in 1950, a location 70 miles farther east in Southern Rhodesia. Abruptly, Harriet lost the familiar places and routines of her early childhood and, most of all, *Gogo's* watchful companionship in her life. Sider family lore recalls that Harriet just as abruptly stopped speaking to her father, apparently blaming him for the uprooting. Harriet's silent protest continued for nine months, during which mother and brother tried to trick and cajole Harriet into talking to her father. Harriet confided in her brother, "When Daddy takes us back to Matopo, then I'll talk to him." Although the Sider family and Harriet recall the standoff with a mixture of wonder and amusement, it embodies some of the important themes of Harriet's future life—striving for rootedness to offset frequent family moves of childhood and adolescence; attempts to find and nurture warm, human attachments; and a keen, persistent, even stubborn sense of justice (and injustice), especially on behalf of people or groups Harriet perceives to be voiceless or powerless.

Harriet remembers preschool years punctuated with transitions and unique childhood experiences. Younger brother Richard was born in 1952 at Wanezi Mission. In the summer of 1954, the Siders traveled to the United States aboard a freighter for their first missionary furlough. Age six at the time, Harriet recalls her excitement about the ocean voyage, her thumb injury when her finger got badly crushed in the stateroom door, and her older brother John's teasing threats to throw her doll overboard.

Upon the Siders' return to Southern Rhodesia in November 1955, Harriet received home-schooling until her family deemed her ready for Coghlan Boarding School in Bulawayo. The Siders made the 30-mile trip to enroll Harriet in January 1957, when she was eight. Coghlan—a whites-only, girls-only, primary school—was run by the British colonial government in the tradition of regimented British boarding schools. Harriet recounts, "I lost almost half that year because of rheumatic fever. I had been at school about two weeks in the second term when I got the most awful cold and sore throat, which turned out to be strep [a precursor to the fever]. . . . As far as I was concerned at the time, going to the infirmary was a fate worse than death." She traveled home for bed rest and recuperation from her bout with rheumatic fever, then returned to boarding school for a third term. A relapse of rheumatic fever sent her home again for the rest of that term. Harriet remembers the frequent bouts of sickness and homesickness associated with her early years in boarding school as well as the caring ministrations of mission health professionals who monitored her condition and her lingering heart murmur.

Despite frequent uprootings, being part of a missionary family had some privileges for Harriet. The family traveled during holiday from school (a six-week break at the end of the school year). Harriet reminisces, "I remember holidays in Pretoria, South Africa (where my brother and I had chicken pox and our family was quarantined), visits to Victoria Falls and game parks, train rides from Bulawayo to Choma and back."[2] Harriet also acquired an extended family of other missionaries and missionary children. "I remember the aunties," Harriet recalls, "[Dr.] Virginia Kauffman, who drew blood many times to monitor my recovery from rheumatic fever; Gladys Lehman, who had a great sense of humor; Edith Miller and Dorothy Gish, who were fun-loving young missionaries; Pauline Frey, who taught me John 3:16. I remember playing Scrabble with Arthur Climenhaga [former Brethren in Christ bishop known for his extensive vocabulary]. I don't think I won!"[3]

In 1957, Harriet moved with her family about 500 miles north to Northern Rhodesia, a neighboring African country now called Zambia. Harriet's parents were assigned to two-year service stints as superintendent and matron at Sikalongo Mission and then Macha Mission. Once again, Harriet attended boarding school, this time in Choma, Zambia, where she completed grade school. Later, as an upper-grade (junior high) student, Harriet was appointed one of several prefects (monitors) at the school. She remembers "feeling unsympathetic toward younger girls who wet their beds and made my life difficult. I'm not proud of that memory."[4]

In 1959, Harriet returned to Southern Rhodesia to spend what turned out to be a transitional year of school and living arrangements at Youngways Hostel in Bulawayo. The hostel provided a home-like atmosphere for MKs (missionary kids) attending school away from home. Regular activities included Bible study, scripture memorization, and piano lessons. During the day, the children attended government schools. Harriet attended Townsend High School. For the first time, she shared a home during the school term with her brother Richard, and with a host of other MKs. She still remembers many birth dates and shared experiences with her peers from this important transitional year at Youngways.

Adolescence Mixed with Re-entry

Lewis and Gladys Sider prepared for a second furlough to the United States in December 1961. This time, the Siders packed all of their belongings into trunks for shipping, because they believed that they might not return to Africa. Lewis reflects in his autobiography that he and his wife intended to settle in the United States to further the children's education, and to reunite with their oldest son, John, who had boarded with relatives in Canada for the previous six years.

Ironically, the Siders' move to the United States, a transition that had been carefully plotted to unite the family and to advance the Sider children's education, became a traumatic time for the whole family. Harriet's father confides, "Taking up residence in the United States again after a long absence can be traumatic, and in our case it really was. . . . It was also traumatic for the children to become adjusted to school life here in this country."[5]

Harriet entered Mechanicsburg High School as a mid-term sophomore at age 13—two years younger than sophomore classmates. She admits to being "academically advanced but socially and culturally clueless."[6]

While her father struggled to find stable, gainful employment, Harriet and her family lived first in the church-owned missionary home on the square in the village of Grantham, Pennsylvania, and later in their own home a half-block away. Gladys Sider, always the resourceful homemaker who had learned to survive on a shoestring budget in Africa, knitted sweaters and fashioned school clothing for Harriet. However, her mother's talents as a seamstress and needleworker did not save Harriet from the stinging awareness of "not fitting in," especially at school. For her first days of school in the United States, Harriet wore the same outfit two days in a row. "I knew within seconds that this just wasn't done," Harriet recounts, "but I couldn't do anything about it, and so I went through the day painfully self-conscious of my fashion gaffe." [7]

From their first arrival in Grantham, the Siders began to attend and become involved in the Grantham Brethren in Christ Church. Harriet recalls her church affiliation, particularly her involvement with youth Bible quizzing, as a life-preserver in a sea of change. At about this time, I became acquainted with Harriet as a fellow adolescent transplant into the Grantham area and into the Mechanicsburg school system. Our association grew from proximity—we lived along the same stretch of Grantham Road; we rode the same bus to high school; and we both attended the Grantham church, where my father had become pastor in the summer of 1963.

Natural affinity sparked an enduring friendship between Harriet and me. In 1963, I transferred to Mechanicsburg High School as a split junior/senior; Harriet was an under-aged senior. We both took piano lessons on the nearby campus of Messiah College (a liberal arts college founded by the Brethren in Christ Church), where our instructor soon dubbed us the "Mozart twins." We joined the Grantham church Bible quiz team, a youth program that involved studying a book of the Bible, then preparing to answer a battery of questions at youth quiz competitions. Harriet and I grasped the opportunity to become recognized as excellent Bible memorizers and quizzers and to become friends with a small core of the Grantham church youth group as part of the quiz team.

When Harriet and I entered Messiah College as day students in 1964, we were poised and ready to blossom as young women in an atmosphere with like-minded peers and nurturing Christian influences. At last, Harriet and her family members were finding a place to belong. Lewis was employed as a civil service worker for the state of Pennsylvania; Gladys worked for the library at Messiah College. Older brother John, a graduate of the college, taught secondary English. Younger brother Richard was a wiry seventh-grader and incessant basketball player. And Harriet had enrolled at Messiah to major in nursing (she soon changed her major to English).

From the beginning of her Messiah College career, Harriet showed a predisposition toward engaging with issues, whether they were campuswide or worldwide. She enrolled in college in the mid-1960s, a period of national turmoil over United States involvement in the Vietnam War. Like other Messiah students, Harriet wrestled with issues about the morality of war and the draft system, and about the appropriateness of civil disobedience toward decision-making authorities whom students viewed as untruthful and untrustworthy.

On the Grantham campus, academic debates about theology and philosophy heated up into conflicts involving faculty members and students. An acute controversy erupted over the college administration's decision not to renew the contract of young philosophy professor Jack Orr because he encouraged students to explore diverse philosophical and theological movements. Harriet was one of a delegation of students who met with the administration to find facts, to discuss issues surrounding the conflict, and to advocate on Orr's behalf. She attempted to mediate dialogue about this and other campus issues from 1965–1968 as staff writer and eventual editor of *Ivy Rustles*, the Messiah College student newspaper, and as a representative to student government.

At times, Harriet felt dismayed about personal attacks and sarcastic comments that campus controversies evoked. Particularly disillusioning for Harriet were some vitriolic postings about the Jack Orr debate that students and faculty placed on the Wittenberg Door—a public, uncensored bulletin board displaying campus opinion pieces. Harriet arranged a meeting with one offending professor, and, voice quavering with emotion, expressed to him her disappointment about his sarcastic tone. Despite the rough and tumble of campus skirmishes, Harriet continued to gravitate toward controversial issues, even delighting in their discussion and debate.

Harriet's attitude toward controversy has continued throughout her career of dealing with church-related issues, and with social concerns like peace, justice, and gender roles. Harriet gamely enters the fray, trying to illuminate various viewpoints on an issue, often expressing her own bias; yet, she feels stung when responses to her discussion or her writing turn personal, hurtful, or pejorative.

Two particularly influential dialogues began during Harriet's Messiah College years. As Harriet began to re-examine her beliefs, she penned a list of questions and doubts about her Christian faith. She gave a copy of this outpouring of thoughts and emotions to Carlton O. Wittlinger, Messiah College history professor, who read and responded sympathetically to the questions it contained. This exchange began a meaningful dialogue between Harriet and Wittlinger that lasted until his death in 1979.

The second influential dialogue began when Harriet met Dale Bicksler, a tall, reserved, sandy-haired classmate with penchants for mathematics and acting. No fireworks, bells, or whistles accompanied their friendship during college. However, they shared a family background of frequent family moves and parents dedicated to Brethren in Christ church work—hers as Brethren in Christ missionaries in Africa, his as a Brethren in Christ pastoral couple. Besides receiving affirmation from friendships and academic achievements during her years at Messiah College, Harriet accrued a new sense of belonging, and a view of herself as a woman who could articulate ideas convincingly, especially in writing.

Harriet headed for the University of Idaho the following fall, with a graduate assistantship (working part time for the university in exchange for tuition) and a continuing interest in English literature. Sheer loneliness propelled her to connect with long-distance friends. She began a friendly correspondence with Dale, who was now on a I-W assignment (a government-sanctioned alternative to military service) in Zambia. In Idaho, Harriet began attending a Nazarene church, where she played the piano for youth meetings and sang in the choir. She appreciated the warmth and friendliness of the young adult group there, but expressed consternation at the Nazarenes' glorification of military service and overt recognition of war veterans.

Marriage and Professional Volunteerism

By the time Harriet completed her master's degree program in 1970 and wrote her thesis on J. R. R. Tolkien's trilogy, *Lord of the Rings*, her correspondence with Dale Bicksler had taken on new life as a serious courtship. Harriet and Dale married in June

1971, and settled first into a Mechanicsburg apartment, then into a country cottage near Boiling Springs, Pennsylvania. Harriet and Dale taught English and math, respectively, in public high schools, and espoused the simple virtues of country life, tending a large garden and picking raspberries for homemade jam. The couple affiliated with Harriet's home congregation, the Grantham Brethren in Christ Church. Daughter Dana was born in 1973, and son Derek followed in 1978.

The young Bicksler family seized a desirable opportunity to purchase a home on Mulberry Street in Harrisburg, Pennsylvania's capital city. Dale began working for Penn National Insurance, located a few blocks away from their semi-detached home. Youthful idealism also motivated Harriet and Dale to move to Harrisburg, where they joined Brethren in Christ Church–related friends and their young families. These urban transplants met occasionally for common meals, sent their children to neighborhood public schools, and encouraged each other to live out their commitment to improving society. Dale put his carpentry talents to good use by remodeling their house and adding to the family's sparse furnishings. One spectacular piece that Dale crafted during their early marriage was a butcher-block dining room table—soon to become home for stacks of Harriet's writing and editing projects.

From this time forward, Harriet calls herself a "professional volunteer." She worked as a part-time assistant at Messiah College, helping to grade students' papers for several professors. She also worked part time at the college post office from 1975–1978. In 1978, Carlton Wittlinger engaged Harriet as a freelance indexer for a Brethren in Christ history he was writing entitled *Quest for Piety and Obedience.*

Harriet's ties to the Grantham church (then located on campus) also grew and deepened during these years. She dedicated nine years to coordinating Grantham's Bible quiz team, often coaching her former college professors' children. While she coached, four Grantham teams won denominational championships. She served as adult Sunday school teacher and church board member (including two stints as secretary), and participated on various committees. Later, Harriet also participated on regional conference boards and served as secretary of the

Susquehanna Conference (a regional division of the Brethren in Christ Church), to which her congregation belonged.

On the denominational level, Harriet launched her career with church publications in an unlikely domain—as editor of the *Prayer Challenge*, a monthly prayer request calendar for missions prayer groups. She continued as editor from 1970 to 1978, drawing upon her background knowledge of Brethren in Christ missions and her gift for concise writing. Harriet expanded her role as a denominational spokesperson by editing the Board of Christian Education page for the *Evangelical Visitor*, the denominational periodical then edited by John Zercher. After Zercher died suddenly in 1979, Harriet took over his responsibility as revision editor for the *Foundation Series*, an Anabaptist youth and adult church school curriculum. Although Harriet began to receive remuneration for these writing assignments, their lasting value came from the network of contacts she was building across the Brethren in Christ denomination, among various Anabaptist and Mennonite groups, and within the offices of Brethren in Christ publications.

A survey of Harriet's official and unofficial contributions to the pages of the *Evangelical Visitor* from 1978 to 1985 reveals the emergence of a very lively strand of interest—peace and social concerns. At first, Harriet sticks to reporting on conferences like the New Call to Peacemaking, and reviewing peace and justice–related books like *Christ and Violence* by Ronald J. Sider. In reporting the actions of the New Call to Peacemaking effort, Harriet's passion for the subject seeps into her writing. She summarizes, "The entire conference attempted to put practical handles for action on to long-standing peace beliefs. . . . Whether it is a new call, an old call, or a recall to be makers of peace, the need for strong, active peacemaking in today's volatile world was made quite clear."[8]

In the December 25, 1980, issue of the *Evangelical Visitor*, Harriet writes a three-page essay making a compelling case for war tax resistance. She examines the issue from many sides and in her own voice proposes, "Another way of demonstrating the sincerity of our belief in peace is to begin resisting war taxes now, before it is legal [as it would have become, had Congress passed the World Peace Tax Fund Bill]. . . . If we believe that war is wrong, then it is just as wrong to pay others to wage war as to do it ourselves."[9] Clearly, in this strongly worded article, Harriet examines the issue of war tax resistance using a prophetic framework. She closes with the vision of Micah, the Old Testament prophet, in which "Nation will not take up sword against nation, nor will they train for war anymore." (Micah 4:3b)

On a more personal level, Harriet wrestled with how pursuing causes such as war tax resistance could affect her marriage and young family. I distinctly remember sitting with Harriet on a beige, overstuffed sofa in her living room discussing what would happen if she and Dale decided to withhold the percentage of taxes that supported the military and the assembling of arms. She agonized over whether she and Dale would pursue their passive tax resistance until the Internal Revenue Service conducted audits or garnered their bank account or paychecks for the missing tax money. Did both spouses believe with equal strength in this cause? In pursuit of an ideal, was it worth disrupting their young family or risking having themselves placed on a government or IRS surveillance list? The contrast between her public and personal reflections upon the war tax issue reveals the tension Harriet often experiences between the theoretical framework out of which her writing springs and her life experiences, from which her doubts, concerns, and human feelings emerge. Harriet balances her responses to issues uneasily between prophetic utterance and human sensitivity.

Peace Interest Expressed in *Shalom!*

Despite the discomfort of fitting theory to reality, Harriet continues to demonstrate a strong commitment to peace and justice in her writing and in her lifestyle. Although Harriet analyzes United States government policies and attitudes toward war, peace, and social justice, her examining lens has a wide angle. By virtue of her Canadian ancestry and her early life as an expatriate living in Africa, she naturally has a more global perspective on issues of war, peace, and social justice.

By 1981, Harriet had become a member of the denomination's Commission on Peace and Social Concerns. In 1984, the Commission (by then subsumed into the Board for Brotherhood

Concerns, or BBC) asked her to edit a newsletter focusing on the themes of peace and justice. She immersed herself in the work of the BBC and in editing its quarterly mouthpiece, *Shalom! A Journal for the Practice of Reconciliation,* from 1986–1992. From 1989 until 1992, Harriet assumed a dual role as director of the BBC and editor for *Shalom!*.

A series of Brethren in Christ denominational restructuring efforts phased out the staff of the BBC and then the Board itself in 1992. However, Harriet and a base of supporters and subscribers doggedly persisted to keep *Shalom!* alive. In 2000, *Shalom!* gained new respectability and a secure future when it was declared one of three official Brethren in Christ periodicals. The journal retained its niche as a forum for peace and social justice issues.

A brief survey of *Shalom!* journals over the past 17 years illustrates the breadth and depth of issues covered within its pages, and of the network of contributors Harriet has cultivated over the years. *Shalom!* has dealt with abortion, aging, peace education, reconciliation, models of discipleship, worship and music in the congregation, Brethren in Christ core values, the church and culture, mental health, and ministries of compassion, among other topics. Contributors to the publication have included college professors, missionaries, mental health workers, Anabaptist-related theologians, pastors, social workers, healthcare professionals, prison ministries workers, social activists, Brethren in Christ and Anabaptist church leaders, and laypersons.[10]

Anabaptist and Mennonite Central Committee Connections

Harriet's continuing interest in peace and social issues has led her to become deeply involved with Mennonite Central Committee (MCC), headquartered in Akron, Pennsylvania. MCC is the relief, development, and service agency of the North American Mennonite and Brethren in Christ Churches. Harriet has served as a board member for MCC (United States section) from 1989 to the present, and was elected chairperson of the board in 1999. During her tenure with MCC, Harriet has traveled to North American and international meetings, and has toured and studied in Bolivia, Brazil, Zambia, Cuba, Mexico, and Southeast Asia.

I caught up with Harriet during board meetings on January 12 and 13, 2001, to see her in action as recorder for the combined MCC North American meeting, and as chair for MCC U.S. A slight arch to her eyebrows gives Harriet an air of inquisitiveness, concern, and deep concentration. Harriet's dark eyes are striking, even piercing, as they dart from speaker to speaker. During this session, Harriet records ideas that come from each brainstorming group in the meeting. She labors over wording, rechecking for accuracy with the original speaker. When reporters fumble for words, Harriet interjects, "I don't know how to put that. I was hoping you'd help me capture it."

As chairperson, Harriet sits with 15 members of MCC U.S., a board made up of a mixture of generations, genders, and ethnic representatives (Asian, African American, Hispanic, and Caucasian). Titus Peachey, an MCC insider who has served as an MCC staff member with Harriet since 1989 observes, "[Harriet] is a calm presence, whether as a board member or a chair. She remains committed to peace and justice concerns. . . ." [11]

Certainties and Ambiguities

Harriet writes and deals with issues because she must. She mirrors the strong sense of calling her father expressed in his missionary reminiscences when he declared, "If I had a thousand lives to give, I would give them all to foreign missions."[12] Harriet's paraphrase applied to her own mission might be, "If I had a thousand words to give, I would give them all to advocate for peace and justice."

Yet, while Harriet staunchly affirms what "ought to be," she deals daily with the struggles and ambiguities of "what is"—marriage, family, parenting, caring for aging parents, church life, friendships, and interpersonal relationships. "Phoebe's Journal," a column written anonymously for the *Evangelical Visitor* from 1984–1992, is Harriet's most self-revealing published work. As each month's deadline approached, Harriet recalls, she grasped something that was happening in her life, her faith, or her family, and turned it over in her thoughts and emotions as a springboard for writing. Her sentences are short and simply worded;

her emotions close to the surface. In a journal entry titled "In the company of old friends," Harriet muses wistfully about her lack of ongoing childhood friendships, "Perhaps that's why friends from early adulthood are so important. . . . I need to hang on to them as links with a past that has been significantly broken."[13]

Another flash of self-revelation appears in Harriet's dedication to a volume she edited titled *Perspectives on Social Issues.* Harriet alludes to the ways in which the "rubber" of her convictions about peacemaking, servanthood, and reconciliation "meets the road" of marriage and family life. "My husband, Dale, is a good sounding board for my ideas. We don't always come out at the same place on issues, but he helps me think clearly and honestly. My children, Dana and Derek, are perhaps not aware of how much they help my writing simply by being around and forcing me to deal with the nitty-gritties of real life when I am tempted to be theoretical and idealistic."[14] Harriet and Dale agree on most matters of lifestyle and personal ethics, and both have a strong social conscience. However, their spiritual pilgrimages have been quite different. While they are both persons of faith, their faith has led them in different directions—Harriet to a point of strong affirmation of basic Brethren in Christ beliefs, and Dale to the exploration of non-traditional faiths. Each partner has needed to allow the other to travel his or her own road, and to give honest expression to his or her own faith.

In another venue, opportunity and conviction led Dale and Harriet to raise their family in urban Harrisburg where, again, convictions faced reality. Dana and Derek grew up in a neighborhood, walked to the bus stop, and attended public schools where Caucasians were a minority (most students were children of color). Some cross-cultural connections were humorous. For example, daughter Dana frequently ate two evening meals—the first with family, the second with a neighborhood friend whose family was Indian. The Bickslers were unaware of Dana's double supper for some time.

On the flip side, the Bicksler children occasionally were targets for name-calling, prejudice, and threats. They experienced a "great divide" between their street-wise, city friends, and their more affluent, sophisticated, suburban church friends. In a book review on the city and the church, Harriet expresses her ambivalence about her own family's commitment to urban living: "During my tenure as staff person for the Board for Brotherhood concerns from 1989–1992, urban ministries was a priority. . . . [We] sponsored a retreat for urban workers and a pre–General Conference event in 1992 called 'Bridge to the City.' Yet, just six months after that event, our family moved to a suburban development, at least in part because of negative factors we felt were stronger in our city context than in the suburbs."[15] In congregational life and in denominational church life, Harriet also experiences an array of certainties and ambiguities. Harriet often has felt understood and respected as a person, and as a proponent of peacemaking, justice, and gender equality. Yet, she has felt distressed when associates, readers, even church leaders have misunderstood or belittled her views, or have pigeon-holed her as a "liberal," or advocate of "social gospel," or "feminist." On the one hand, Harriet admits, she welcomes conflict when dealing with controversial ideas or issues. On the other hand, she hates conflict in relationships and finds it excruciating.

Harriet candidly describes her Brethren in Christ experience in the editor's preface to the Summer 1996 *Shalom!*. When friends and relatives who have chosen to leave the Brethren in Christ Church ask Harriet why she stays, her answer often mentions "how the church is 'family' and provides a place to belong and a sense of identity." She affirms that "in its best moments, the Brethren in Christ Church articulates an understanding of scripture and theology that intuitively makes sense to me." Admittedly, Harriet's frustration is great "when that understanding is twisted to justify behaviors that don't square with what I believe God wants and Jesus teaches." Harriet concludes, "When I am critical of the church or speak out on certain issues, it is because I very much want the Brethren in Christ Church to really be the church in the right sense of that word."[16]

In the context of denominational life, Harriet experienced a monumental personal and vocational crisis in the early 1990s when denominational restructuring phased out the BBC and Harriet's directorship. For the first time since she began accepting voluntary and then paid positions in denominational ministry, Harriet found herself looking for secular employment. What would be the secular counterpart and outlet for her faith-based passion for peace and social justice, Harriet wondered. In 1992, she began working part time at the Office of Mental Health for the state of Pennsylvania in Harrisburg. At that time, Harriet started editing two publications for the agency, a task that has evolved into her current full-time job as publications specialist with a state-funded institute that provides continuing education opportunities for children's mental health workers.

During the past ten years, Harriet has rewoven the important themes of her life—a craving for roots, a desire for continuing and nurturing relationships, and a thirst for peace and justice. She has pursued these personal goals and ideals on two levels: as an unflagging advocate for peace, justice, gender equality, and, more recently, children's mental health; and as a participating member in the "real world" of family, relationships, and church life.

By this time, Harriet's theoretical framework for issues that she cares about is well developed and aptly articulated. However, her practice of those principles is tempered with human compassion and tolerance. Long-time college friend and correspondent Jane (Light) Raser reflects in a recent interview, "I value Harriet's friendship immensely because she is so open in sharing her joys and struggles—nothing seems to be off limits in our friendship. . . . She embraces me in my joys and struggles—I don't have to filter my thoughts before expressing them because I know [Harriet] accepts me in all my imperfections." [17]

Witness a concluding vignette from Harriet's life, and of our friendship of 30-plus years, that illustrates the interplay between real and ideal in Harriet's worldview. On March 12, 2000, Harriet and I sat together in the emergency room of Harrisburg Hospital, engaged in an all-night vigil as my mother received treatment for a health crisis. We sat on tan stools chatting and waiting for events to unfold. We talked about being the "baloney" in the "sandwich generation" between our own children and our aging parents; about the struggles and triumphs of our teenage and young adult children; about tidbits of news concerning mutual friends from college or church; about our career goals and career changes. Harriet's theoretical framework of social concern was there, undergirding our night vigil. Yet, Harriet's warm, supportive presence and her acceptance of the players and the parts in this unpredictable drama were also there. We sat there comfortably suspended between the worlds that Harriet inhabits—the world of striving toward ideals, tempered by the world of embracing what is real.

A Mother to Many

Katie Sheets Bollinger

by Eva Gramm Brubaker*

On a blustery day in 1879, wind skipped across the wooden planks of the weather-beaten platform outside the Harrisburg, Pennsylvania, train station. Groups of women and children huddled together exchanging tearful goodbyes and wishes for a safe journey. The men loaded household goods, farm equipment, animals, and feed into many freight cars on the tracks.

Katie Sheets, a six-year-old girl, held tightly to her mother with one hand while clutching her favorite doll in the other. Her long pigtails tied with bright blue ribbons peeked out from under her warm headscarf. She was sad to be leaving some of her friends and all that was familiar to her. But she was also eager to climb the train coach steps and see a new land float by her window.

The singing began softly, gaining momentum, the melodic notes of "God Be With You 'til We Meet Again" expressing anticipation of a new life for this Brethren in Christ group. Embraces and farewells were suddenly punctuated by the shrieking whistle and escaping bellow of the steam from the train engine. The train chugged slowly away from the station in a rhythmic clickety-clack, headed to a faraway land of

*Eva Graham Brubaker has been a partner with her husband, John, in Christian ministry for over four decades. She lives with her bishop husband in Upland, California. She has three children and three grandchildren. As a child, Eva became acquainted with Katie Bollinger when both she and Katie were part of the Franklin Corners, Illinois, community.

untamed prairies, wide-open spaces, unknown dangers, and a different lifestyle in Kansas.

A Kansas Childhood

Katie was born April 19, 1873, in Lancaster County, Pennsylvania, one of seven children of John and Martha Nissley Sheets, members of the Brethren in Christ Church.[1] Katie's great-grandfather was born in Switzerland in 1776 and immigrated to the United States before he was married.[2]

Upon arrival in Kansas, the Brethren in Christ immigrants constructed in Abilene a building called The Emigrant House. The families lived in this temporary structure until they obtained their land and erected houses. John Sheets was soon able to buy 240 acres in the settlement, first known as Bethel Community, from the federal government for $6.00 an acre. Later he added an additional 240 acres on which he constructed substantial buildings.[3] In response to the government's requirement to plant a grove of trees on the new homesteads, Sheets planted an orchard of fruit trees, as well as other varieties. A grove of trees still stands on the old Sheets farm.

Katie's father was ordained to the ministry in 1885, and became one of the early ministers of the Bethel church after a building was constructed in 1887. Sheets thought that a trade center with staple commodities would help the community by saving neighbors the 12-mile round trip to Abilene. For this purpose he constructed in the early 1890s a building on the north edge of his farm which became a country convenience store that contained everything from darning needles to threshing machines, but no tobacco. In the early 1900s, the first area telephone was installed in the store, which also became the local post office for a time. The family store became an important part of Katie's life during a number of difficult years.

Katie had numerous friends and cousins living in proximity in the early Kansas settlement. They shared many happy, mischievous times together. Katie's daughter Avas related the following incident: "She [Mother] followed the injunction from the Bible, 'Whatever your hands find to do, do with all your might.' She really got joy out of life. She had a cousin about the same age—their mothers were sisters—who lived about one-half mile from her. What one didn't think of, the other one did. They had heard that one of the older brethren had said they were proud. So these girls set out to prove they were not proud. They came to church dressed as plain as they could, wearing red or blue bandana handkerchiefs (used by the men in the fields) round their necks. They came into church—oh, so sanctimonious, and sat in the front row. . . . They felt that they had proved their point."[4]

Another story, told by Alvin Hoover, also illustrates Katie's carefree, playful spirit. Alvin's mother-in-law, Barbara Sheets Brandt, often visited her cousin Katie's home when the girls were young. On one occasion, the two girls were given the chore of pulling weeds in the garden. "The girls really wanted to play together rather than work. So, the girls set out to impress Katie's mother with their industriousness. They made themselves look like they had worn themselves to a frazzle doing the weeding. They proceeded to smear their faces and hands with axle grease, then rubbed plenty of powdery dirt on their faces. The next step was to run around as energetically as possible to look all sweaty, hot, and grimy."

Katie's father was highly respected in the broader community and known as a community-minded man. John Sheets was often asked to conduct funerals of non-members in the community. In the church he was known to be impartial. This became apparent in the divisive radical holiness movement in Kansas. Martha Sheets is remembered as a gentle, composed woman, who often responded to fractious situations by saying, "Oh, if we all just had more love."

As a child, Katie was happy and secure, enjoyed a stable family situation, and had a great zest for life. She related that the happiest event of her life took place at age 11, when she gave her heart to the Lord.[5]

Katie's Spiritual Journey

Although Katie was raised in a Christian home, she knew that godly heritage was not saving faith. She was 11 years of age when she promised to serve Christ all the days of her life. Her response may have been a direct result of an extended revival meeting, possibly held at the Bethel church. As she later wrote: "I had not wandered away in sin, as perhaps many others, who were farther advanced in years, yet I knew that unless I would become a true child of God, I could not be saved. Neither did I realize that great change of heart as I have heard others tell of. But, oh! The joy and happiness that I was permitted to feel in my soul, I can never express." [6]

Later, however, her spiritual vitality declined. She became distressed over taking something that did not belong to her. When her father inquired why she seemed troubled, she at first hesitated and then told him the story of her wrongdoings. "Oh, how ready he was to forgive," she relates. "He put his arms around my neck and tried to encourage me to be faithful." Later she writes, "I have found that true obedience to the Spirit of God brings us more real pleasure and enjoyment than anything this world can afford." [7]

In 1895, it became evident that the Holy Spirit was moving among the people attending Bethel church. Audible expressions indicated a hunger for God. One Sunday evening stood out in Katie's memory. Then a young adult, Katie described the events of the evening in this way: "As for myself, my hunger for God was inexpressible. How could I tell it? As I stood to my feet and tried to give expression, I saw God's great hands. There He was holding in His right hand a pitcher of water, and in the other hand He held a funnel, and from this pitcher He was pouring water into this funnel. The water overflowed and all came straight down on me. The tremendous amount of water coming from so small a pitcher was miraculous. I fell helplessly backward and shouted praises of God. No one present had ever witnessed such a scene. I myself did not understand what had happened. Brother Brechbill said, 'Let us pray.' My husband came and knelt beside me. The meeting lasted until 2:30 a.m. Then John Sheets (my father) said, 'We are not through, come to our house tomorrow evening and we will finish up.'

"I remember prior to this experience how God had let his flashlight focus right down on my heart one day at my home, and there was the whole catalog of sin laid bare. My heart was black. I abhorred myself. I said, 'Oh, I did not know all this.' I now knew beyond a doubt that the work was done and God the Father, Son, and Holy Ghost had moved in and was now on the throne. As I went about my work I found myself standing still in awe. Then I felt the hand of God on me and I heard Him say, 'I have baptized you with the Holy Ghost and with fire.' "[8]

Events like these did not go unnoticed. There was much skepticism and division about the work of the Holy Spirit during this time. Some persons were "dealt with" by the church. At a subsequent General Conference at the Cross Roads church in Pennsylvania, much time was spent discussing the pros and cons of this movement. At one point during Conference, Katie herself was instructing a seeker when another woman beside her said, "Didn't you hear you are not to talk that way anymore? "[9]

Marriage and Clouds of Sorrow

Accurate records of Katie's teen and young adult years are very limited. It may be assumed that Katie attended a one-room country school for her primary education. Unlike one of her best friends, Sarah Bert, Katie did not have the opportunity to obtain advanced education to fulfill her hopes of becoming a teacher.

During this period of her life, however, Katie met her future husband, John Gish Bollinger. John's grandparents emigrated from Switzerland to the United States in 1828 when John's father was seven years old. They had first located in Indiana, then moved by wagon to Iowa. There they stayed for a time with the Gish family. John's father, Melchior, and Mary Gish married and settled in Iowa. The family later moved to Kansas with their family of six boys and two girls. John, one of the sons, was born in 1869.[10]

When the Bollinger family moved into the community near Abilene, John apparently caused a stir of excitement among the young ladies. Sarah Bert, in particular, took a fancy to this young man and thought a relationship with John would be "natural" since both of them were planning to go away to school for training to become school teachers. Katie was a little more self-effacing. Although impressed by and attracted to young John Bollinger, she seemed to feel that nobody would ever want her. In the course of time, it was Katie on whom John cast his eye. Sarah's hopes vanished when, following a church service, John and Katie walked out of the meeting together. Nevertheless, Sarah and Katie remained lifelong friends.[11]

Apparently John was out of the area during part of their courtship days. The way in which he signed his letters to Katie indicates the progression of their relationship. A letter of July 8, 1891, is signed, "I remain ever yours, from John to Katie." In a letter of June 20, 1892, he writes, "With this letter I would tender my kindest affection to the one I love and esteem above all others." Later he makes a statement possibly referring to wedding plans when he talks of "dress goods": "All I have to say is this: while I believe I would like to have things nice and pleasant, yet I think it would betray a weakness in our spiritual labors should we have everything too grand."

The last letter of August 17, 1892, reads as follows (quotation unedited): "Yours of the 12 rec'ed on Tuesday the 15th and it was indeed welcome. Katie until that time I could hardly realize that we would enter the relation we intend to. But it is becoming more and more apparent to me and I am permitted to feel more as if we stood at the threshold of a new and unexperienced life and one that I look for a happy one at least I believe its enjoyments will exceed those of the present one. Of course this to a great extent depends on ourselves both our actions to each other to ourselves and to others. I do not mean to say we will be void of all trials, by no means but yet in all these if we are free and open hearted to each other there will be a calm and sure retreat. And above all I feel as if we will have the blessing of Divine Providence."[12]

John and Katie were married on September 6, 1892, in the Sheets' home, with Katie's father performing the ceremony. Katie felt that her new home was the happiest on earth.[13] John also was very happy with his new home, especially since he had been orphaned at age eight. He was very supportive of and active in the local church. Unsuccessful at finding a teaching position in the country, he was hired by Katie's father as a clerk in the family store.

In due time, John and Katie were happily preparing their home for the birth of their first child. However, anticipation soon turned to mourning when their infant son died at birth. The second child, daughter Avas, was born in December 1894, and another daughter, Alma, in early November 1897. During the summer, John became ill; his health progressively deteriorated until he was too weak to continue his work in his father-in-law's store. Katie's load was heavy as she cared for an infant and a very ill husband. John and Katie, with many others, prayed fervently for his healing, but in vain. Katie related their last hours together: "Now as we bid each other farewell that last midnight hour, we knew the separation for this life had come. In his dying hour he tried to encourage me by saying, 'Your God will help you through,' as I sat with him with a broken heart and feeling that I just could not live without him. He committed me with our two little girls to the Lord. And I knew he would soon be entering the Pearly Gates of Heaven and be forever with the Lord—which was far better." [14] According to grandson J. Bert Carlson, John died of tuberculosis in the doctor's office.

As Katie followed her husband's body to his burial place, she was deeply conscious of the overwhelming and sustaining grace of God. The verse "Not my will, but thine be done" helped her to submit to this tragic event in her life.[15] Nevertheless, her sorrow was deep and the weight of responsibility for two very young daughters was daunting. During the winter months she moved into her parents' home and later sold her house.

Katie talked about another "midnight hour" when infant Alma needed attention. As she was trying to comfort Alma, she was overcome with an indescribable sense of loneliness. As she walked the floor with a crying baby, the heavy weight of loneliness and sorrow seemed too much to bear. Recalling how the Lord had seen her through other situations, she reached for her Bible. It seemed to open by itself to Isaiah 54: "My eyes fell on the words in verses 4–7. As I stood there reading these words, it seemed to me all heaven was interested in my 'need' and God himself was talking. There came over into my being an overwhelming of the Lord and wonders of God Almighty. My loneliness was gone for days—I would just want to be alone with my Bible, reading this message from God over and over again. 'For the Lord your Maker shall be a husband to you.' I call this Chapter 54 of Isaiah my love letter from heaven." [16]

The Call to Service

Katie's difficulties did not end with the death of her husband. At one time she was in bed for weeks with typhoid fever. Her lips were parched; she was unable to feed herself. She was aware of the seriousness of her illness and knew that death was near unless God himself intervened. She had glimpses of God and the brightness of his glory. On the one hand, she was ready to leave the world behind, but the thought of her two little girls kept her holding fast in faith for healing. Many people prayed fervently for her. One Sunday afternoon she was sitting up in bed, after hardly being able to move a hand, shouting and praising the Lord. Others in the room felt the unusual power of the presence of the Holy Spirit as well. Katie recalls, "With this unspeakable blessing of Divine Healing, there came also the revelation of God's will to my heart concerning my future life. I knew my work was not yet finished." [17]

In her parents' home, Katie felt well cared for and surrounded by love as she endeavored to come to terms with her grief. In addition to caring for her two small daughters, she helped her father in the country store. But as much as she enjoyed the work, she was restless regarding her future. She became increasingly heavy-hearted. Often she prayed, "Oh, if only I had a place in this wide world where I could take poor motherless children and do for them just as I do for my very own. Oh, if only I had a home." She felt she had so much love to give above and beyond what she showered on her own little girls.

She had a growing desire to help other widows and orphans. One evening after closing the store, she followed a cow path to her father's orchard. There, under a large apple tree in the center of the orchard, she began to pour out her heart to God. She knew God understood her troubled spirit. She later wrote, "As I prayed my faith seemed to mount up. I had not prayed long until my faith touched God, and in a clear, audible voice God said, 'Mount Carmel Home.' I arose to my feet and stood in holy awe. Though it was eventide, it seemed like it must be the dawning of a new day." [18]

Katie's burden lifted. She felt a new sense of direction as she continued her walk home. She immediately wrote to Abram Zook of the Mount Carmel Home. His response was confirmation of her faith. He said in his letter, "We have been praying all summer for a worker."

A Mother to Orphans

Establishing homes for orphans was generally a new venture at this time and not very well received or supported. Little did Katie realize how important her role would become in this pioneer venture of faith.

In the early nineteenth century, caring for orphans and homeless children was a growing social concern. Such care was often given by private institutions. The caregivers were usually compassionate individuals who felt that they were "doing God's work." In 1879, a petition was brought to General Conference for permission to buy land in Kansas to be used to benefit the poor, widows, and orphans. But the purchased land was lost in an economic depression and no orphanage was built in that area. However, orphanages were being started in other places by the Brethren in Christ, including in Lancaster County, Pennsylvania; Thomas, Oklahoma; and Harrisburg, Pennsylvania.

The beginning of Mount Carmel orphanage near Morrison, Illinois, is largely attributed to Sarah and Anna Bert, sisters serving at the Chicago Mission, who wanted a place for homeless children in Chicago. Abram and Roseanne Bowers Zook, who lived near Morrison, approximately 100 miles west of Chicago, without knowledge of the prayers of the Bert sisters, offered their house for the care of homeless children.

Roseanne, herself an orphan, had become an heir to an estate soon after her marriage to Abram in 1879. They purchased 40 acres of land and built a 13-room house in 1893, which the Zooks made into an orphanage in March 1900. Abram and Roseanne, with their four children, continued to live in the house while caring for orphans who were placed there. The first 12 children were all from Chicago.[19]

Katie, with Avas and Alma, ages nine and six, arrived at Mount Carmel Home on September 7, 1903. Abram Zook was waiting with a two-horse lumber wagon to take them over 10 miles of mud road to the Home. One can imagine the long, rough ride in the slippery mud, with mother and girls hanging onto each other, hoping the old wagon would not tip over. They were met at the door around 9:00 p.m. by two workers, May Donaldson and Matron Myrtle Zook. All the children were in bed at this hour, but were up early the next morning, waiting expectantly to get a glimpse of their new "auntie."

Katie was given responsibility for the kitchen and dining room. She made three meals a day for 25 to 30 children and several workers. She was quickly introduced to all the modern "inconveniences." The kitchen had been a laundry (a lean-to shanty) with rough planks as flooring. It contained two open shelves, one tiny cupboard, a cistern pump, no screen door, and a very inadequate cookstove for heating and cooking. Through the bitterly cold Illinois winters, their feet were never warm, and their dishcloths froze while they were making meals.[20]

Mount Carmel was started as a "faith work," but many times the workers' faith was severely tested. Katie tells of the time the flour barrel was nearly empty and there was no money with which to buy more flour. The children and workers were called together and the dire situation explained. Immediately, all knelt to pray for their "daily bread." That evening, a sack of flour was delivered to their door. The next day more flour came. Now they had not one but four barrels of flour in the attic storeroom. Katie reported, "We never knew the barrel of flour to run low since that day."

Many other situations tested their faith. At one point, a child was too ill to take to the doctor over the ten miles of dirt road. The staff gathered around the little boy, anointed him with oil, and prayed earnestly for God to touch his body. Soon he rallied and asked for something to eat—completely well again.

Katie was eventually given even more responsibility as matron and later as superintendent of the orphanage. She is remembered for her many wonderful qualities by staff and the children who were placed in her care, even though she always worked under much pressure. Never were there enough workers to share the heavy workload.

Katie felt it was very important for each of the children to have chores commensurate with age and ability. She assigned jobs for a month at a time and rotated the work. She endeavored to teach two main things to the children: how to love and how to work, so that they would not leave the home without a set of well-developed skills.

Katie was not an easygoing taskmaster. She had high ideals and expectations for quality work. Ruth Adams Kitner knows firsthand that if beds were not made properly with "hospital corners," Katie would take all the bed sheets and covers off the beds, and require the children to remake the beds until they did their work properly. Boys as well as girls rotated duties in the kitchen and dining room, learning to work at a variety of chores. Ruth remembers Sister Katie, as she affectionately became known, as a "wonderful mother." Katie became a mother to over 100 different children who moved through the home during her tenure of 35 years.

Katie's philosophy of discipline was that "prayer was more effective than the switch." Ruth remembers that when she gave her playmate Mildred a stunning blow, Sister Katie sent her to her room to pray until she could ask Mildred for forgiveness. Ruth was sent to pray three times before she was willing to say, "I'm sorry. Will you forgive me?" Another time, Katie was dealing with a very recalcitrant boy and feeling quite defeated because her efforts at discipline were not making any noticeable difference. After much thought and prayer, she decided to try another method. She met the little boy in his room and discussed his behavior, suggesting that because he was still being very naughty, she was feeling as though she had failed him. He was told to go to the orchard and get a switch and come back to the bedroom. Undoubtedly, he thought, Katie intended to use the switch on him, but, instead, she told him to give her the whipping. He began to cry; it took repeated insistence on Katie's part until the boy finally carried out his punishment on her.

The children were taken regularly to all Wednesday and Sunday services at the Franklin Corners church. Illness was the only reason someone could miss a service. They were expected to sit with their hands in their laps and their feet directly ahead of them. Any misbehavior in church resulted in going without Sunday dinner.

Avas and Alma, as part of the orphanage family, were also taught the rigors of work; they shared in many of the sacrifices, and were assimilated into the same lifestyle as the other children. This could not have been an easy adjustment for Katie or her two daughters, but, in time, both daughters became immersed in the work of the orphanage alongside their mother. When Avas married Carl Carlson, she moved with her husband to the inner-city work at Chicago Mission, while Alma remained as a constant companion and worker for Katie.

In 1927, Katie was relieved of her duties as matron. Some individuals felt that she was beginning to show signs of aging and stress. To the consternation of many in the immediate community, the Board of Trustees asked her to resign. She complied with grace and dignity, even though this must have been a deep blow to her indomitable spirit and her definite call to service. She decided to return to Kansas.

Faithful in Kansas

Back in Kansas, Katie and Alma moved into the Sheets home near Abilene and attended the Bethel church. Kenneth Hoover was their pastor for a year. He remembers Katie as a strong woman, a leader, a completely "in charge" type of person.

Katie and Alma were both very faithful in their commitment to the life of the church. Katie always informed Deacon Alvin Hoover when she or Alma would not be at the service. They never missed without having a good reason. At a point when the congregation was between pastors, Alvin and Naomi Hoover and the Bollingers were often the only two families in attendance.

Chris Frey remembers Katie as a wonderful Saturday morning Bible school teacher in Abilene. Parents dropped their children off at the Abilene church while they did their weekly shopping. "She seemed to me to be very old," Chris comments, "like the grandma that I never had. She was very kind and gentle, and I remember her never getting upset with us children, many of whom were boys, and I am sure lively like most boys."

After a few years of life again on the Kansas prairie, Katie received a letter from the superintendent at the orphanage. The home was desperately in need of help, especially with the mountains of mending that accumulated with so many children. After much prayer and still not settled with a decision, Katie and Alma decided to lay out a "test fleece." They would talk this over with their deacon, Alvin Hoover; if he did not voice any strong objections, they would accept the invitation. Alvin listened carefully (not knowing about the test), and said, "I certainly don't object to your going, even though this would not have been my first choice for you." This was the confirmation they needed.

Service in the Golden Years of Life

Katie and Alma were inseparable. They went together in tandem, "like a horse and carriage." They made the move back to Illinois to take up residence in a house beside the Franklin Corners church. Although the specific reason for this move was to help with mending for the orphanage children, they continued to live unselfishly and to serve in many diverse ways.

Living next door to Katie and Alma were LeRoy and Cora Walters, who became the newly married pastoral couple to the Franklin Corners congregation in 1942. Cora related that from time to time Katie taught her domestic skills, much appreciated by Cora because her mother had died when she was a teenager. Pastors were paid meager salaries at that time and often both pastor and wife needed to work part time to meet family obligations. While Cora was working in the area hospital, Katie and Alma cared for little LeRoy, Jr. Cora felt very confident in leaving LeRoy with Katie, because Katie was "awfully tender" with him. During a later Walters family visit to Illinois, Katie taught LeRoy's younger siblings, Mary and Beth, how to craft dogs out of soap and washcloths and fish out of soap and netting.

After the Bollingers returned to Illinois, my parents, Clarence and Elsie Gramm, moved our family from Pleasant Hill, Ohio, to a farm across the road from Mount Carmel Home. My parents felt called to support the ministry of the orphanage and church at Franklin Corners. I was ten years old when I first learned to know Sister Katie and Alma.

I remember her as being short in stature, amply rounded, very approachable, and kind. Her soft, warm hugs were given freely and enveloped my whole being. Her eyes often twinkled with laughter waiting to bubble forth. She had a quick wit and keen sense of humor. Often she laughed and cried at the same time in telling or hearing a funny story or experience. One sensed that she was a person of intelligence and wisdom, someone who had encountered a wide range of life-changing experiences. Yet she displayed a truly humble, serving spirit, void of arrogance or condescension. You knew that she cared and was deeply interested in you as a person. She was especially concerned that each person made the right choices in life and knew the Lord as personal Savior.

This interest in people is illustrated by the role that Katie played in the conversion of Louis Cober, who became a minister in the Brethren in Christ Church. "In late November 1949," he relates, "Earl Sider of Ontario, Canada, was concluding a series of revival services at the Franklin Corners church. As the morning service was concluding with a hymn of invitation, Sister Katie came to me and asked me if I would like to go to the altar. I resisted and did not go.

"That Sunday afternoon several of us teenage boys were in the barn at the Mount Carmel Home building hay tunnels and crawlways. Intending to 'make fun' of the morning service, I spoke of Sister Katie's plea for me to go to the altar, but none of the boys laughed. Finally one of them said, 'Louis, if you would have gone to the altar, I'd have gone, too.' Three others agreed.

"I was immediately overtaken by conviction and an awareness of the impact of my decision. I determined that if an invitation was given in the evening service, I would go to the altar. As the evening service concluded, the invitation was again given. I waited until the last line of the last chorus and then stepped into the aisle and headed for the altar. As I went, I could hear the footsteps of others following me." This event in Louis Cober's life became even more poignant in the summer of 1950 when the community was stunned by the drowning of Tom Harding in a local creek. Tom was one of the boys who followed Louis to the altar to receive salvation that previous November.

Sister Katie always had a ready smile and saw the best in people. She possessed a gracious spirit, choosing to encourage rather than to harbor a critical spirit. The Bollingers always carried a deep love for mission work both at home and abroad. As a young woman, Katie was present in the General Conference (the highest governing body of the denomination) meeting at the Bethel church when the first $5.00 was placed on the table for foreign missions. Katie and Alma regularly prayed and wrote many letters to missionaries. At Christmas they always enclosed "something special" in the envelopes: sometimes it would be plastic bags, since they were not available overseas, or a small homemade gift.

In the best sense of the term, Sister Katie and Alma were crafty. They knew how to turn bits and pieces into useful creations. Their giving of themselves went far beyond their mending for Mount Carmel Home children. Their hands never seemed to be idle. They crocheted, worked with a community sewing circle making quilts and comforters, and baked goodies for many people. Katie even concocted a secret recipe for vanilla. She sold the vanilla, contributing the profits to missions. I still cherish the red and black comforter they made for me as a wedding gift.

Among my well-remembered yearly events were the long days spent in Katie's garage or in the orphanage kitchen, canning sweet corn to be sent to the Chicago Mission. We froze at least 100 quarts of the donated corn in one day. It was hard, messy work for a pre-teen, but also fun to be a part of these community events and to listen to adult conversation.

In her retirement years, Katie received a number of honors for her service at Mount Carmel Home. At age 80, she was the featured guest on NBC's "Welcome Travelers," once on the radio program and twice on the television program produced in Chicago. As the special guest, she was presented with hospitality gifts for herself as well as the orphanage. To her surprise and delight, one of the gifts for the home was an Amana freezer filled with frozen food. In 1961, the Twin-Co Business and Professional Women's Club in Sterling, Illinois, chose her "Woman of the Year." The award was a surprise for this 88-year-old lady. In recognition of this honor she received over 125 letters and cards from friends and former orphanage children, in addition to a bouquet of yellow roses and other gifts.[21]

Katie's ninetieth birthday on April 19, 1963, was another milestone, celebrated with a large party given in her honor. Those who could not attend sent over 200 cards and letters. She received many lovely gifts, plants, flowers, and the warmest wishes.[22]

I remember well the love and care my own parents exhibited toward Katie and Alma during those years. We lived on the farm just across the county line road from the Franklin Corners church and the home of Katie and Alma. This county line meant that we could not telephone back and forth to the Bollingers without paying long-distance tolls. My mother especially was concerned about keeping close contact and being available to them when help was needed. Soon after we moved to Illinois, the telephone system was modernized by changing from hand-cranked telephones to rotary phones. My father, Clarence Gramm, was able to buy three or four of these old hand-cranked phones at $5.00 each, with the intention of using them between our house and the barn. However, it also seemed like a great way to avoid toll calls to the Bollingers, so Dad also put one in Katie and Alma's house. He rigged up a system to run a line from our house down along the fence row of the cornfield and across the road to the Bollingers. We then had our own two-party private line at no cost for very short-distance calls. (I often wondered later about the legality of this—but it was fun and proved to be very convenient.)

At the End

In December 1964, Katie suffered a stroke that affected her speech and the use of her right arm. Her indomitable spirit and strong faith, however, did not deter her from being concerned about others and their spiritual vitality. She often asked Alma, "Is everyone in the fold?" Her health improved somewhat over the next year or so, but her outlook for the future was expressed in these words: "As I look to the time of the end here on earth for me, and think of being with my Lord throughout all eternity, there is a yearning in my heart to be with him."

On December 13, 1966, her life on earth came to a close and her yearning for God was fulfilled. She had requested that Psalm 17:15 be read at her memorial service: "I shall be satisfied when I awake with Thy likeness." Her last journey took her back home near Abilene, Kansas, to be buried beside her husband and infant son in the Bethel church cemetery.[23]

She was held in the highest esteem in the community and wherever she was known. Her life was characterized by a ready smile, a compassionate heart, a gracious spirit, unselfish love, cheerful generosity, and a deep abiding faith in God. These qualities she fully bestowed on many orphans who came to know and love her as a "Mother in Israel."

Enduring Change, Retaining Faith

Ernestine Begay Chavez

by Eunice Stoner*

In the Navajo culture, relationships, especially family relationships, are very important. Ernestine Chavez, who grew up in this culture, has often experienced broken relationships, although not by her choice. From relationships to cultural adjustments, she has endured separation and forced changes in many areas of her life. In the midst of these circumstances, Ernestine has found that her relationship with God supports her and gives her strength, because God does not abandon her.[1]

An Unconventional Beginning

From her childhood, Tl'éech'i deezbaa' (Ernestine's Navajo birth name) experienced the hardships of broken family connections. She was born on December 24, 1924, in the Kimbeto area of New Mexico, about 15 miles southwest of the current site of the Navajo Brethren in Christ Mission. Her mother died one week later. Navajo families are matriarchal—children, at birth, become part of the mother's family clan (husbands and wives are usually from different clans). Because of this custom, Tl'éech'i deezbaa's grandmother would have been next in line to raise her, rather than her father. But her grandmother had died in 1911.

---

*Eunice Stoner has lived and worked in New Mexico and Navajoland since August 1970. She currently serves with her husband, Ben, at the Navajo Brethren in Christ Mission. Eunice enjoys singing, playing the piano, and reading. She first learned to know Ernestine through contacts at the mission, and now the two share a close relationship. Eunice's parents live in Pennsylvania, so in New Mexico she calls Ernestine her mother.

So T1'éech'i deezbaa's great-grandmother, of the same clan and living in the same family camp, helped to care for the infant.[2] Dlínázbaa', the great-grandmother, raised T1'éech'i deezbaa' with the help of the child's aunt, Louise Werito.

T1'éech'i deezbaa' had an unusual childhood. Without a nursing mother to provide nourishment for her, her great-grandmother and aunt fed her a mixture of coffee, canned milk, and sugar, purchased at the local Kimbeto trading post. Years later, her physician was surprised to learn that she started drinking coffee as an infant. Her aunt Louise, who gave birth to a daughter shortly after starting to care for T1'éech'i deezbaa', was able to nurse both girls for a brief period until a neighboring trader provided a nursing bottle for T1'éech'i deezbaa'.

The family lived in a canvas tent, moving often to find pasturing land for their sheep on the open range. Sheep-herding, an important source of livelihood for the Navajo tribe, became a significant part of T1'éech'i deezbaa's early life. Between the ages of four and five, she began herding sheep on her own. Sometimes the grass on the plain was so high that she could not see the sheep. And herding could be dangerous. Once, while chasing her aunt's goats into a corral, a coiled snake appeared directly in her path. Without thinking, she kept running and jumped over the snake, which was preoccupied with eating a rabbit.

Introduction to a New Culture and a New Religion

At six years of age, T1'éech'i deezbaa' and her cousin, Ahii'názbaa' (Louise's daughter), traveled 75 miles with a government white man to the Ignacio Indian Boarding School in southwestern Colorado. The first time the white man visited T1'éech'i deezbaa's reservation, the girls hid in the "wash" (a dry river bed) at their great-grandfather's prompting. They had never seen a white person before and had never heard any language spoken other than Navajo. Since their family used a horse and wagon for transportation, the unfamiliar sight of the white man's car intensified their feelings of fear and uncertainty. This first attempt to transport the girls to boarding school failed.

Now, one year later, they faced many foreign experiences as new members of the school community. Immediately upon arrival the girls received English names, since English was the required language for the classroom. School officials gave Tl'éech'i deezbaa' the name Ernestine; Ahii'názbaa' became Annabelle. Their physical appearance changed too. For the first time, their long, black hair was cut. They also had to wear Bilagáana (white people) clothes instead of the squaw skirts and blouses of the Navajo people. Exposure to this new way of life included discovering and learning to use clocks, calendars, electricity, and running water. The imposed cultural changes deeply affected Ernestine and Annabelle with feelings of sadness and fear. Glad to be together, they felt some comfort from knowing that the school treated other Indian girls the same way.

With assimilation to a new culture came an introduction to a different religion. Two missionaries in Ignacio (a Navajo man and a white man) held Sunday school each week for interested students. During Ernestine's third year at the school, the men began to explain the concept of salvation. The Navajo man, J. C. Morgan, asked the pupils to refrain from worshiping traditional idols and attending "squaw dances"—traditional Navajo healing ceremonies—and to avoid Navajo medicine men. He explained that Christians believe there is only one God. At first, Ernestine had difficulty grasping this new teaching with principles very different from the religion she knew. She became afraid when she learned that God watched over her all the time, believing he would "burn" her if she did something sinful. Perhaps Morgan understood this when he invited the students to receive Jesus; he cautioned them from rushing into a decision. Ernestine decided to accept Jesus—somehow, she really believed that he loved her. Morgan baptized her soon after her conversion, and she received her own Bible.

After staying in Ignacio for the entire school year, the girls traveled home by way of a large army truck. Each summer, Ernestine returned to Dlínázbaa', who she called "my old mother." When she returned home after becoming a Christian, she was anxious to tell Dlínázbaa' and her family about Jesus, as Morgan instructed her to do. They listened and did not scold her while she talked.

During summer breaks, Ernestine learned many things from Dlínázbaa' by watching her perform certain tasks over and over—the traditional Navajo method of teaching children.

Ernestine learned how to dry the meat of sheep, elk, deer, even horses, by slicing it, salting it, and hanging it over a rope. She also helped with butchering, since this task is typically a woman's job. When butchering, Ernestine did not waste any part of the animal, not even the eyeballs, which could be chewed like wads of gum. She also learned how to make fry bread and tortillas from wheat flour bought at the local trading post. There were no recipes to follow—she discovered the proper ingredients and technique for baking bread by watching Dlínázbaa'. Although she continued sheep-herding, as she had done in her childhood, she now learned how to shear the sheep, card and spin their wool, and weave the wool into rugs, saddle blankets, and sash belts. Other chores included hauling water and chopping wood. Ernestine remembers, "I was not bored at home. There was always something to do."

Dlínázbaa' raised Ernestine with strict discipline and love. Some Navajos thought her old-fashioned method of child-rearing paralleled Solomon's teachings in Proverbs. Dlínázbaa' did not raise Ernestine alone. Ernestine's aunts, also members of her clan, assisted with parenting. Her father, Nez Begay, contacted her often and provided socks, shoes, and yard goods for her clothing. Nez Begay's relationship with Ernestine was unusual: when a child's mother dies, the father is often excluded from the child since the child is not part of his clan.

Broken Relationships and New Beginnings

When she turned ten years old, her beloved Dlínázbaa' died. Dlínázbaa's advice to Ernestine before passing away was simple: "Remember all that I have taught you. Don't drink and do bad stuff." Immediately after her death, tribal members wrapped her body in blankets and buried her under large rocks. According to custom, the family grieved for four days. After that period of time, Dlínázbaa's name could not be mentioned, and no one could grieve her loss or look at her burial site. Ernestine's love for her great-grandmother was so strong that she went to look at the burial site after the four-day period. Then she cried until her emotions were spent. Feeling much better, she thought about her relationship with Jesus and remembered that he was with her, even though she had lost Dlínázbaa'.

After her great-grandmother's death, Ernestine stayed in the homes of her mother's sisters. She continued attending the Ignacio school during the school year until she reached the age of 13. After that, her father decided that she should have someone else to take care of her. He arranged her marriage to Charlie Burns. Charlie owned cattle, horses, and sheep, and Ernestine's father believed she would be well cared for.

Ernestine strongly objected to the marriage. She was only 14—she couldn't be sure of Charlie's exact age, but knew he must be between 25 and 30 years old. Also, she had enjoyed her school experience and hoped to go back to the classroom in the future. But her efforts to convince her father to wait failed. On the day of the ceremony, Ernestine shed many tears and even tried to run away. Acquaintances had to virtually throw her into the brush-covered shelter where the ceremony would be held. Her father and her uncle then performed the traditional Navajo ritual to join her and Charlie together.

Ernestine received little training or preparation for married life. She remembers her great-aunt explaining that the new sleeping quarters for the couple would have two sheepskin blankets on the ground, but only one quilt for a covering. Understanding the implications of this, Ernestine desperately wanted to take her blanket to the shack where the sheep slept.

Even after making the initial adjustments to her new life, Ernestine still expressed her displeasure at the marriage. Charlie often went to talk to her father about their difficulties. Eventually, he left and traveled to Idaho to work on the railroad, but not before the couple had two children. Ernestine was 17 years old when she gave birth to her first child, Nancy. Several years later, their son, Vern, was born. Charlie never returned to live with Ernestine and the children.

Two years after Charlie left, Ernestine left New Mexico to join Bessie Sandoval, her great-aunt, and Bessie's husband, Julian, in Idaho. The Sandovals, like Charlie, worked for the railroad. Julian recruited workers and Bessie cooked for them. At Bessie's invitation, and with the encouragement of her aunts—who agreed to keep Vern—Ernestine traveled to Idaho with her daughter. After one week of cooking with Bessie, she moved to the end of the railroad, seven miles outside of the local town. Alone, she cooked three meals a day for 30 men.

In the midst of her duties, she met railroad worker George Chavez. George had served with the Marines during World War II as a code-talker (Navajo recruits were in demand after the attack on Pearl Harbor, since they could create a military code language using their native tongue). He had also acquired some baking skills while serving in the military, so the Sandovals asked him to assist Ernestine. Bessie and Julian thought Ernestine needed help with cooking and security while she worked alone during the day. Ernestine and George enjoyed spending time together, and eventually decided to get married. Much to Ernestine's surprise and delight, she discovered that the state government did not recognize her earlier marriage to Charlie, since no official papers were signed at the time of the ceremony. This was particularly gratifying since she had never wanted to marry Charlie. With the Sandovals' encouragement, George and Ernestine moved home to New Mexico, marrying in May 1951.

Daughter Janet was the first to join the family. Eight more children followed: Loretta, Melvin, Irvin, Julia, Winona, Alvin, George, Jr., and Lisa. Ernestine tried her best to train her children in the ways she learned as a young girl, modeling her discipline after the methods of her great-grandmother and aunts. Ernestine's daughter, Janet Harris, remembers how her mother often told the children legends and stories from her own childhood. Janet comments, "I appreciate my mom for the way she raised me and taught me from childhood. She taught me to go to church, and she lived by what she learned at church. She taught us that Jesus loved us. She put the Lord first in her life. Mom's favorite verse is from I Thessalonians 5:16–17: 'Pray continuously through all circumstances. And rejoice always.' She stood on that faith all those years."

Connecting with the Brethren in Christ

After returning to New Mexico, Ernestine and George moved to Farmington—45 miles from the Brethren in Christ Navajo Mission—in the early 1950s. George provided for the family by working at service stations and a large gas company. Ernestine worked small jobs like cleaning houses and washing dishes at local cafes so she had money to give in church offerings.

On many Sunday mornings, Ernestine and her children walked to the Christian Reformed church in Farmington. In the afternoon, they attended the service at the Brethren in Christ mission; then the children returned to the mission school for the week. George seldom accompanied her.

The Brethren in Christ Navajo Mission provided a much-needed hospital and school. Several of the Chavez children were born in the hospital. And since Ernestine learned about Jesus while attending school, she sent her children to the mission school so they could be introduced to God. She supported their schooling by helping the mission to make applesauce from donated apples, going along on a school chorus trip, even serving as a dorm supervisor in later years. Unlike Ernestine's experience at Ignacio, some of her children were prohibited from using their native language, and had their mouths washed out with soap when they did so. Many schools, including the Brethren in Christ mission school, restricted the use of Navajo, in part because of government regulations concerning the acculturation of the Navajos. This was difficult for Ernestine and for her children to accept.

Having the mission close by provided opportunities for Ernestine to grow in her own faith. She especially enjoyed the camp meetings held at the mission in earlier years. Many Navajos attended the meetings, traveling by horse and wagon, and camping out in the open. Services were held mornings and evenings under a large brush shelter; attendees sat on the ground during the services. The camp meetings could last as long as ten days. The mission provided some of the meals, but the Navajo women provided one big meal each day, cooking together over an open fire.

Ernestine's spiritual growth continued through educational opportunities at the mission. The Navajo language was not written down until the early 1900s, and many Navajos, including Ernestine, did not know how to read the words they spoke. Two Wycliffe Bible workers, who helped complete the first translation of the Navajo New Testament, came to the mission to teach the Navajos how to read. Under their training, and with instruction she received from the Christian Reformed church in Farmington, Ernestine learned to read the Navajo language. She developed a love for reading and singing in her native language. Ernestine can sing high notes using her "head voice"—something very few Navajo women do. (Traditionally, Navajo men and women sing in perfect unison, with the man in his falsetto voice and the woman in her lower throat voice.)

In the 1960s, the mission offered several short-term Bible courses. Through this teaching, Ernestine came to realize that she called herself a Christian because she was good. With that realization, she rededicated her life to the Lord, making it clear that her salvation was a result of God's work, not hers.

Sharing Her Faith

Ernestine's love for God is strong, and she welcomes opportunities to talk about her faith. While raising her children, she prayed a blessing with them before meals. Often her prayers went on for five to ten minutes, or longer—this was a special opportunity for her to talk with God. Her children frequently tired of the long blessing and begged, "Mom, let's just say the Lord's Prayer."

At a regional gathering of Brethren in Christ congregations in the Western states, Ernestine's bishop, Don Shafer, invited her to share a brief testimony with the group. Much to the surprise of the bishop, she talked freely, sharing for at least 30 minutes in her comfortable way. In her home congregation, she is known for sharing long testimonies and prayer requests, often about family and friends.

Her unreserved, talkative nature serves her well at church gatherings. She enjoys attending Brethren in Christ conferences when she has the opportunity to do so. Even though she often knows very few people, she likes being with other Christians and gets acquainted with them quickly.

Ernestine is devoted to her congregation, the Navajo Brethren in Christ Church. Church member Faye Francisco comments, "She's there nearly every Sunday, even though she doesn't have her own transportation [she does not drive or own a vehicle]." Faye's husband, Ernie, talks about her dedication:

"Thick or thin, she's there. She comes with enthusiasm. She is ready to sing and pray, ready to be at church and to worship."

Church membership is important to Ernestine. As she says, "Being a church member gives you the right to say something. If you're not a member, you can't say anything." Through her membership, she serves the church in many ways. At various times, she has assisted with cleaning, singing, the church board, and the Navajo language Sunday school class. She brings ingredients, and sometimes the entire meal, for fellowship dinners after church. But her presence and her testimony are as important to the congregation as her service. Ernestine makes others feel welcomed, especially young people. She is quick to greet them and shake their hands. An acquaintance comments, "She brightens up the room when she's there. She's able to cope with problems, especially alcoholism in her family."

Ernestine is most fulfilled spending time with God and with her family, church members, and friends. She especially enjoys interacting with other believers. Her deepest longing is for her husband and her immediate and extended families to know that God loves them. When she thinks about her burden for her family—about the alcoholism that afflicts her husband and some of her children, and about her limited relationship with one of her sons—tears come to her eyes.

The struggles of the past and the challenges of the present have not destroyed Ernestine's character or her faith. Through cultural adjustments, coercive situations, and broken relationships, she remains faithful to her relationship with Jesus as a Navajo sister in the family of God.

Serving with Wisdom and Wit

Dorcas Mildred Slagenweit Climenhaga

by Martha M. Long *

As a little girl, Dorcas Climenhaga admired two ministers' wives. Both gave their children loving care and extended warm hospitality to people in their homes. Dorcas hoped that she would grow up to be like them.[1] Little did she know then that she, a girl from a somewhat remote church district, would one day become the wife of a man who was a pastor, missionary, and later bishop, and in her own right make significant contributions to her family and denomination.[2]

Hard Work and Humor

Dorcas Mildred was born on July 7, 1919, the fifth of eight children of David Andrew and Cora Edna Slagenweit. She grew up on the family farm near Martinsburg, Pennsylvania, where she learned the rigors of farm life, and worked hard at household as well as outside chores. In addition to baking cakes, cleaning the house, sewing, ironing, and preserving food, she sometimes papered room walls in the spring. Industrious and skilled with her hands, she plied her needle mending and patching garments for the family. Her outside chores included yard and garden work, and she helped with barn chores, sometimes milking seven or eight cows at a time by hand and participating in an

*Martha M. Long is an assistant professor emerita of English at Messiah College. A resident of the Messiah Village community, she has served as a deacon for 24 years at Grantham Brethren in Christ Church. In 1960, Martha learned to know Dorcas as a neighbor in Southern Rhodesia (now Zimbabwe). Through the years, they kept in touch.

occasional butchering.[3] Not only did she expend energies at home, this petite young woman also periodically helped the neighboring Stoltzfus family and her older married siblings with cleaning and washing.

The Slagenweits were a closely knit family who enjoyed one another. Dorcas was loved and respected by her siblings. On one occasion her small stature and strength were tested as she suddenly witnessed an angry brother throw a pitchfork at another brother. Spontaneously, she grabbed the culprit by the arms, and sternly lectured him about the danger of what he had just done. He did not resist her and calmed down.[4]

The family also related to Dorcas with a sense of humor. Once while driving on the turnpike with her brother Andrew, Dorcas suddenly realized she had accelerated to 80 miles an hour. She asked Andrew, "Did you know I was going that fast?" "Yes," he replied. "Why didn't you tell me?" she pressed him. "I just wanted to see how fast you would go," he answered.[5]

Life on the farm was not all work for Dorcas. Spiritual and social life revolved around the church. On winter evenings, she often attended revival meetings in the community, sometimes at other churches as well as at her own congregation in Martinsburg. At these events, Dorcas socialized with friends and made acquaintances with those outside her home community. She also enjoyed traveling a few hours to the annual young people's and Bible conferences held at Messiah Bible College (now Messiah College), in Grantham, Pennsylvania.

As Dorcas's social circles grew, so did her appreciation of music. Before her family owned a piano, she looked forward to visiting a friend's home to play that family's piano. She remembered vividly the day that a piano came into her parents' home and the thrill of her first formal lesson. Dorcas also enjoyed singing and sometimes was a song leader in church services. She sang in the high school glee club and performed solos at a family wedding.

Even as she thrived on the musical and social activities of high school, Dorcas's graduation was delayed for two reasons. Since her mother was sickly, she needed help to care for Davy, the youngest of the family. At that time, her parents also did not see the need for high school education, so she repeated the local eighth grade three times to meet the state's age requirement for school attendance. Later, her parents changed their thinking, and she attended Morrison Cove High School. Her request to complete high school in three years was denied by the principal. By now, she was six years older than the average student.

While in high school, Dorcas developed speaking skills by engaging in school activities. She was elected president of the freshman class and gave an address before the class on February 1, 1940. She also participated in an oratorical contest and won second place. Her diary indicated, however, that she felt she didn't receive first place because of her gender.

Finding Her Wings in Young Adulthood

With her lovely voice and attractive looks, this young woman caught the eyes of young men from various church districts and dated and corresponded with several of them. Her dating interests did not go unobserved. Five days after taking a walk with a young man at Grantham, she received a card from a female friend telling her that this young man had measles. Despite her friend's observation, a relationship with the young man continued for several months.

In December 1938 a correspondence commenced between Dorcas and David Climenhaga, to whom she had been introduced four months earlier. On first sight at a tent meeting at Granville, Pennsylvania, in August, he had been smitten by the pretty girl leading singing attired in a yellow dress. He asked his brother Joel who she was. Joel replied, "If you're getting any ideas about her, forget them. [Some fellow] has her all sewed up." [6] Although this was intimidating, David continued to think about Dorcas. An active courtship developed as this very shy young man pursued her. In February 1939 at the Bible conference in Grantham, she had opportunity to speak with him, and he met her parents. Afterward, a May letter delivered a snapshot picture of David.[7]

Their first formal date occurred at the 1939 General Conference held at Grantham. Accompanied by eventual missionary couple Amos Ginder and Verna Faus, they drove to Mechanicsburg, Pennsylvania, for ice cream at Rakestraw's ice cream parlor. For David, who had never dated before, the experience "was heady and earth shaking." When Dorcas spilled ice cream on her dress, David gallantly produced his handkerchief for her to clean the spot; she took the handkerchief home and laundered it.[8]

David proposed to Dorcas at the annual Young People's Conference at Grantham on August 11, 1939. For this special occasion, he had chosen to walk with her on the Asa and Anna Climenhaga "trail," a special pathway through the woods. First, he informed her of his call to serve the Lord in Africa, where he had been born, and she responded that she felt led to give her life in Christian service. After this momentous event, Dorcas's diary entry of this day was surprisingly discreet: "David presents me with two books as parting gifts. Spent one short hour with David. (Memories precious.)" On an anniversary in later years, she showed David the entry and explained that if anyone read her diary, she wanted to keep the memorable safe in her memory.[9] For his part, David marveled that this popular young woman would agree to become his wife.

During their correspondence and, eventually, formal dating, Dorcas's diary entries about David became much more expressive. After their engagement, she wrote of longing to see him and having "precious moments" when he was able to visit her at her home. Their engagement extended over three years while she completed high school, and he began to study at Beulah (later Upland) College, a Brethren in Christ institution of higher education, in California. They visited each other during summers and also on a few special trips.

In the midst of this romance, Dorcas received an opportunity to change high schools. C. N. Hostetter, Jr., president of Messiah Bible College, heard about her desire to accelerate her high school program and invited her to attend the school. She told him that she had no money to pay for Messiah's tuition. He said she should come to the school, and he would see that her expenses would be cared for. President Hostetter kept his word. At the end of her senior year, in 1942, Dorcas received a receipt for her school bill which said, "Paid in full." She was filled with gratitude, but never knew who paid that bill.[10]

Cross-country Marriage

Finally, after graduating from high school in the summer of 1942, Dorcas prepared to move to California, where she would marry David. She wondered why her mother did not assist in helping her pack suitcases, because her mother had helped her brother Andrew to pack when he prepared for marriage. The distance troubled her mother; she knew that Andrew was coming home after marriage, but Dorcas was not. Dorcas traveled by train to California, and, upon arrival, she worked for a wealthy family in Pasadena and lived in their home.

On Thursday evening, October 22, 1942, David and Dorcas were married in the Beulah College Chapel. David's older brother Arthur officiated. Dorcas wore a white cape dress, the same one she had worn at her graduation from Messiah Academy (the high school connected with the college).[11] After the ceremony, they walked to Arthur's home for a reception.

At the time of the wedding, David was a senior and Dorcas had entered her first year of college; there was little time for a honeymoon. But they did take a three-day trip to Los Angeles. Even on their honeymoon, the young couple exhibited a concern for others by picking up a hitchhiker on the trip. But they soon deposited him along the roadside again because he was drunk.

With modest resources and busy schedules, the couple began housekeeping in a small cottage in Upland. Both bride and groom resumed classes on the Monday morning following their wedding. Soon David became a professional blood donor to earn extra money. Following each donation, Dorcas served him liver at dinner. After he almost fainted one day from weakness, she declared, "That's enough of that; no more blood donations!"[12] Married life did not stifle Dorcas's cocurricular involvements. An energetic young woman, she participated in student council and the gospel team. She also was news editor for the student newspaper, the *Echo*. In addition, she sang in Ladies Chorus and joined the Music Club.

Following his graduation from college, David and Dorcas took one step closer to their goal of serving God overseas. They moved to Waukena, California, to assume the pastorate of the Brethren in Christ church there, fulfilling the requirement of the Foreign Mission Board for them to engage in service at home prior to taking up overseas work. They pastored at Waukena for three years.

During this time, Donna Faye arrived to bless David and Dorcas's home on February 13, 1945. In a letter to David's mother, Dorcas wrote details of Donna's birth and David's love for his daughter. She added, "David certainly has proved to be a loving and considerate husband; I know some of the women around here are surprised at all the things he does for me. . . . David really is exceptional in his ability and willingness to help." [13]

Along with pastoral duties at Waukena, David and Dorcas were 4-H club leaders one year. They also entertained friends and parishioners in their home. To support the family, David taught in nearby school districts. During their last year at Waukena, Dorcas taught for five weeks in the elementary school because there was an influx of migrant children. She took a "first and second grade transient overflow room," which was "a chance to clear our bill," David wrote to his parents.[14] The school supplied Dorcas with a classroom, desks, and papers but no textbooks. Undaunted, Dorcas did the best she could.[15]

As they taught and pastored, both David and Dorcas wrote letters to their families, keeping them informed about their work and their numerous activities. This became a pattern which extended throughout their lifetime. One time when it was his turn to write to his parents, David tried to persuade Dorcas to take on the responsibility, but she claimed that wasn't included in their marriage vows. "She promised to 'love, honour & cherish'; but not write letters. . . . She feels that she's already done the 'for worse' part of it by writing entirely too many letters for me already," he wrote.[16]

Their last year at Waukena became a transitional time for David and Dorcas. As a good organizer, Dorcas began planning what their needs would be overseas. By then, the mission board had projected a date for their departure to Africa. This was reflected in their Christmas gifts that year. David gave her a wristwatch that she would appreciate in Africa, and she gave him a raincoat.

Dorcas's practical nature kept her busy sewing dresses and slips for herself and Donna. Because of shortages of some materials during World War II, Dorcas had trouble purchasing stockings. She wrote to family asking them to buy some if they could. Stockings "do get past the mending stage, too," she stated.[17]

Mission Years in Northern Rhodesia

After a summer on the East Coast spent visiting both their families, speaking at various churches, and busily making preparations to go to Africa, they were finally cleared by the mission board for the trip. They departed from New York, December 12, 1946, accompanied by other missionaries. Even during the long trip, Dorcas kept her sense of humor. At one layover, Dorcas found the coffee to be horrible. She laughed because it "looked strong enough to stand without the aid of a cup. . . . Then they had it sweetened, and how I dislike sweetened coffee!. . . . All in all, it tasted like the worst kind of medicine."[18]

They arrived at Matopo Mission on Christmas Day. There were teas and celebrations for the new recruits and visits to other mission stations. Within three days of arrival they saw every missionary in Southern Rhodesia (now Zimbabwe) and wondered where they would be placed. In this new environment, Dorcas was confronted with one of her fears: after observing a snake being killed, Dorcas asked for prayer to conquer her fear of snakes.[19]

David and Dorcas were assigned to Sikalongo Mission in Northern Rhodesia (now Zambia) to replace Elwood Hershey and his family, who were due for a furlough. Upon arrival there, schoolboys marched to greet them with songs. They had a few weeks with the Hersheys, then were left in charge of the mission along with two single women: teacher Anna Eyster and nurse Rhoda Lenhert.

Mission responsibilities were weighty tasks for this young couple. David had oversight of the property and management of workers. Dorcas, now matron, kept busy with family needs, including meals for the single missionary women who ate with them. She was hostess also when missionaries from other stations came to visit and do business, or when local people came with needs or inquiries. In *My Story, My Song: Life Stories by Brethren in Christ Missionaries,* Dorcas wrote, "Gradually I learned to speak the language, to garden, to butcher, to separate milk and make butter and to cook and bake on a little wood stove. It was a great day in 1948 when the mission received a kerosene refrigerator, sent out from the United States by a friend of the missions."

Dorcas soon learned there were limits to what she could do. One day a man was brought to the dispensary with his hand severed. "I almost felt sick!" she said. "This is no job for us who know nothing about nursing." [20]

Nonetheless, Dorcas made intentional efforts to relate well to the Africans. She welcomed help in understanding the culture. On one occasion, a Zambian boy was sent to Dorcas for a bath. Puzzled, she asked him to repeat the request. Anna came to the rescue and interpreted "bath" as being an English expression for a tub.[21]

At intervals Dorcas visited local villages and conducted women's meetings at which she taught some domestic skills that were new to them. She demonstrated how to bake bread and biscuits, to make soap, and gave lessons on child care. But she left basic medical care instruction to the nurse. While working together with the women in homemaking, Dorcas used the occasions to discuss spiritual life.[22] Due to her soft demeanor, the Zambians nicknamed her Kanziba, which means "little dove."

David and Dorcas maintained a good relationship with their co-workers. "We are here to work with our coworkers; not to pull away from them, so if the single sisters desire the present [breakfast] schedule continued, that's what we will probably do," she declared in an April 12, 1947, letter to the Climenhaga parents.

There were times when life at Sikalongo lacked the social interactions that Dorcas enjoyed. On July 6 she wrote, "One thing is sure—missionaries in the north go on their own companionship. . . . We like Sikalongo a lot, but we do miss the social visits with other people. I'm surely glad I have a *lovable* husband, Ha!"

Family Tragedy and Growth

Since obstetric care was at a distance from the mission, in February 1948 Dorcas went south to Matopo Mission to await delivery of her second child. Before she arrived at the hospital in Bulawayo, baby Dorothy Lee arrived on March 31, two and one-half weeks early. David immediately went south to bring mother and daughter home.

Months later tragedy struck—on November 11, 1948. Baby Dorothy had malaria, and in Choma the doctor's efforts to treat her seemed futile. To seek more specialized care, David and

Dorcas left at night by train to take her to Livingstone Hospital. Dorothy died soon after the train departed from Choma. They transferred at the next station and returned to Choma at 3:00 a.m. The doctor himself met them. He then drove to Macha to inform the missionaries of Dorothy's death, and the parents went immediately to Sikalongo for the baby's funeral.

Ruth Hunt Byers, a Macha co-worker, still recalls hearing the rasping sounds of nails being pounded into a coffin being constructed. When ready, Rhoda Lenhert and Anna Graybill lined it with white material. A service was held, and baby Dorothy was buried in a small plot beside missionary Myron Taylor's grave.

Grief stricken, Dorcas suffered quietly. She kept herself very busy with her routine tasks and spent extra time sewing on a hand-cranked machine for her family. However, this was not sufficient for working through her grief. Sometimes she felt she was becoming very sick and she would tell herself, "Now Dorcas snap out of it."[23] On one weekend at an outstation with David, she told him about having various pains and being unable to sleep. Not recognizing her symptoms of grief, he felt she was imagining these ailments. Her struggle with depression continued until she was able to talk to a medical person who explained grief responses and gave her six pills to help her sleep at night. She never took the pills because her depression lifted after she gained a deeper understanding of the process of grief.[24]

Two years after Dorothy's birth, Dorcas was pregnant with her third child. This time Verna Ginder accompanied her to Livingstone, where they stayed in guest huts waiting for the birth. Daryl Ray was born at Livingstone hospital on May 30, 1950, and the family rejoiced in having a son.[25]

Following seven rigorous years in Africa, the Climenhaga family returned to the United States for furlough. Besides doing deputation (describing their mission work to various churches and generating enthusiasm for Brethren in Christ World Missions), they spent a year and a half visiting both sides of the family. They returned to Africa in 1955.

Mission Years of Maturity

As seasoned missionaries, they had the role of introducing younger recruits into the mission program at Matopo, where they now served. A newly married couple, David and Laona Brubaker, became an extension of their household and immediately felt at ease upon arrival in 1957. They noted that "[Dorcas] always seemed to treat missionaries and Africans respectfully, with friendliness and taste. She readily built relationships with household help to where joking was done appropriately and comfortably."[26] A most gracious hostess, she inducted David Brubaker into the British custom of serving tea properly: to married ladies first and according to seniority.

Dorcas used her talents in a variety of ways in addition to maintaining her role as matron in charge of household affairs. She gave haircuts to her husband and also to some of the single I-W young men until she asked David to stop telling them that she could do it. When Daryl was ready for school, she taught him and Priscilla Book, daughter of missionaries Alvin and Thata Book, in their first year. Donna was then in boarding school in Bulawayo.

On one occasion, Dorcas presided as hostess to the Governor General of South Rhodesia when he came to Matopo Mission. He addressed several classes during his visit and then asked her, "How did I do?" She felt he was a man of sensitivity and humility despite being British royalty.[27]

During this second term in Africa, Denise Elaine was born on June 8, 1957. At this time Donna, then 12, had rheumatic fever and was bedfast for six weeks. Some months later David was in bed for three weeks because of a stomach ulcer. Extra busy, yet uncomplaining about the extra care and added work, Dorcas was able to maintain her equilibrium as she kept the mission smoothly operating.

While on holiday in Tanzania in 1958, David bought Dorcas a wedding ring from an Indian trader who crafted it in their presence. Traditionally, rings were considered jewelry by the Brethren in Christ, who frowned on wearing them; but South African people didn't understand this tradition and questioned the lack of a marriage symbol for women. For several years, Dorcas wore it only while traveling and on selective occasions.

Early in 1959, David was assigned by the mission board to be a bishop of the church in Africa and general superintendent of the mission, so they returned home for a short furlough before his intensive service began. Prior to returning to Africa in April 1960, they faced the difficult decision of leaving Donna to continue her education in the United States, residing with David's brother Arthur and his wife, Arlene. Dorcas's heart was torn at leaving her firstborn behind, even though Donna would be living with relatives.

Their five years living in the bishop's house in Bulawayo were very different from their previous terms. Their home became headquarters for numerous guests whom Dorcas graciously hosted. With the structure of the African church changing, many committee meetings occupied their time and space. In addition, on many weekends they camped at rural schools and churches to conduct services and baptisms. They sometimes slept under the open sky or in partly enclosed buildings. Dorcas took these rugged weekends in stride as she cared for her children in rustic conditions.

Despite her active life, Dorcas always kept her family uppermost in her heart, and lovingly, patiently cared for them. She enjoyed informing relatives of her children's antics and growth. When needed, she disciplined them mostly through dialogue, often asking questions to draw out their feelings. Rarely did she resort to physical punishment, as David sometimes did with spanking. Yet they did not contradict each other in disciplining.[28]

New Service Opportunities in the United States

In 1965, their overseas service came to an end. They had served God in Africa for nearly twenty years. Soon, David accepted the pastorate at Fairland church in Cleona, Pennsylvania. Here, Dorcas kept busy as homemaker, Sunday school teacher, and leader in youth and women's activities. She also became employed as office manager in a Brethren in Christ doctor's office. She was an efficient organizer, a good listener, and able to calm irate patients. Her maturity and controlled temperament commanded respect and became a role model for all the staff. Her employer regarded her as an outstanding office manager.

While in the pastorate, Dorcas spoke at missionary meetings and mother–daughter banquets. On one occasion, she addressed the topic "Ladies and the Great Commission," declaring, "Down through the years God has reserved a special place for women in the fulfillment of his plans and purposes. . . . There is a woman's touch which God uses. . . . Our field of service is unlimited. Opportunities are everywhere."[29]

Beginning in 1966, Dorcas served thirteen years on the denomination's Women's Missionary Prayer Circle (known as WMPC). She was assistant chairperson one year and then served her remaining years in office as president. In that capacity she sat on the denominational mission board representing WMPC. From 1978–1979, she edited the *Prayer Challenge*, a publication which focuses on guided prayers for missionaries.

In 1972, David became bishop of Central Conference and the family moved to Nappanee, Indiana. According to Arthur Climenhaga, Dorcas was "an outstanding bishop's wife," never pushing to lead but leading when given the opportunity. She became involved in Christian Holiness Association (CHA) meetings, and in 1979 was asked to serve as president of the CHA Women's Commission. In that role, she gave leadership to the publication *Sounding Board.* Her ministry expanded as she became involved in women's retreats within the denomination and for other groups. She created a "Women's Page" that was included with David's monthly "Central Conference Star" newsletter to pastors. She almost always had some little story or illustration from which she drew words of encouragement or wisdom for pastors' wives to ponder.

She wrote once about seeing a little girl wailing loudly on the sidewalk in Nappanee. When Dorcas inquired what was wrong, the child said the cars were going too fast and she couldn't cross the street. So Dorcas took her hand and safely led her across to the other side, and the girl happily went home. Dorcas concluded, "Most of us know we can't go it alone. We have found the security of walking with God."[30]

Another time, she cited a six-year-old neighbor boy who told her that he was glad she lived next door. "Little expressions of love sorely needed everywhere are so easy to give," she observed.[31]

Her homey illustrations also pointed toward ever-expanding visions. She told about building air castles while hand-picking potatoes on the farm during her childhood. "Nothing could stop us" from planning for the future. "[Now] we're learning that we must live joyfully and expectantly, turning our eyes to the new door of opportunity which each New Year sets before us."[32]

Although Dorcas took on more responsibilities, she did not hesitate to cancel or postpone events in favor of supporting her children at special times in their lives. For instance, she discontinued writing a "Women's Page" one month to give attention to her daughter's graduation. Two years later she canceled the page again to focus on preparation for her daughter's wedding. She heartily accepted her children's spouses. Her daughter-in-law, Lois, regarded her as a very affirming and empathetic mother.

Dorcas befriended everyone. Friend Esther Ebersole felt that she "had the ability to make everyone feel special, like you were a special friend of hers." Mabel Frey viewed her as a dear, kind, hospitable missionary "First Lady." And Martha Lady said that Dorcas sometimes served as the voice of single missionary women, conveying their concerns to the overseas bishop. Many sought Dorcas for counseling; she was a great peacemaker and listened to both sides. She knew how to sift information, did not gossip, and kept confidences. When several people were asked who Dorcas's "best" friend may have been, there was always a pause in their reflections because she was a friend to many people. Only Rhoda Lenhert's name was mentioned several times, but with hesitancy.

From her youth, Dorcas maintained a deep spiritual commitment. Throughout her life she depended upon prayer and, on occasion, sought God at altars. Numerous times she requested prayer, whether speaking or writing, and was careful to express praise when requests were answered.

In September 1984, after David's term as bishop had expired in July, he and Dorcas moved to Guelph, in Ontario, Canada, where he pastored the Cross Roads Memorial Church. In important decisions such as whether to accept a new pastorate or to become bishop, Dorcas allowed her husband to make the decision and fully supported him in it. He never felt she was a "driver" urging him to do things her way.[33] In fact, their son sees that their personalities complemented each other. With his travel background and experience in the wider world, David gave Dorcas a forum in which she could spread her wings, utilizing her gifts. She provided stability in their marriage along with a keen sensitivity and understanding of human nature. Their son, Daryl, said that his mother probably influenced his father more than he did her.[34] They both daily attempted to dissolve tensions which cropped up between them.

Entering the Retirement Years

After almost three years in Canada, Dorcas and David moved to Messiah Village, a retirement community near Mechanicsburg, Pennsylvania. There, Dorcas continued to have an impact on the lives of others. She accepted part-time employment in the Messiah Village Commons Office as receptionist and continued to minister to people as she attended to their needs. Many still recall her influence with fond memories.

Although a woman with healthy self-esteem, Dorcas had a few personal sensitivities. Donna recalls that Dorcas never liked to show her teeth when having her picture taken. She seldom displayed anger, but Denise observes that there were times that she retreated to her bedroom, possibly to gain control of her feelings. If something seemed ludicrous or disagreeable, sometimes she was heard saying "fiddlesticks." When she needed to undergo heart surgery, she hesitated about telling people that she was going to the hospital. She was probably reluctant to express her feelings because she did not want to draw attention to herself.

When David suffered from deep depression, she visited him faithfully in the hospital and never wavered in affirming him. During his recovery she encouraged him to try new things such as baking cookies, and told others how proud she was of his efforts. She maintained an even temper, a *kanziba* (little dove-like) demeanor throughout difficult times.

Establishing a Legacy

Dorcas was an intelligent, strong woman who exemplified Christ in her family life as well as in public. She was liberated without having to assert herself. Her spontaneous giggle and sense of humor was a lubricant for friends and co-workers throughout her life.

On their thirty-eighth anniversary, David commented, "What a wealth of memories! It has not been all better, or richer, or ness either. The girl I married was pretty. The woman, who is not now that girl, who is my wife, is beautiful." [35]

Several weeks before her death, awaiting surgery and looking toward the future, Dorcas again applied her organizational skills and showed David how to do laundry. Her heart surgery was successful; however, infection set in and claimed her life. Dorcas died on Mother's Day, May 12, 1991, while still in overall good health. This was a tragic loss for the family, as well as to the immediate and broader communities. David acutely felt the blow of this loss. Daughter Denise felt robbed of her best friend. Sister-in-law Ruth felt like she lost a sister. Nearly ten years later, upon the mention of Dorcas's name, a spontaneous heartfelt cry came from a pastor's wife, "Oh, I miss her so." [36]

Even after many years, Dorcas's legacy of wit, wisdom, and love continues to echo in the memories and inspire the actions of those who knew her.

A Journey Shaped by Life's Experiences

Eloise Dawn Smith DuBose

by Beth Saba*

Since before the American Civil War, Valley Chapel Brethren in Christ Church has ministered in the community of Canton, Ohio. In 1830, Brethren in Christ families emigrated from Pennsylvania to form a fellowship, and by 1866 they had constructed the present building, the oldest in the denomination. After World War II, African Americans began moving into the area, but at first they sent only their children to the church. Soon, African American adults appeared at the services. At its next meeting the church board decided that if African Americans were to be accepted, they must be fully accepted. "The Valley Chapel members were highly disciplined in terms of separation from the world 50 years ago," current pastor Charles Burkett observes, "and racism was seen as one of the world's vices."[1] There was and is a structured commitment on the part of the congregation to be guided by the scripture, which teaches that in Christ all are one. It was in this historically integrated group that Dawn DuBose took membership in 1984.[2]

Formative Years

Eloise Dawn Smith was born in Warren, Ohio, on March 13, 1954, to Norman James Smith and Virginia Eloise Smith

*Beth Saba, recently retired, was a teacher in the public schools of Clark and Franklin Counties in Ohio. She has served on various boards of the Brethren in Christ Church on both the regional and General Conference levels. She has been a friend of Dawn DuBose for over 15 years.

Proctor. Known by her middle name, Dawn was the only progeny in the couple's brief marriage. When she was eight months old, her parents divorced and Dawn's mother returned to Alliance, Ohio, to live with her parents. Dawn was raised by her paternal grandmother, while her father left to serve in the armed forces in Italy for two years. When he returned from Europe he remarried, and Dawn went to live with him and her new stepmother, Sonya. To this union were added two children, Cynthia and Peter. Dawn didn't realize until she was much older that they were her half-sister and half-brother. When Dawn was in second grade, her father divorced again. The three children were raised by their father until he married for the third time when Dawn was in junior high school.

Dawn's father was a strict disciplinarian who thought that children should not question parental authority. She learned early that she should abide by her father's guidelines. He had a fun side and often got down on the floor and played with the children, but his discipline was accepted as final. As a result, she did not openly question why her father had custody of her instead of her mother. In a time when custody was almost always awarded to the mother in a divorce, Dawn was baffled by her circumstances.

After he left the armed services, Dawn's father worked at many jobs. One of the most creative was his "pick up and delivery car wash." He had been laid off from a local company, Packard Electric, and believed that the community would benefit from having a person available to pick up a vehicle, wash it, and return it to its owner. Later he became a *World Book Encyclopedia* salesman, which gave him many contacts in the Warren educational system. None of these efforts were large money-making endeavors, thus the three children never had an abundance of material goods. They always had enough to eat, but they did not wear trendy clothes. Their clothing was conservative, and purchased to be handed down for others in the family to use. Dawn remembers that her father would prepare her school lunch, which, instead of a Twinkie like everyone else had, included a sandwich of bread, butter, and confectionary sugar, with a banana for dessert.

Her relationship with her mother was often strained. Dawn deeply loved both parents, but knew that one of them would suffer more pain than the other because she could live with only one of them. Since her father had custody, she visited her mother on weekends and shared some holidays with her. On two occasions she deeply injured her mother emotionally. The first time she was 14 and old enough to choose parental custody. Her mother drove to Warren with no advance warning. When Dawn returned from baby-sitting, her mother was waiting and had packed most of Dawn's belongings for a lengthy Christmas holiday visit. In the confusion which followed their quick departure, Dawn knew that the time she had been dreading had come. She had hoped she would never need to make a choice between the two parents. She had an exciting holiday with her mother, but knew that her home would be with her father.

The second occasion occurred when Dawn made a quick decision to attend the Bible Leadership Training School in Calgary, Alberta, soon after high school graduation. She had attended one quarter at Kent State University, and had gone to a music camp in Ontario, Canada, at the invitation of her Uncle Bernie. He and his family were moving to Calgary and he suggested that she consider going with them. The decision was made in less than three days. She called her mother from the airport in Youngstown, Ohio, to inform her. Dawn's decision was difficult for her mother to accept. Even though she and her parents have a close relationship now, they do not talk much about the past. As Dawn puts it, "Just like some people do not discuss religion or politics, my mother and I do not discuss the past."

In addition to the impact family life had on her, Dawn was molded by church, public school, and music. From the time she was an infant she was carried to church. One of the first churches she attended was a liberal Methodist church, which was, as Dawn says, "predominantly white, and when the Smith family wasn't there, it was white." On one occasion the church was invited to a private swimming club for an afternoon of recreation. As the cars pulled through the gate, all were welcomed; but when the Smith auto arrived, the entire group was asked to leave, the weak explanation being that the group did not have an appropriate reservation. Although they felt welcomed at this Methodist church, the family eventually left to attend the church of well-known evangelist Kathryn Kuhlman, where Dawn's father had been asked to play bass in the church music ensemble.

In time, the Smiths became friends with the McCrarys, who were involved with the music program in Kuhlman's church. The congregation was large, Pentecostal, and had a huge choir. Often the first hour was only praise and worship. Usually the children were sent out when it was time for Mrs. Kuhlman to preach. But one Sunday the children stayed. Dawn was sitting with Mrs. McCrary on the main floor. At the end of the service, when the invitation to receive Christ was given, Mrs. McCrary leaned over and asked Dawn if she had ever invited Jesus into her life. Her question led 11-year-old Dawn to walk down the long aisle to take her first steps of faith. From that time on, church became her life. She attended the Kuhlman service Sunday mornings with her family and then traveled with the McCrary family when they sang at other churches.

The Kuhlman group, which met in the Stambaugh Auditorium in Youngstown, Ohio, emphasized a strong salvation message and physical healing. Dawn soon was exposed to other teachings, such as speaking in tongues, in the churches she visited with her father or the McCrary family. She often returned to the altar to make sure she was saved. By junior high school, Dawn began to see the importance of studying God's Word. It became a daily habit for her and her sister Cynthia to read it together. These times with God's Word and the fellowship she experienced in church helped to fill the vacancy of not having a mother in the house. She did not have the consistency of a mother's touch to guide her, but was close to her spiritual family. "I could survive," she says, "if I had good friends in church."

Public school had its own set of challenges. Dawn admits that she was never a good student; she did just enough to slide by. She endured school, believing herself "poor, plain, homely, and shy." From her earliest years, she did not fit well into the black community. She felt that she was shunned because she did not behave like others in the community. Her early ancestors, just out of slavery, became teachers and from that time on, certain standards were demanded of the family in speech and verbal expression.

Her maternal grandmother lived in a Slovakian neighborhood; the most contact Dawn had with blacks outside her family was in her church. When her father returned from Europe, they moved into an area having an equal mixture of races. As a five-year-old, she impressed the black community by asking the neighbor gardener in distinct, precise language, "Are you planting the garden?" She had to learn how to adapt her speech to her environment in order to get along. When she went to high school, she talked little because she sounded like a white girl, which would have meant being called an "Uncle Tom."

In both church and public school, music became a lifeline for her. Even before Dawn was born, her father and his brothers had formed a quartet called the Songsmiths. Dawn's father Norman, Gene (his identical twin), and brothers Bernard and Nathan were later joined by Marcia, Gene's wife, and Marcia's mother when Nathan left for the armed services. Eventually, after Marcia's mother died, the children of the family (Dawn, sister Cynthia, and cousin Vera) began to join the public appearances of the Songsmiths. Appointments came through contacts that Dawn's father made in his car wash business and later through his encyclopedia sales position. They performed at churches, Christmas programs, Fourth of July picnics, company celebrative occasions, and other special events.

The Songsmiths did not read music well, but harmonized beautifully. Dawn, Marcia, and the little ones were almost always chosen to sing the melody. Her father and uncles and other members of the family provided the harmony, with her father playing the bass viol. The only other instrument was the piano, and their only piano player was high school student Jim Garber, who at first could only sight-read. The Songsmiths taught him how to play by ear. Dawn relished these performances. She attributes her abiding interest in music and her attitudes toward worship to these early experiences.

In high school her involvement in choir and another music group, The New Tomorrows, helped her to survive the loneliness she experienced. The discipline of rehearsals and the joy of performance helped to fill the void caused by having few friends. Her teachers liked her. She believes her speech helped her sound educated, sometimes leading teachers to give her grades she did not deserve. She did not receive much help from home with her studies and often crammed or finished assignments on the bus. Dawn admits that even today, she is often motivated to complete a task out of deadline pressures or frustration.

During her first quarter at Kent State University (Warren branch) she and her father often visited a nightclub, where the group Hot Cargo sang. Destiny, the parent company of Hot Cargo, invited Dawn to audition with them. After a successful audition, she joined a new combination called New Image, which consisted of two female and six male members. She began going on the road singing primarily in hotel lounges. The only other Christian in the group was the drummer. Dawn talked about this group with the woman minister of the church she was now attending. The pastor's advice was to pray to make sure she was in the right place. Even though the costumes were not risqué and the music consisted primarily of romantic lyrics and was not suggestive, Dawn left the group after a year.

She began to seriously consider returning to college, entertaining the possibility of studying at Ball State University for a degree leading to work with the hearing impaired. Instead, she chose to go for a year to the Baptist Leadership Training School in Calgary, Alberta, where her uncle had taken a position. Intermittently, for the next four years, she attended Kent State but never graduated with a degree.

The school at Calgary cemented her love for God's Word. She believes her intentional walk with the Lord and unquestioning acceptance of circumstances are rooted in her love for and obedience to the Word and her strict upbringing with a loving, authoritarian father.

Marriage and Family Commitments

By this time Dawn had begun to pray that the Lord would bring into her life the man she was to marry. She had two conditions for her marriage—one biblical, the other parent-honoring. First, the man must be totally committed to Jesus Christ; second, he had to be African American. The paternal side of her family had a history of mixed marriages; she believed if she was ever to make peace with her mother, she would need to marry someone in her own cultural group.

She was now approaching 28 years of age. While at Kent State she was active in InterVarsity Christian Fellowship. A friend from this group introduced her to Morris DuBose; both Morris and his friend worshiped at Valley Chapel. Morris, too, was waiting for God's choice in a mate. When he came to southern Ohio for regional church conferences, he chose to stay overnight in private homes. While staying with the Saba family in Springfield on one occasion, the Sabas teased him about a future Mrs. DuBose. He smiled tolerantly and said that God would bring him exactly the right person.

Theirs was a whirlwind romance. They met in March 1982, Morris proposed in May, and they were married on August 28.

As a wife, Dawn accepted wholeheartedly her husband's leadership as head of the house. The passage from the book of Ruth in the Old Testament was recited at their wedding. Dawn remembers that it was "serious stuff" for her, not just a nice passage to read at a marriage ceremony. "Whither you go, I will go" meant that she would attend the same church as Morris.

Her first impression of the Valley Chapel Brethren in Christ Church was like a "step back in time." She had never before met so many women who could bake bread, create beautiful quilts, can and preserve everything they grew in their own gardens, and sew or craft just about anything. Immediately, she felt welcomed by the congregation. The members accepted their marriage and supported them in their decisions, even more than their biological families. The church members' gifts to them were hand made and of beautiful quality. Even though this outpouring of giving made a strong, beautiful impression, Dawn admits that to this day she still isn't into the "make it from scratch" routine.

Since both she and Morris were older when they took marriage vows, she had expectations that maturity would help make the marriage more manageable. She confesses that during the first year she cried a lot. It was quite an adjustment for this single, strong-willed woman to become a helpmate to an older, although godly, man. Today, both she and Morris are occasionally asked to counsel young married couples; while they do much listening, they are also honest and open in sharing their own experiences both then and now. Morris has taken some courses in counseling, but Dawn states that her knowledge comes from the school of hard knocks. Nevertheless, her listening skills have been honed. She has a gift "for distilling the essence of situations and for not getting bogged down in superfluous details."[3]

Four children were born to Dawn and Morris in the eight years following their marriage—Morris III in 1984, Ivana in 1986, Philip in 1988, and Nicholas in 1990. Dawn believed that large families were a trust from the Lord, but after four, she said with a smile, "I decided to tell the Lord I wasn't going to push His trust further." She reflects that motherhood has stretched her, although children are her real joy. Her supervisor at Pets Marketing noted that Dawn's priorities are her family and instilling godly family values: "This was most evident during last year's company Christmas party," he says. "Every year I invite employees and their spouses to my home for the holiday. This past year, Dawn, after leaving the party to pick up her children from caroling, found time to return to my home with her children to sing Christmas carols to everyone."[4] They made a lasting memory for all who attended the party that year.

Dawn sets a good example for her children, teaching them the values of responsibility, politeness, work, and study. For several years she home-schooled her children, and believes that the results of that opportunity will have eternal consequences. One of the benefits of home schooling is the ability to direct the children in Christian family principles as they go through the subject material. When as a family they made the decision for Dawn to return to the workplace to supplement Morris's income, the children were placed in public schools. Dawn enters into parent-teacher conferences at the public schools with confidence, knowing that she understands her children's learning strengths and weaknesses just as well as the public school system does.

In her view, she and Morris are raising "spiritual warriors for God's army." They have created their family to be guided by Jesus, and to be committed to each other—husband and wife, children and parents. The two oldest are excited about Jesus and are interested in Christian service of some kind. In fact, Ivana wants to be either a missionary or an evangelist.[5] The younger two are growing up in the Lord, interested in bringing others to youth events.

Valued Ministry

Dawn's service in the Brethren in Christ Church began with her marriage to Morris. She did not become a member until Morris was elected deacon and Morris III was dedicated. Dawn had always viewed herself as non-denominational. She "was hard pressed to see where in the scriptures membership in a denomination is necessary." But Dawn concludes that as one walks with the Lord, he or she is moved on to the next level; thus, membership may be a needed implementation of one's personal commitment to the body of Christ. Before she became a member, she was active in many ministries of Valley Chapel; after she became a member, she continued to serve in any capacity to which she was called. Her special gifts include music, both as a performing artist and as the worship and praise leader for the local congregation, as well as events relating to evangelism and missions.

Dawn has a heart for the spiritually lost, and wants the Brethren in Christ Church to be on the cutting edge with people-grabbing outreach programs. She says, "Brethren in Christ World Missions is doing a better job reaching the lost than we are here at home." She suggests missionaries going on scouting expeditions to reach the unconverted where they are. "When was the last time we went on a scouting expedition?" she asks. Church members seem to be satisfied with "old carpet, hard pews, and invitations to join us. We need to get out and scout."

The music she brings to the church, both locally and at large, is inspirational. Her love for Jesus Christ is evident in her preparation, whether she personally is performing solos or singing with her family, leading praise and worship for the congregation, or opening a board meeting. Charles Burkett, her current pastor, notes, "Valley Chapel is no stranger to worship wars. Being worship leader, she hears lots of irreconcilable enthusiasms from those she leads. She chooses not to react, but attempts to be faithful to good convictions about worship while attempting to accommodate those who are disgruntled."[6] She once told the pastor that she intentionally listens to music that she does not enjoy. This, he believes, helps her to live "outside the box." Listening to styles of music beyond her own tastes shows her high level of commitment to others. Burkett concludes, "She is not political. She honestly approaches conflicts with strength and wisdom. She seems to believe that good solutions don't need to be compromises if one thinks carefully enough."[7]

Her approach to other church-related issues is identical to the one she employs with music. Her pastor says that "she looks for solutions that have integrity, not merely looking to please people." [8] In the summer of 2001, Dawn worked through a conflict that involved her family and the local church. Ivana, who was only 14, wanted to go on a short-term mission trip. The sponsoring group was not Brethren in Christ. Those two facts caused the church to question the viability of her plans.

Dawn and her prayer partner Debra both had children who wanted to go on the mission trip after visiting an Acquire the Fire booth at an interdenominational conference. When the application process bogged down and the church was not supportive, Dawn prayed about the situation. She asked Ivana to reconsider: perhaps the timing wasn't right. Some support money was coming in, including funds from some church members, but there was a deadline to meet. Dawn wondered if Ivana would wait until the following summer; the monies she had collected could be put in escrow. Ivana wanted them to pray that if God wanted her to go, he would provide all needed funds. The deadline was extended, and the money came in. Her mother had cautioned her, "Don't get excited until you have all you need." When she had acquired all of her funds plus some extra, she asked her mother, "Can I get excited now?"

Now Dawn had to deal with the realization that her 14-year-old daughter was going to Africa, and no family member or close friend would accompany her. The song entitled "Do You Trust Me?" became her guide. She actually believed that her daughter might not return. Dawn felt she was on an Abraham mission, sacrificing her only female offspring for the cause of Christ. She did not share her concerns with Morris, but she prayed daily for Ivana's protection, her mission, and her health. The one crisis that Ivana had was inability to breathe on a bus trip because of diesel fumes. Ivana later told her mother that as long as she sang, she could breathe. Dawn believes that her prayer of faith in God's provision for her daughter made the entire experience a powerful witness for all who met Ivana. She gave total praise to

God when Ivana came home. "Through it all, I've learned to trust in Jesus; I've learned to trust in God," was a refrain that graced her attitude that summer.

As Pastor Burkett states, "She handles stressful situations very well. She takes a lot of flack, but generally handles it quite well, looking for solutions that are sound, rather than simply looking to escape criticism."[9] Prayer convicted her that God was leading this venture even if the church as a collective whole did not approve. This reaffirms the opinion of Dawn's mother that her daughter approaches all phases of her life by asking for God's wisdom.[10]

In addition to being active in her local congregation, Dawn is a member of the denomination's Board for World Missions. After briefly serving as secretary on the Central Conference Board for Brotherhood Concerns, she was invited to join the mission board in 2000. The invitation frightened her. Dawn jokes about her problems with short-term memory; at times she can't remember whom to pray for unless she makes a list. What she could contribute was a recurring question. Perhaps they were looking for a female perspective from another ethnic viewpoint. If that was it, so be it.

She remembers her first meeting with the board. Her first impression was that they certainly did not spend much time in prayer before they made major decisions. She thought they should have prayed for an extended period, "at least two hours," before undertaking business of such magnitude. She is convinced that the Lord has a sense of humor to put her on this board, but being a part of the Brethren in Christ for the past 17 years has heightened her interest in missions.

Being part of a church that has its cultural roots in Pennsylvania Dutch country has had its drawbacks for the Morris DuBose family. Regrettably, instances of racial discrimination have occurred. Dawn and Morris were delegates to the Central Conference one year after they were first married. As was customary, a delegate could request to stay in a home or make a reservation at a motel. Morris and Dawn requested to stay in a private home. They were placed in a motel, even though there were plenty of spaces open in area homes. The son of another African American member of Valley Chapel moved out of Ohio to another state and looked for a Brethren in Christ Church to attend. He wanted to be part of their ministry, but had to convince the elders that he was actually a member of another sister church. He wrote home of his experience, and the Valley Chapel members felt dismay at his treatment.

On the other hand, Morris and Dawn strongly believe, as do most members of Valley Chapel, that to be intentional in reaching out to one race over another is wrong. They have advocated reaching out geographically, but not only on the basis of race.

Dawn believes that the Brethren in Christ Church has much to offer those who are searching for the truth in Jesus. She appreciates the importance the denomination places on the Bible, and doing what it says to do. She likes the emphasis on simplicity and its effect on her. She constantly asks herself, "Where am I going? Where do I need to curb back, so that I am not too much of the world?" Having not had a lot of material possessions as a child, she feels at home attending a church that "doesn't have any Lincolns or Cadillacs parked in front of it." She especially is impressed with the church's focus on missions and the sacrificial giving of the members to support it. Finally, she loves the evidence of hospitality in the church. She observes, "If a church had a single gift, as individuals do, the Brethren in Christ would be known for their hospitality."

Dawn supports more elasticity in worship styles. She wants the church to be adventuresome when reaching out to younger people (in northeastern Ohio, the churches consist mostly of older people). "If we want to draw all people to worship," she says, "we need to figure out how to make the boundaries elastic." The church needs to learn how to express praise using all the senses. She especially enjoys reading about David's abandonment before the Lord in dance when the Ark of the Covenant was returned to Jerusalem. His was a joyous expression in which he used his whole body. Dawn wants to see the church express joy using all that God has created for his pleasure.

For Dawn, all of life's experiences are preparation for what God wants to do next in her life. Because of her childhood background, she is comfortable being a minority person in a predominantly white denomination. A good friend, Delaine Niesley, who attends the Fairview Brethren in Christ Church, marvels that

Dawn and Morris have remained in the denomination, but is thankful for their continued dedication. Many southern Ohio churches have learned to love the family because of contacts made at Memorial Holiness Camp each year, or because the family has been hosted by Brethren in Christ families during the annual Central Conference. Delaine and her husband are impressed by an act of service that occurs each time they come to the southern Ohio area churches. The entire DuBose family makes certain that they visit a couple in southern Ohio who hosted Morris over 20 years ago. This couple is now suffering from health problems and does not get around well, so Morris, Dawn, and the children go to them.[11]

Dawn DuBose would say that she is a pilgrim, walking with Jesus, learning from her mistakes, but always looking for ways to move forward. Those who know her best reflect that "she is able to see through the difficulties and find the good and positive things."[12] She maintains a hectic schedule serving God, loving and spending time with her family, and at times "coping with adversity." [13] Her pastor, Charles Burkett, remarks, "It is always real with Dawn, and never trifling. She takes real joy in her service, and honest interest in people. She is wise, intense, and deeply spiritual." [14] She is a Brethren in Christ woman of the present with a legacy for the ages.

Loving Bridge-Builder

Anna Espenshade Forry

by Lois Jean Peterman*

The neighborhood children gathered for a summer Bible school at the Florin Church of the Brethren near Mount Joy, Pennsylvania. A young Brethren in Christ girl about 12 years old, wearing a simple homemade dress and prayer covering, stepped forward to sing for the assembled group. Unaccompanied, her voice clear and sweet, she sang:

I'm walking arm in arm with Jesus,
I'm trusting Him to lead the way;
I know if I will only cling to Him
He'll never let me go astray.[1]

As she sang this chorus, Anna Forry did not know how clearly it would describe her journey. She was already walking the path of faith, and God was skillfully shaping her life to impact others as a loving bridge-builder.[2]

Growing Up in Two Families

Anna Miller Espenshade was born into the Wesley and Anna Espenshade family on October 13, 1930. Her Grandmother Miller,

*Lois Jean Peterman and her husband, Roy, served as a pastoral couple in Anna's home congregation, the Mount Pleasant Brethren in Christ Church. Lois Jean grew up on a farm in Lancaster County, Pennsylvania, studied at Messiah College and Greenville College, and has worked alongside her pastor-husband for 43 years. Her current passion is grandparenting her five grandchildren.

a midwife, attended her birth in the small Espenshade house near Deodate, Pennsylvania. Her birth occurred at the height of the Depression, when many families were struggling financially.

Her father was a custom butcher, barber, farmer, and carpenter—he could, in fact, do well at almost any type of job. He worked hard to provide for his family's basic needs, so the children also learned to work hard at an early age. He seldom gave affection or compliments, and he allowed no nonsense as a strict taskmaster and disciplinarian. Anna's sister remembers, "All we knew was work, work, work, and not being allowed to do things other kids did."[3]

Anna's mother was a very attractive woman—photos show Anna's remarkable resemblance to her, even as a little child. Anna remembers Mother Espenshade as the "world's best cook" and as the center of stability that helped her children cope with the harsh realities of their lives. Many years later, Anna's mother acknowledged that she hadn't welcomed her pregnancy with Anna during those Depression years. She was already caring for five children in a tiny house without indoor plumbing and modern conveniences. She also shared the burden of making ends meet by raising garden produce, dressing chickens, and baking pies and cookies to sell door to door weekly in town. And she struggled with a growing conviction about her need for God. During this pregnancy, both of Anna's parents made a public confession of faith.

After Anna's birth, an epidemic of scarlet fever brought additional stress into the Espenshade family. Anna, thirteen months old, had just recovered from the fever when twin sisters Geraldine and Pauline joined the family. Overwhelmed with caring for their children, Anna's parents needed help. Consequently, Anna lived with several other families during her first two years. Other siblings also stayed with neighbors or relatives at various times as the family eventually grew to ten daughters (one stillborn) and four sons. This practice of "farming out" children was common in earlier years when a family was under extreme stress from the death of a parent, an extended illness or epidemic, or a financial crisis.

At the age of two, Anna went to live with Harry and Anna Fishburn. The Fishburns had noticed Anna at a church meeting.

Captivated, they spoke with Anna's parents and expressed their desire to bring Anna into their home as a foster child. Recognizing an opportunity for help with raising their large family, the Espenshades agreed, but they made it clear they would never give up any of their children for adoption.

Although the Fishburns had no biological offspring, Anna Fishburn loved children. Little Anna became one of three unrelated foster children who grew up in the Fishburn home. Harry Fishburn was a deacon in the Mount Pleasant Brethren in Christ Church. As highly respected and active members there, he and his wife modeled devout, service-oriented lives. They adhered strictly to the standards of the church and dressed their family conservatively.

Anna understood from early childhood that the Fishburns were not her birth parents. As she grew older, she made frequent visits to her birth family. The visits excited Anna, but she often struggled to reconcile the differences between her birth family and her foster family. She felt uncomfortable, for example, because her long stockings, simple homemade dresses, and later her "plain clothes" made her appear different from her Espenshade siblings. During her summer visits, she looked forward to being allowed to wear bobby socks instead of long stockings. She also sensed that her birth family treated her as an honored guest rather than as a family member, which made her feel like she didn't really belong. Some of her siblings resented that she had special opportunities they didn't have. During one memorable visit Anna accompanied Mother Espenshade as she peddled her produce and baked goods door to door. This was a very special event for Anna, since it included lunch at a restaurant and a day alone with her mother.

In spite of her struggle to belong, Anna loved her birth family. Her visits with them included some pleasant memories. The Espenshades spent little money on toys, but Anna and her sisters and brothers created their own games. There was an old, worn-out Essex automobile on the farm, and the children would take imaginary trips in it. During the winter, they used the bumper to go sledding.

The Espenshade girls enjoyed singing. Father Espenshade liked music, and they had a piano in their home even though musical instruments were not used or permitted in many Brethren in Christ congregations. When the Espenshade girls accepted invitations to sing at neighboring churches, their father took them to the appointments, obviously proud of them. He bought an "extended" car so the family could travel together. (Earlier, some of the children rode to church with their parents, while some rode with other church members.)

During the years when the Espenshade home did not have an indoor bathroom, Anna and her sister Helene often made trips to the outhouse together. While there, they perused the Sears catalog and planned their dream houses. Years later, Anna decorated her first kitchen in red and white, just as she had dreamed she would.

When Anna returned to her Fishburn home after visiting her birth family, it was like entering a different world. Life seemed more serene and revolved around pleasing God. The Fishburns expressed this desire to please God through conscientious behavior, service in the church, loving family relationships, and a simple lifestyle. Father Fishburn was usually very serious, but he impacted Anna's life more than any other person. She felt the influence of his quiet demeanor, his desire for excellence (even his handwriting was a work of art), and his organizational skills. His faith was an important part of his daily life, reinforcing his family prayers and his public testimony.

Mother Fishburn was a fun-loving complement to her husband. She cherished her foster children and found creative ways to bless their days together. Summer brought picnics in the meadow and wading in the creek with neighbor children. An unused goat pen became a playhouse for Anna and her friends. Mother Fishburn could also enjoy a good practical joke (a relative observed years later that Harry Fishburn probably found it difficult to keep his wife's humor under control),[4] like the time she hid an onion inside a homemade chocolate Easter egg.

Shaped by a Third Family—the Mount Pleasant Church

As a member of the Fishburn family, Anna attended the Mount Pleasant Brethren in Christ Church regularly. She listened to the singing and testimonies every Sunday, often sitting with Father Fishburn in the "amen corner"—the section of front, corner pews intended for church officials (deacons, ministers, and the bishop). She also attended Sunday school, and was an eager learner in teacher Velma Martin's class. Velma's junior and teen girls thrived under her love and care, which reached beyond the classroom to regular class meetings in the Martin home. These occasions became highlights in Anna's memory and served as a model for her own teaching in the future.

Anna's childhood in the Fishburn home and her regular attendance at the Mount Pleasant church drew her to accept Christ at age 12. Upon baptism and joining the church, she began to wear the traditional plain garb: simple cape dresses and a prayer covering with long ribbons. The little girl who wished for "store bought" dresses, like her friends, instead wore simple garments made by Mother Fishburn.

Conscientious Anna also struggled to understand the church's teaching on sanctification. Ministers often presented sanctification as an emotional, life-changing encounter with the Holy Spirit, after which one was no longer troubled by unholy desires, failures, or doubts. The constant self-examination to see if she had truly reached this state of holiness became a heavy weight. Anna often went to the altar, but became disappointed when she didn't feel differently. "Looking at myself inwardly and checking myself spiritually, I was afraid to claim what I didn't know I had," she remembers.

When Anna began to understand that God's spirit was already at work in her life, she found the courage to yield her life fully to him. She felt comforted by the realization: "It's not how much I have of him, but how much he has of me." God's peace came to her heart, assuring her that God would complete the process of making her his holy child.

The Mount Pleasant church brought a new kind of blessing into Anna's life as she learned to know B. Musser Forry. During her childhood years, this young man of purpose and integrity, four years her senior, developed into an active and faithful church member. Musser drove his father's car to Young People's Meetings—major social events for Brethren in Christ youth—and regularly transported other church teens who needed a ride. Anna was among his passengers, and Musser especially enjoyed the times when she rode in the front seat with him. He was a bashful farm boy, but Anna's warm personality and spiritual life attracted him.

Musser and Anna both became models among the Mount Pleasant youth, willingly accepting opportunities to serve in the church. Both sang in the Gospel Light Chorus (a regional chorus) and in quartets. Anna became secretary of the church youth group. She was growing in the ministry and leadership skills that would bring opportunities to be a good neighbor and a bridge-builder.

Anna also distinguished herself as an outstanding student and leader at the Mount Joy High School, holding a class officer responsibility each year. "It's almost a wonder they wanted me because I was plain," Anna reminisces. When she graduated on May 21, 1948, Anna was class secretary, second highest in her class of 37, and one of the three honor students to give a speech at Commencement.[5] One of the persons proud of her accomplishments that evening was Musser Forry, who had begun dating her just two months earlier.

A New Family, A New Vocation

After high school, Anna struggled to make decisions about her future. She enjoyed science, and dreamed about someday studying nursing and becoming a registered nurse. But with no money to finance further schooling, the door seemed firmly closed. There was also the question of how her new relationship with Musser would fit into such a plan.

Two and one-half years after her graduation, Anna and Musser both felt God leading them together in marriage. Musser had a large-scale agricultural operation on the farm his grandfather previously owned. He and Anna lived in a house adjoining the farm. Anna ended her work at a local dental office to help with farm operations.

They planned a simple wedding for October 21, 1950, in the Mount Pleasant church. Father Fishburn proudly walked down the aisle with Anna. All of the Espenshade family were also present. Even surrounding this special day, she struggled with how to make both of her families an integral part of the event. In one of the complexities of this situation, Anna later wondered if she could have included more of her birth family in the wedding party, and if she should have asked her birth father to walk her down the aisle.

After the wedding, Musser and Anna traveled to Niagara Falls for a short honeymoon. All too soon, the honeymoon days passed and Anna was thrust into a new world as a farmer's wife. She found the demands of farm life overwhelming, especially in those early years. When life became hectic during the busy season, everyone worked hard. Musser and Anna raised acres of potatoes and tomatoes, and hired migrant workers to help with the task. Anna did laundry for the workers and took them to town for groceries. One year, while pregnant, she helped plant tomatoes three times before the plants survived and grew. Daily and seasonal tasks like gardening and canning and freezing also consumed her time. She even learned how to drive the farm tractor.

Anna remembers the frustration she felt at that point in her life. She reflects, "I think I wondered if I really belonged here [on the farm]." She missed employment outside the home, and began to feel like she had no marketable skills. But Musser needed her on the farm, and she couldn't follow both callings. Her nursing dream died painfully, especially when she felt most keenly that she was doing a poor job on the farm and that she was not really qualified to be a farmer's wife.

She coped with the discouragement and feelings of inadequacy in several ways. Initially, she kept her emotions inside, not letting them show. In time she recognized her need to be open and to verbalize her struggles. Anna also recognized that she made a commitment to life on the farm when she married, and she determined to persevere. Instead of pitying herself, she tried to fulfill her responsibilities without complaining. And, as she turned her focus to the people around her, God responded by giving her opportunities to bless other lives.

New opportunities to serve the Mount Pleasant congregation started to appear. Anna began teaching Sunday school classes and put her whole self into her teaching. She especially enjoyed working with junior high and teenage girls. Remembering how important class meetings were to her during her own teen years, she regularly invited her students to her home. This sometimes meant that she and Musser would have to pick up the girls and take them home again, driving within a 20-mile radius. Years later, former student Darlene Keller remembered her teacher with pleasure: "Models are very important for teens. . . . You served as a model for me of the woman I wanted to become. I wrote essays about you in school, thought about how you would approach the problems I encountered, and studied your actions, your words, even your hair and dress! I'm so thankful to God that such a model was provided for me. . . . Just the other day, I was thinking about our class meetings at your house. How glad I am to have been one of your Sunday school girls!"[6]

As a result of Anna's efforts to make Sunday school an important experience, she became Mount Pleasant's first female Sunday school superintendent. Patiently, and with persistence, she worked to develop more opportunities for the Mount Pleasant children and youth. She was instrumental in helping to begin a junior church program (a worship service for children). Anna also promoted a weekly club outreach for children until the congregation responded positively to the idea. Then she went to work canvassing the neighborhood for potential attendees, building the club program into an important outreach that continues today.

When Anna and Musser learned their first child was on the way, they welcomed the news—both looked forward to having a family. Anna was excited about the opportunity to use her energies in a new vocation, motherhood, and about having her own children to love and teach. On May 4, 1952, their first child, Dennis, arrived. Brother Gary joined the family in 1954; Daryl, their third son, was born in 1957. Those early years of motherhood gave Anna many unforgettable memories. One son used the electric sweeper to vacuum out the contents of the toilet bowl. On another occasion, he locked her out of the house. Another son poured a bottle of concentrated detergent on the living room sofa.

As a stay-at-home mom, Anna had many opportunities to serve her children. She read books to her boys with such enthusiasm and animation that the stories came alive. On Sunday afternoons, she often played softball with the rest of the family. And she found special ways to express her love for her sons. The boys each received a birthday party when they turned 16. As they transitioned into adulthood, Anna spent many hours praying for them and encouraging them through each new stage in their lives. Before leaving home for married life with his new bride, Gary found a note in the last lunch Anna packed for him. In the note, she shared her mixed feelings at his leaving, her love for him, and her joy in the knowledge that he had chosen a wonderful wife.

More Open Doors

While raising her family, Anna's ministry opportunities at Mount Pleasant continued. In 1955, Musser purchased an organ for their home. As Anna learned to play it, she received frequent requests to bring her organ to the church to perform for weddings and other special occasions. When the Mount Pleasant congregation purchased an electronic organ in 1965, she became the primary organist and continued in this major music ministry for more than thirty-five years.

When the congregation elected Musser to a deacon role in 1957, Anna took seriously her promise to support him in this calling. At that point, she clearly remembered the discomfort she felt as a child when deacons made their annual home visits to inquire about the spiritual health of every church member. Wanting to encourage and bridge gaps in a more positive manner, she and Musser developed their own unique pattern of care. Taking the list of members they needed to contact, they began giving out invitations to visit and share a meal in their home. Anna's natural gift of hospitality grew and blossomed, members responded to her love and caring, and Musser and Anna received much satisfaction from their ministry. Musser is quick to say that "Anna was more of a deacon than I was!"

Their service as deacons often went beyond expectations for the role. When they became aware of two single sisters who lived together but were no longer able to care for their personal needs, Anna and Musser tried unsuccessfully to find an opening for them in a nursing home. Concerned for their welfare, the couple visited the sisters and invited them to stay in the Forry home. They lived with the Forry family for several weeks until they could move to the nursing home.

Musser and Anna served faithfully as a deacon couple over a 30-year period. But whatever the need, in and out of the congregation, people found in Anna a gifted leader and a willing servant. In 1973, when a Christian Women's Club (CWC) organized in Mount Joy, Anna was eager to become involved. She chaired the club for a period of time, then continued serving in a wide array of roles: prayer coordinator, contact coordinator, and Bible study hostess, among others.

Gathering with Christian women from various churches gave Anna many opportunities to bless a wide circle of ladies. Unconsciously, she built bridges to many lives in the group as a leader and model for the women she served. She remembers sensing that God was teaching her to become more sensitive to the needs of others. A letter of appreciation from club member Betsy Wolgemuth describes Anna's gifted service: "I wanted to let you know what your gentle leadership, your peacefulness, your kindness meant to me. I especially appreciated the way you handled conflicts and stress. I have only met a few people in life like you—they, too, were godly people. With all the stresses and changes Mount Joy CWC has been through the last few years, I know why God kept you there at the helm, calmly guiding the way. Thank you!"[7]

Anna even found ways to connect her love of nursing with service to others. Although she never pursued a formal nursing degree, she became a Red Cross hospital volunteer. Meeting and ministering to other people in this way still invigorates her after 31 years.

A Faith Tested

The 1970s brought many unforeseen changes to Anna's family. Dennis and his wife, Kristy, moved from California to work on the family farm. Later, Gary and his wife, Lynne, moved from Mount Joy to join Dennis and Musser in farming. Son Daryl graduated from R. G. LeTourneau University in Texas with an associate's degree in aviation technology. After finding work as an airplane mechanic at a local airport, he moved home to live with Anna and Musser. Although Daryl was often quiet and reserved, Anna treasured the times when she could listen as he talked about his goals and dreams and his desire to find God's path for his life.

On Sunday, April 2, 1978, Daryl left the house after a home-cooked meal, eager to see his girlfriend, Penny Coyle, for an afternoon visit. Later in the day, Penny's foster mother called Musser and Anna with the urgent news that the children had been in a car accident. The Forrys dashed to the hospital and found Daryl unconscious. The doctor's grim words were brief: "His brain is dying." Daryl lived until evening as his parents watched by his bed. Mount Pleasant pastor George Bundy arrived to share their grief; his presence was a great comfort. Penny survived only a few more days. The intoxicated driver who ended the lives of the young people was hospitalized with a broken leg.

Trying to make sense out of the blur of those grief-filled days and the reality of Daryl's death, Anna tried to put together pieces of the puzzle. "I had been praying that the Lord would draw me closer to him"; she wondered if this experience was a part of God's answer. She thought about things Daryl had confided to her—his uncertainty, for example, about his friendship with Penny—and wondered if this accident was God's way of sparing Daryl and the family from future heartache. She believed that God "must know something we didn't." Psalm 18:30 comforted her and Musser again and again: "As for God, his way is perfect." "I could easily have been bitter," she muses. "I often wonder, what if Daryl were still here? But the Lord gives me peace when I question the way circumstances went."

Anna struggled to keep her focus on positive results from the devastating loss. She and Musser were very grateful for their good memories of Daryl and for the certainty of knowing that he was with God. They were thankful that he did not live to face irreversible mental and physical damage. They recognized, too, that Daryl's sudden death spoke deeply to the young people of the Mount Pleasant church. And Anna knew this experience had changed her: she would always, from this time on, have a greater sensitivity to the hurts of others.

Typical of her character, Anna used her grief to build bridges to other needy people. She felt a desire to personally contact the intoxicated driver who caused the fatal crash. Several weeks after Daryl's death, she went to the post office to obtain the driver's address and directions to his house. She found him at home with his wife and four children. He had little to say and showed no remorse. Nevertheless, Anna told him that she held no bitterness against him, and that she hoped God would give him the strength to make that fatal drink his last one.

Anna reached out to other people struggling with grief, like her sister Dorothy, who lost a ten-year-old grandson in an accident. Dorothy felt a new closeness to Anna, for she knew Anna had experienced the same feelings of loss. Anna's letters comforted her. Dorothy comments, "She gave me a different outlook on heaven. We talked about God, and I felt I couldn't blame him [for what happened]." [8]

Before Daryl's accident, Anna and Musser had agreed to serve at a Brethren in Christ boys' camp (Spring Lake Retreat) in a rustic New York setting. Now, fresh with experiencing the loss of their son, Anna questioned the timing of the opportunity. While traveling to New York, they stopped for worship at an unfamiliar church. To Anna's surprise, a girl from the congregation—remembering her from a Bible school class—came to greet her. Anna sensed that God was confirming her ministry in New York through this unexpected meeting with someone she had ministered to in earlier years.

Anna and Musser needed this assurance many times in the next ten days. Anna served as the Bible teacher; Musser served as an equally needed maintenance expert. Their mission field was a group of inner-city boys, many of whom were already in trouble with the law. It was an unforgettable week of difficult challenges, which included a pillow fight riot and the spraying of fire extinguishers. One camper brought a snake into Anna's class. At the height of frustration, Anna recorded in her diary one day that she hadn't felt like teaching. But God provided strength and endurance for the day's lesson; some of the boys even sat up front on the teacher's platform so they could hear better. With increased sensitivity from Daryl's death, Anna was able to relate to these young boys, and she and Musser went home with a new burden for inner-city children.

Walking On

Anna's whole life continues to be characterized by gracious caring. When friend Vivian Shank delivers an Avon order to Anna, Anna often insists on setting an extra place at the table so Vivian can stay for lunch. When Vivian faced major surgery, Anna took her to the hospital, then brought her to the Forry home to recuperate until she could cope alone. Vivian comments, "I can't say enough about her. She's so special. She's no phony. She really walks with God."[9]

More evidence of her warmth comes from entries in Anna's diaries, which chart the meals and other acts of caring she has provided for those in need. When the husband of an acquaintance became terminally ill, Anna made a final visit to his home, concerned about his spiritual state. He affirmed his faith, an answer to her many prayers through the years. When Anna and Musser built a new home, they included a small apartment so that Mother Fishburn, now widowed, could spend her last five years under Anna's loving care.

For 51 years Anna and Musser have been walking with God together. Early in their marriage they set out on a path of daring financial stewardship. One year they decided to give 100% of their profits to God's work; although their faith was tested by a bad hailstorm, they were able to fulfill their goal. Determined to keep their promises to God and to each other, they have experienced God's strength and rewards, even in the hard times. Anna is quick to affirm, "The Lord's been so good to us, and much credit goes to my wonderful husband." Anna and Musser are now investing their lives in the Mount Pleasant church, returning blessings to the congregation that shaped them.

Looking back, Anna sometimes wonders whether she has accomplished all that God intended for her life. She is keenly aware of not achieving everything she had hoped to do. Anna does know that her deep desire is "to be a bridge-builder and to leave footprints that others can follow." Out of her own hurts—as a child caught between two families and two worlds, as a young woman struggling to find her place in life, and as a mother grieving the loss of a son—she continues to follow God's direction by lovingly ministering to the needs of others.

A Gracious and Independent Spirit

Beth Laverna Winger Frey

by Mary Frey-Engle*

Beth Frey's home from birth was Mtshabezi Mission, 55 miles southeast of the city of Bulawayo, in what is now Zimbabwe. Along the Mtshabezi River for perhaps a mile on both sides, the leaves high in the eucalyptus trees whisper in the dry breezes. Walter O. Winger, a missionary from Ontario, planted these "gum trees" shortly after he arrived at the station in 1911; later he would use them for beams in the roofing of the original mission church. Walter's children and later Beth's children remember the rustle of the tall trees during happy hours spent playing at the river when it flowed. These happy hours were harbingers of a near lifetime of joyous and fruitful service that Beth would give in the land of her birth.

Parental Influence

Beth Winger Frey grew up to resemble her father in many ways, and to a lesser extent, her mother. For 36 years, Walter O. Winger was the superintendent and her mother, Abbie Bert Winger, the matron of Mtshabezi Mission in Southern Rhodesia (Zimbabwe since 1980). Beth was born there on February 13, 1919, in a three-room, pole-and-mud house with a roof of grass thatching. She was the couple's third child and their first daughter, a particularly prized baby. She was walking at eight months, a promise of dynamic things to come. She understood the story

*Mary Frey-Engle is a family therapist with Catholic Charities In-Home Intensive Services, Lancaster, Pennsylvania. She is Beth Frey's daughter.

of Christmas, "For God so loved the world," before her third birthday.[1] A particular experience of personal conversion was not something Beth spoke of, so she must have simply grown up accepting and believing in Jesus Christ.

Beth's first ten years were spent at Mtshabezi, sometimes lonely after her brothers went to boarding school. But hers was a relatively carefree childhood of running around barefoot, never overly burdened by schoolwork. She absorbed the rhythm of life on a large mission station and the languages, names, and ways of the Africans of Matabeleland, an area in Southern Rhodesia, whose people speak Sindebele, a dialect of the Zulu language. In their early childhood, Beth and her siblings were equally fluent in Sindebele and in English. Their father was first and foremost interested in preaching the gospel and building relationships with the Africans. His Sindebele pronunciation was never perfect, but he understood the people and the nuances of their idioms, and they understood what he was saying. Beth told her children that many Africans spoke of her father with respect and affection for years after his retirement from the field as "our brother, a missionary who walked beside the people, not in front of them."

Walter's unflagging partner in the work, Abbie Bert, had first come to Southern Rhodesia in 1905, 21 years old and single, but after a few years had returned to the United States for health reasons. There at a service focused on missions she met Walter Winger; they started and for years maintained a correspondence with each other. Their correspondence culminated in their marriage, at the close of the farewell service at Messiah Home that marked their departure for New York City and a ship bound for Africa. Beth would remark, many years later, that Abbie, in a break with tradition, wore the first white wedding dress in the Brethren in Christ Church.

Abbie had numerous responsibilities. She ran the mission's main house; supervised the female students, the Sunday school, the mission's teachers, and a mother's club that she began; taught her own children until they went to boarding school; gardened on a large scale (vegetables enough to feed the students and staff, and flowers—her pride and joy); and even found time to design, build, and upholster furniture. Walter planned and managed the operation of the station, preached the Sunday sermons, officiated at numerous weddings, and rode horseback to local villages to evangelize. He farmed enough maize and peanuts to feed the population of Mtshabezi and to sell. He built classrooms, dormitories, the main house, the library, and the church. Clearly, the Wingers were dedicated and industrious missionaries. Their energetic life would later be reflected in Beth's personality and work.

To some extent the parents' single-minded commitment to the work of the mission kept their children at the periphery of their lives. Beth was to write to her fiancé a few months before their wedding: "I suppose to most people I'm rather self-sufficient and sure of myself. I wasn't always that way—of all us children, I suppose I was the most 'clinging vine' type. Then we were shoved out on our own and in desperation I built a wall of self-sufficiency around myself—nor would I allow myself to care too deeply, for I dreaded partings and separations."[2]

Their father had a great ability to show affection to his daughters, and Beth felt her father's love and respect. Her secure attachment to him may be a major reason for Beth's success in defining her own life and making her own decisions, and in many ways following the same path of service as her father, without loss of individuality. She could differ from her father's opinions without making it a matter of rebellion. Although Beth's siblings felt she held a special place in her mother's regard, Abbie was not as emotionally expressive as Walter, and Beth experienced a certain detachment or coolness from and toward her mother. This did not mean, however, that Beth discredited Abbie's considerable talents, nor the benefit of her strict instruction in cooking and sewing or the economical and efficient ways in which Abbie managed the station headquarters that was the main house.

To Boarding School

At age eleven, Beth went to Evelyn High School in Bulawayo. Compared to life on the station, this was not so simple; it required a significant cultural adjustment, as well as an adjustment to more rigorous schoolwork. Beth made this first major shift in a life that would be filled with adjustments. The white Rhodesian students found missionaries odd and were baffled by their motives for, as they put it, "living out in the bush, spoiling the natives," a way of thinking that was foreign to Beth's world until then. Little things like wearing nightgowns rather than pajamas, too, left her with a sense of being conspicuously different from other students.

The school system and culture were British, which had a lifelong influence on Beth and her brothers and sisters. The children's sense of the British identity was shaped also by their Canadian father's pride in being a member of the British Commonwealth and a self-described "loyal subject of the Crown." He was pleased to be laboring in a land that was also part of the Commonwealth, and was keenly interested in King George V and all of the other Windsors.

During these boarding school years, Beth learned to know a number of young people who met for Bible study in Bulawayo. Several of them remained lifelong friends, thanks to her habits of letter writing when far from friends and of hospitality when near. Many years later, some attended her wedding at Mtshabezi Mission. One of these, Ossie Conolly, teasingly informed Beth that he was bringing champagne for the occasion. (He did not.)

Education and Teaching in America

A second culture shock in Beth's life came in 1935, when the Wingers took their family of eight back to the United States. Beth said of this time, "Our excitement tended to dwindle when we children discovered that we were no more Americans, in the States, than we had been white Rhodesians at the British boarding schools we attended."[3] The Winger family visited Brethren in Christ congregations to report on the work in Rhodesia. At these services, 16-year-old Beth gave the 15-minute talks her father required that she present. It was in this setting that Glenn Frey first saw the slender, attractive Beth Winger, with her dark hair, olive-toned skin, and the graceful bearing bred into her by her tall, ramrod-straight father.

Beth's sister Ruth, younger than her by nine years, remembers a revival service during this furlough, when she was just seven years old. Ruth's life until then had been spent at Mtshabezi Mission, so this kind of a revival service was a new experience. The fervor and emotion of the preacher's call to the lost stirred this young child, bringing confusion and some tears. Beth was an affirming presence beside her, explaining that the invitation meant that she could give her heart to Jesus. With Beth's encouragement, Ruth accepted Christ as her Savior. As they left the church that evening, Ruth remembers Beth telling her that things would look different to her now, that even the stars would seem brighter.

Within a year, Walter and Abbie returned to Africa for what turned into a 12-year term due to World War II. They took their two youngest daughters, Elmo and Ruth, with them, while Beth and her three brothers—Bert, Mark, and Paul—stayed behind in the United States. Their father strongly believed in education and urged them to pursue this goal, but they were responsible to find the financial means to do so on their own. A mentor and benefactor—whom Beth always loved and honored—entered her life in the person of C. N. Hostetter, Jr., who found scholarship money to augment what she could earn for school expenses.

Beth graduated from Messiah Academy and Junior College, in Pennsylvania. At Messiah, Beth came to feel that she belonged. For three years she had a home: she participated in college ministries, served on the *Clarion* (yearbook) staff, and worked in the kitchen. To raise funds for schooling beyond the associate's degree, Beth planned to work as a domestic servant. But when Lottie Martin, a resident of Elizabethtown in Lancaster County, Pennsylvania, offered her room and board in exchange for work and a loan for tuition, Beth was unexpectedly given the means to go directly on to senior college at Elizabethtown, from which she graduated in 1941 with a B.S. degree in elementary education.

Much to Beth's dismay, she discovered that the teaching certificate was unavailable to her because—born in Southern Rhodesia of a Canadian father—she was not a United States citizen. Fortunately, that fall a teaching job opened up at the private Training School in Vineland, New Jersey, where for two years Beth taught retarded children and adults, a rich experience that she said changed her life. She was moved by the nature of the students; she learned the error of calling or treating mentally retarded adults as children, and became more aware of the dignity and spirit of human beings. In the fall of 1943, she returned to Messiah Academy as a teacher.

Beth's sense of elegant dress developed when she enrolled at this time in summer and Saturday classes at Drexel Institute of Technology. She took courses in dress design and flat pattern making. She had a flair for this work and was even tempted to go into the field of clothing design and fashion. More than one person at Drexel told her that she was such an excellent "clothes horse," too, that she could have worked as a model if she had chosen to do so. With a hint of pleasure at the compliment, Beth would say on the rare occasions when the subject came up, that she believed such a choice would have meant going against God's will for her life.

Beth's sense of style was not without its benefits and enjoyment. She liked pretty lingerie, she sewed and wore nice clothes, and she wore them well. But fashion was not a main feature in her life. In a similar way, Beth sometimes said she was by nature lazy and could have been a real "lounge lizard," whereas she actually worked almost all the time (mentally or physically, in this way resembling her mother). She found difficulty in resting and relaxing. Beth appreciated fine craftsmanship—from fine art to fine linens and crystal—but she was not passionate about objects. As a mother, she had a rule for herself not to scold her children if they accidentally broke a valuable item in the home.

Beth taught at Messiah for five years, enjoying fellow faculty, the community, and students. Also, she made a home for her two teenage sisters, Elmo and Ruth, when they came to the United States two years before their parents' return. During all the years she spent in America, however, Beth's sense that God was calling her to work in Africa "crystallized," as she put it. She had avoided personal relationships that would keep her from following her sense of God's guidance to the mission field, a kind of selectivity that carried with it the possibility of heartache. Her holding firm for years to her sense of vocation is an example of Beth's uncommon inner clarity about her priorities, which were rooted in her understanding of God's priorities for her.

Returning to Africa

Beth returned to Africa in 1948, knowing about life in mission work and expecting to love the life of a single missionary. Back at Mtshabezi, the place of her birth, Beth taught and worked with students in the Christian League Service (similar to Girl Scouts, with an emphasis on camping). In these first years, she also shot more than 20 snakes, a feat that impressed her children and grandchildren greatly. She reestablished a women's club which met in the school buildings for sewing, knitting, crocheting, and cooking classes. The members decided to name the group "Lomalanda," which means a tall, straight pole on which the white tick bird or egret sits, and the African name the people had given to her father.

Beth would say, "God's plans are not ours. In 1952, mine were completely changed with Glenn Frey's arrival in Rhodesia." Glenn was assigned to Mtshabezi Mission. He and Beth did not immediately "click," as he would say, but then one day after a missionary picnic, Glenn helped Beth down off the high back of the truck and "it hit [him] like a ton of bricks." He could not eat for a week. They began a well-chaperoned courtship, both 33 years old, and in September of 1952, they were married. Beth made her own dress, simple and beautiful, and carried a graceful bouquet of white carnations. Her mother wrote, advising her not to have a "fussy" wedding. Her father had written to Beth before the wedding, after meeting Glenn's parents (his spelling and punctuation are retained): "I was amused on Sunday just as we left, Father Frey was talking to Mother and I, and said Glenn was in with a number of girls, but couldent feel to marry any of them, but now how romatic; here he goes to the Wiles of Africa, and finds one who has been waiting for a suitable chance, and finds one to his liking, it is very complimentary to you Beth, and I am just pleased that you dident rush into matrimony sooner, for he is a very fine man by all I can see, and will take good care of you, and also I believe will make a good mission Supt. so things are working out just right, and I am very much pleased with it all. . . . [I]n many ways your position is the same as with your mother and I, as she was in Africa first, knew the language and the people better than I did, so you will do your best, and God will help. God bless you good Beth, and with lots of love I close. W.O. Winger" [4]

Beth sent this excerpt to Glenn, with the note, "Don't take this all too seriously. Isn't it nice that he approves so much?"

Partnership: Personal and Vocational

Beth's eldest daughter, Laureen, remembers her mother saying that in their early years at Mtshabezi she was always careful to defer to Glenn, who was unfamiliar with the mission and the people. Beth was completely fluent in Sindebele, knew a great many of the people and lines of kinship around Mtshabezi, had grown up "in the system," and was sure of the right way to do things in Rhodesia. Glenn was quieter, calm and gentle with Beth, patient with her self-confessed tendency to be too critical, too "fussy," and too conscious of what others thought. Beth gave Glenn her trust, but not without a bit of an inner struggle, for she had been very independent.

The couple gradually worked out the differences between them, which arose in their first year of marriage from a clash between Beth's inbred notions of British propriety and Glenn's earthier Lancaster County background. Table manners and English grammar were the two most obvious areas of friction. In addition, Beth's idealism about life and perhaps about her role may have made marriage seem a step down from the life of the self-sufficient, single woman. The way Glenn put it was, "I went out to the mission station and pulled her down out of the clouds." To which Beth would retort, "It was purely a matter of propinquity!" Glenn accepted and enjoyed Beth's "glitter," as co-worker Mabel Frey described Beth's socially gregarious nature. Beth enjoyed Glenn's lovely, light humor and his solid, unpretentious rootedness. Their commitment to each other was deeply founded; they prayed together every day of their shared life, were true partners in work, and, by the end of their lives, were devoted and joyful spouses.

The newlyweds were the ready-made superintendent and matron team at Mtshabezi. They moved into the main house. Beth's model for her new position had, of course, been her mother. As Abbie had done 30 years before, Beth managed a large household and working staff, and a large garden, which always produced an abundance of flowers along with vegetables for students and staff. Wherever she lived, Beth had flowerbeds, even if only one row along the house. All her life she arranged bouquets of her flowers for her home.

A big difference between her mother's and Beth's styles as mission matrons was that Abbie had not entertained company. "We are not here for that," her daughter Elmo recalled her saying. Beth was always—from 1952 through to the morning of the day of her death—continually and almost famously, a great hostess. She loved entertaining, thrived on company and conversation, and on providing simple, good food served with elegance. Teatime on the station was a morning ritual over which she presided with natural ease.

Of the two terms of superintending at Mtshabezi, Beth would write: "Our 12 years of service there were rewarding. There was love and gratitude from co-workers and the people we served." Beth and Glenn shared a love and enjoyment of the African people and the land itself. Superintending the mission resembled in almost every point what had been Walter and Abbie Winger's responsibilities. They were on call round-the-clock for teachers, missionary staff, students, and people from the surrounding countryside who came to their door to sell goods or to seek their counsel.

Beth was as uncompromising and forthright as her father had been in presenting the gospel to whomever she met. She was attentive and supportive toward students who were at times caught in the conflict between indigenous moral values (for example, polygamy) and the mission's values. For Glenn, the climate and the relaxed pace of life in Rhodesia were entirely congenial, and the "jack of all trades" nature of the work matched his gifts and his temperament. Among other things, he built a new church, a structure that fulfilled his hopes for it and was a lasting joy to him.

In June of 1953, they listened to the coronation service of Queen Elizabeth over Glenn's short-wave radio. (These radios were a lifelong interest of Glenn; he tuned in whenever possible to the news broadcast by the BBC.) In September of that year, the couple's first child, Laureen, was born. Three more children—Mary, Heather, and Eric—were born in Bulawayo during these Mtshabezi years. Beth taught her children between other tasks in her busy days. At age seven, the children each left the station for Bulawayo and Youngways Hostel, the home-away-from-home for Brethren in Christ missionary children while they attended the government schools. Beth had been instrumental in the formation of Youngways, with her memories of less-than-comforting aspects of government hostels in her youth. For Glenn, the absence of the children was one of the more painful experiences of his missionary life in Rhodesia.

Out in the Villages

After a brief furlough in the United States, Glenn and Beth agreed to return to Rhodesia in 1964 for a five-year term, provided they could work "out among the people" in the bush rather than manage a large mission station. Happily, their assignment was to rural evangelism. In addition, Glenn planned and supervised the building of Ekuphileni Bible School (established to train African students for the ministry), where the family found a home base. Beth found rural evangelism a "rich experience" (one of her most frequent expressions). As they visited outstations and villages, they witnessed people opening their hearts to God's love, some "backsliders" returning, believers studying the Bible, and parents enthusiastically attending Family Life Conferences they offered at outstation schools. They held occasional retreats for local pastors and the regular evangelists (some of whom traveled and camped with Beth and Glenn) during which they offered encouragement, Bible study, and guidance. Beth described the couple's lifestyle, now mainly as campers: "We started with a tent, which was pitched at every new place where we stayed for meetings, village visitation, and teaching. In about 1967 we were assigned to Mobile Bible School, for which we spent four weeks at each place. At this time, a small trailer was considered more appropriate than the tent. It was a blessing to be able to cook at table level rather than in a three-legged pot on the ground. We were almost embarrassed by the trailer, which seemed so plush next to many of the homes of our African friends."

She and Glenn can be pictured walking into a village, being offered stools or a grass mat in the shade of a tree, and exchanging greetings in Sindebele. Beth recalled the gentle opening of a typical conversation that had a clear-cut agenda.

After a proper pause, the Freys would tell why they had come. "We are looking for people."

"Yes."

"Yes, we want to tell them of Jesus. Do you know him?"

"No, we don't know him."

"Would you like to hear of him?"

"Yes, you could tell us of him."

And Beth and Glenn would tell the gospel story. All sat quietly. Then came the question: "Father, would you like to give your heart to Jesus?" Both father and mother gave their hearts to Jesus and came to the afternoon Bible study and to church the next morning, all aglow.[5] This work of being present and available "out among the people" made the last full term in Rhodesia probably the most rewarding one for Beth.

Beth's love of the native Rhodesian people was deep, born with her, nurtured through lifelong friendships. Her love was not an idea or an ideal, but an attachment that was part of who she was. Bekitemba Dube has told of the funeral of his grandmother Ziga Sibanda (nee Ndlovu) shortly before Beth and Glenn left the country. Bekitemba had just finished high school. Imbued with the highly politicized views of the late 1960s and early 1970s, he had come to expect little real good from the whites in his homeland. At his grandmother's funeral, however, he saw Beth crying openly, and recognized that her grief was real. He describes how this was like a window opening for him at that moment, an illustration that the radical politics he had learned during his high school years did not necessarily apply to all white people. Naka Bekitemba (his mother) and Beth were such close friends that Bekitemba came to think of Beth as his "umama omdala," that is, "elder mother" all his life.[6]

The Family in the United States

In 1971, Laureen was ready for college. Beth had always been determined that the whole family would return to live in the United States when this time came. So they left Africa, where most of Beth's life had been spent. The family settled into Glenn's family home at Washington Boro, Pennsylvania, for probably the most difficult adjustment Beth ever made. She said years later that she was "feeling like an alien." Not only that, but now there was a whole family to care for, along with the work of visiting congregations. Teaching part time at Messiah College helped Beth feel more at home.

Always sensitive to the human need of the moment, she responded in 1974 to the flight of Vietnamese refugees, thousands of whom were placed at Fort Indiantown Gap, in Lebanon County, Pennsylvania. Beth welcomed interested persons to go with her week after week to help at the bases in whatever ways possible. Her heart was soon touched and won by two teenaged sisters and their brother. Within weeks, Nga, Nam, and Hong Nguyen came to live as part of Beth and Glenn's family for several years. Even after the Nguyens moved out into their own homes and lived in Florida, the bond remained strong between them and their American mom and dad.

Glenn was called to be interim pastor of the Speedwell Heights Brethren in Christ Church in Lititz, Pennsylvania. This was an assignment that was at first a struggle, but was finally rewarding for both Glenn and Beth. Many lasting friendships were formed there. Beth was settling in, but she needed some challenge that would ground her further in the familiar yet unfamiliar environment of central Pennsylvania. She enrolled in the master of psychology program at Millersville State University. She would write, "Launching into academia U.S.A. 36 years after I had completed college was a traumatic venture. It was, however, a broadening and stabilizing factor. I rubbed shoulders with the non-Christian group. I learned to communicate with folks 'out there' and found that I could hold my own as an ordinary person in the marketplace." She had gone to graduate school with the goal of personal growth, but the master's degree she earned in 1979 was soon to play a significant part in the next stage of Beth and Glenn's life.

Paxton Street Home

The new creative venture that Beth now entered was the creation of a home in Harrisburg, Pennsylvania, for disadvantaged people. The location was the former Messiah Home, a retirement center which in 1978 had moved close to Mechanicsburg, Pennsylvania, and was now known as Messiah Village. In 1980 the property in Harrisburg came back to the trustees of Messiah Village because the buyer had not paid the mortgage.

Beth describes how she and others became involved in the new project: "At this time, a number of concerned people with me among them felt that the old building would be an excellent facility, if refurbished, in which to start a home for disadvantaged persons. Everyone agreed that it would be good, but the bottom line was dollars and cents. The ad hoc committee that was formed was granted permission to work on the building, pending a decision as to disposition by the Board of Benevolence in July. Volunteers cleaned, repaired, and kept 24-hour security on the place. In July, the board inspected the building, affirmed the work done, then voted to sell it. We were alarmed and dismayed, even though we had known this could happen."

Within two days, the team came to the conclusion that they must incorporate and try to buy the building, with a down payment of $100,000 within three months. The Village board voted to let these five dreamers try. Amazingly and miraculously, the money was given, the last of it arriving just hours before the deadline. The group of five and the Village board agreed: Paxton Street Home would open, and would pay a further $400,000 within four years. Beth continues: "As we faced opening, we were informed that we must have on staff a mental health professional with a graduate degree in a mental health field. There I was, with my M.S. in psychology. I had not had a 'heavenly vision,' but I had followed a strong inner urge. I was humbled to realize that though I had not sought it, I was prepared to step into an administrative role. The procuring of staffing, furniture, and utensils would fill several chapters. God was faithful. The support from the local organizations and foundations after we got started was a saga of its own. To God be the glory!"

Beth and Glenn moved into the building as soon as the first deadline was reached, and launched into a vigorous campaign of recruiting volunteers, going from church to church, calling everyone they knew. Beth had the gift of communicating both a vision (in this case, for the poor and disadvantaged) and the practical needs its realization entailed. Her words, her energy, and her commitment had the effect of galvanizing people to join the work—to give time, material goods, or money. Glenn would say, "Beth gets the vision, and I help her realize it." As the supervisor of maintenance, Glenn worked tirelessly and oversaw scores of volunteers in the task of restoring the building to a habitable state. His attention to details and his quiet, gentle approach to people were a great support and balance to Beth's role. Her reliance on him for innumerable details is suggested by a note she wrote on the back of a framed picture that hung in their bedroom at Paxton Street Home: "Dearest, Would you please change the eyelets and wire. I L U."

Beth, as director, shaped a program for a community that was Christ-centered, recognized the dignity of every person, and gave those who needed it a home, where they were cherished as members of a family. In readying the big building for full occupancy, "everyone cleaned toilets," including the director. For Beth, love was action. She wanted the 80-room house to be clean and beautiful, each resident having his or her own room with curtains made for it. Meals were to be served in a dining room in which flowers were placed on each table, along with china and new flatware.

In every way possible, staff members were to recognize the dignity of each resident. Beth did not care about her degree in psychology, or the directorship. What mattered was that the people be loved and be given a chance to know the Lord. In all her dealings with state agencies, Beth was forthright about this being a Christian home. She gave psychology short shrift most of the time, focusing her efforts on persuading people that Jesus was the answer for their needs, sometimes seeming almost relentless in her efforts. Much to the staff's relief, she would rely to some extent on a professional psychiatric nurse or social worker to bring the necessary perspective to working with some of the mentally ill residents.

That Beth's single-mindedness bore fruit may be illustrated in the story of Dwight. Dwight was an angry, bitter, profane, older man, who spat constantly, verbally and literally. He became critically ill and was hospitalized. Beth visited him and said, "Dwight, you are dying." He agreed. For the last of innumerable times, Beth asked Dwight if he wanted to ask Jesus to come into his heart. Dwight prayed with Beth for Christ to be his savior. He died two or three days later, but even the nurses remarked on the complete transformation in Dwight, from anger and harshness to joy and courtesy.

If Beth erred, it was on the side of grace, always giving residents the benefit of the doubt, expecting and looking for improvement. As Roanne Funk, a psychiatric nurse on staff in the first years, states, "Beth had high expectations for people, high expectations of herself, and high expectations of God. She believed God was able to do anything." According to Brian Funk, a member of the staff, even when the needs of a prospective resident's mental health were clearly beyond the extent of the staff's preparation, she was not inclined to turn anyone away at the beginning.

The rule was that new residents would not be admitted on the weekends, when only a skeleton staff was on duty. Brian and Roanne remember a Saturday night when Beth broke this rule and insisted that the couple cooperate with her in admitting a woman—homeless, disturbed, and truly "down and out"—when she came to the door. Beth could be powerful in getting what she wanted from all people—when she was convinced that it was the right thing to do—calling into force all her considerable verbal gifts of persuasion and persistence. Brian and Roanne went along with her intention this time, against their better judgment. Such was Beth's commitment to the purpose of the home that staff members did not want to disappoint her. However, her will could not always dictate or override decisions that staff needed to make in their personal lives. Beth could hardly bear it when Roanne left Paxton Street Home at the time of the birth of her first child, but Roanne was firm in her decision, and Beth accepted it.

Gradually, as the home grew and gained psychiatric professionals on staff, admission could become more focused and more closely considered. Still, there were times when the fit was not good and did not improve. Beth hated confrontation, hated to tell any resident that they must leave the home. But it was sometimes necessary to do so, thus she did what she so often did—recognized a gift in someone that could meet a need. In this case, it was Brian, who was kitchen manager and became in many ways Beth's right hand in dealing with difficulties with residents, because he had a gift of handling people, saying hard things in gentle, non-antagonistic ways. Beth freed Brian so he could recognize and expand his innate talents as a communicator and a leader.

She gave trusted staff members freedom to shape their parts of the program, set standards, and make decisions. The entire staff began the workday with an hour of group devotions, led by each person in turn, in which they shared needs, supported and cared for each other, and sang together. Beth held staff needs as priority, and nurtured members in the motherly way she had with anyone whom she recognized was hurting or in need. While expecting the best of people, including herself, Beth did not expect perfection. As she often said, "We all have our feet of clay."

Beth's mind was active, constantly engaged, learning, connecting, looking about at the world, reading, writing articles for the denominational magazine, the *Evangelical Visitor*, and writing many letters. It was difficult for her to realize that some things, such as choices her children made, were beyond her control and must be let go. Much, if not most of what Beth did—including entertaining in her home—followed an agenda of reaching people for God and for good. She was purposeful, poised for action. She found difficulty in relaxing and often in falling asleep, and in letting her mind rest. Nevertheless, she did not rush; she had personal grace, was calm of speech and movement, and could listen closely to a person and a conversation while, for example, cooking dinner. During her three years as director of Paxton Street Home, she welcomed young people who sought counsel, and spent many hours talking with individuals in her office. Beth continued to grow throughout her entire life, deepening in perception, able to consider, and reconsider, to stretch beyond old ways of thinking and take in new ideas.

At 65, after three years as director, Beth would say, "God clearly said to me, 'You've done what I sent you to do; move over.'" Her legacy and Glenn's live on at Paxton Ministries, which in June of 2001 celebrated its twentieth anniversary.

Youngways Guest House

Following their service at Paxton Street Home, Beth and Glenn returned to what was now called Zimbabwe, responding to Bishop Stephen Ndlovu's invitation to refurbish and run another building, the former Youngways Hostel, as a guesthouse for travelers through Bulawayo. They spent what she called three "rich" years there, greatly enjoying the country and people after an absence of 16 years. Beth wrote in a January 1988 letter to friends and family, "We said we were coming as helpers and we see ourselves in that role. It may be a load of supplies to be taken to the Mtshabezi Hospital, a supply of groceries to feed a volunteer group, helping fellow workers get settled in, or listening as a coworker shares burdens and then praying together. We enjoy the 'crowds' who come through the home and then we enjoy the days of tranquility to catch our breath and do a few more needed things before the next group."[7]

Beth also saw the stopovers of executives from para-church organizations at the guest house as "frequently a cause of blessing to the Brethren in Christ Church itself." Beth and Glenn, with their years of experience and old friendships, now living in a new Zimbabwe with majority rule and a shrunken missionary presence, were "the force that is bringing the expatriates—and the Africans in many cases—together," commented church leader Owen Alderfer and his wife, Ardis. The Alderfers called Beth and Glenn "the glue that binds the individuals into community."[8] The Freys left their beloved Africa, finally, and returned to live in Pennsylvania at Messiah Village in 1990.

Continued Service in Retirement

Beth and Glenn were happy in their version of retirement, enjoying their children and grandchildren, and delighting in the community of friends, many of them former co-workers on the mission field. Their children teased them about their social whirl, as they were usually entertaining or being entertained, had just begun serving as deacons at the nearby Grantham Brethren in Christ Church, and were involved in a small-group Bible study. They provided a home away from home by opening their basement apartment to missionaries on furlough and friends passing through, and were open to all requests for counsel.

Saturday morning, May 29, 1993, Beth served a bountiful breakfast to four guests. It was a joyful occasion in which the conversation centered on heaven, and on the expectation of seeing one another and loved ones there. Beth and Glenn then packed up and left for New York, where they were to attend a wedding. (The bride was the granddaughter of their old friends, the Winchees, a Chinese couple who had operated a store at Stanmore Siding, a few miles from Mtshabezi Mission.) Around noon, their car inexplicably crashed into the abutment of a bridge near the town of Bethel in Berks County. Beth died instantaneously, and Glenn followed her ten hours later.

In the days and years since their deaths, the shock to friends and family of the double loss may have softened, but the gap their deaths left remains. Their absence is a sorrow, especially for their children who are the parents of five grandchildren, two of whom Glenn and Beth never met. Their deaths were mourned by those who had known them, in Zimbabwe as fully as in the United States.

Beth lived in a variety of places and among a broad range of people, but her life was bounded by certain loyalties and loves. She was born and reared in the Brethren in Christ Church, first in Africa, on the mission station to which she returned as an adult. Here she married Glenn Frey and worked together with him, and here their four children were born. In addition to missions and Africa, Beth had a heart for the poor and disadvantaged, eyes that recognized the social need in the world around her, and the will and energy to respond. She was committed to family and friends, most of whom were within the Brethren in Christ Church. She worked hard and was gifted, but it was God's working through her that enabled her to overcome limitations and even to surpass herself.

Mopping Up and Moving On

Dorothy Jean Gish

by Anna M. Yeatts*

In November 1993, Dorothy Gish spent two weeks in Tahiti taking a much needed rest and contemplating her future. That fall, Messiah College, where she was associate dean for faculty development, had unexpectedly lost its academic dean. Dorothy had been picking up that work as well as managing her own responsibilities, resulting in an exhausting semester. Before she left for Tahiti, the college president, D. Ray Hostetter, had asked Dorothy to be acting dean of the college. This would not be an easy task: the college faculty was divided; hurt and distrust reigned. Dorothy was happy in her current position and reluctant to assume a new, difficult assignment.

With the need to make an important decision in mind, Dorothy embarked on the trip to Tahiti not only to rest and recuperate, but also to take time to seek God's guidance about the job offer. Several times in the past, when Dorothy had been asked to take challenging assignments, she had set aside time to look for God's leading. She accepted new positions only when she was certain they were God's call. This response had become a pattern in her life.[1]

---

*An active member of the Grantham Brethren in Christ Church, Anna M. Yeatts works part time in the college day-care and is an adjunct faculty member in the Department of Biblical and Religious Studies. Through teaching in the Messiah College community, Anna became acquainted with Dorothy Gish.

Birth of a Traveler

Tahiti is a long way from Messiah College, but by 1993 Dorothy was a seasoned world traveler. Her passion for traveling, however, was not ignited until young adulthood. During her sophomore year of college, she ventured out of Pennsylvania for the first time when she traveled to New York City. Through subsequent trips, Dorothy learned to appreciate the richness of other cultures, and international travel became one of her passions. Her first trip abroad was on a freighter to South Africa as a new missionary in 1958; many trips followed, so that by the time she retired in 1998 she had visited more than 80 countries.

Dorothy began her life in rural Lebanon County, Pennsylvania. Born on June 9, 1935, Dorothy Jean Gish was the oldest of six children. Since her last three siblings were born between her eleventh and fifteenth birthdays, she remembers providing care for them. In fact, her sister Karen Sellers says that people sometimes assumed Dorothy was the mother of their sister Mary because she was always taking care of her.

Dorothy remembers "always cleaning up" in her childhood; she enjoyed organizing and rearranging her room. Rather than playing with dolls, Dorothy climbed trees, built with lumber, and played store, putting the merchandise in order. She preferred working in the house to farm work. Karen remembers that Dorothy was always reading; a nearby woods, with a small stream which had big rocks to sit upon, was a favorite reading place.

Academic and Spiritual Growth

Although education became Dorothy's life work, her formal schooling began somewhat haltingly and required many adjustments. During first grade she broke her leg by falling down a coal chute and missed six weeks of school; then she got chicken pox and missed another two weeks. By the time she finished grades seven and eight in one year, she had moved with her family three times, changing schools with each move and attending a one-room school at one point. Eventually, Dorothy enrolled at Hershey High School, where she was placed in the top college preparatory section. Even as she excelled in her studies, she floundered socially at times. She was the only farm girl in her section, rode the bus, and wore the customary prayer covering of her church. At times she felt like the only Christian at school. With these differences to set her apart, Dorothy experienced lonely high school years. The one person with whom she could identify was Ruth Eckert Engle, a Brethren in Christ classmate and friend from Lawn, Pennsylvania.

During these years, Dorothy began the practice of an early morning quiet time when the rest of the family was working in the barn and she was alone in the house. Dorothy recalls, "It was hard. We didn't have central heat and the house was cold." Early morning devotions have remained an important discipline in Dorothy's spiritual life.

As a young child, Dorothy attended the United Christian Church. Dorothy's friend Mary Jane Davis, who also grew up in the United Christian Church in Lebanon County, remembers their culture as rural and agricultural and not particularly valuing education, especially for women. Within this context, Dorothy later proved to be an exception to the church's expectations for women by pursuing further education.

When the family moved to a rural area near the town of Palmyra, Dorothy's grandmother, who was a member of the local Brethren in Christ Church, introduced Dorothy to her denomination. Attending this church, Dorothy, a fifth-grader at the time, developed a close relationship with her Sunday school teacher, Catherine Basehore Hoffman, who took an interest in her, invited her to tea, and had a great impact on Dorothy's spiritual formation. Dorothy became a committed Christian teenager who later joined the Shenk's Brethren in Christ Church, regularly read the Bible, listened to "Back to the Bible" on the radio, and anticipated a life of Christian service. A missionary to China quickened her interest in missions and opened her to the possibility of education for service.

In 1952, after Dorothy graduated from high school at age 16, she had hopes for further education in preparation for mission work. Finances proved to be a daunting obstacle: her parents, who had six children, three under age six, were in no position to offer financial help for Dorothy's education. She had been accepted at Prairie Bible Institute in Alberta, Canada, an adventurous option for an almost-seventeen-year-old who had never before traveled outside of Pennsylvania. Yet she needed to work for a year to finance her education. Her first job at a shoe factory was soon followed by one in which she cleaned and later sold chickens.

Before the year was over, Jacob Kuhns, a faculty member at Messiah College, learned of Dorothy's ambitions and offered her a scholarship to the college, which at that time was a two-year institution. Dorothy accepted, then completed a bachelor's degree in 1957 at Greenville College in Illinois, with dual majors in psychology/education and philosophy/religion, including Greek courses.

Education in a Different Field

Dorothy had an interest in going to Cuba as a missionary, but when that door was closed by Fidel Castro's communist revolution, the Brethren in Christ Mission Board invited her to teach in Africa. As became her pattern, Dorothy accepted this new challenge but asked for one year to prepare for it.

After interviewing at two local school districts, she was offered a teaching position by both, beginning what would become another pattern in her professional life: not seeking employment but having the Lord open doors to professional positions. In her class in the Elizabethtown (Pennsylvania) School District, Dorothy had 40 first-graders "straight off the farm." Her two goals for the year were that her students would like school and learn to follow directions. Returning to the area in later years, Dorothy was gratified to discover that almost all of these first-graders had graduated from high school even though they could have dropped out at age 16 to work on the farm.

With her year of teaching and preparation completed, 23-year-old Dorothy left the United States for Northern Rhodesia, Africa, in the summer of 1958. She immediately began service as headmistress at the Macha Secondary Girls' School. Henry Hostetter, executive secretary of Brethren in Christ Missions, had instructed Dorothy that her task in Africa was "to work yourself out of a job." Six and one-half years later, when Northern Rhodesia became an independent nation and was re-named Zambia in 1964, she had done just that by turning her work over to Zambian teachers she had mentored. A new chapter of her life was about to begin.

Dorothy returned to Pennsylvania, and, after working for part of one year, began graduate school at Pennsylvania State University in September 1965. She won an assistantship to fund her studies and managed to save money. When she received her master's degree, Dorothy was not ready to go directly into doctoral studies. True to her pattern, she needed time to make this personal transition. She returned to Zambia for two years of voluntary service as hostel mistress and teacher of English and Bible at Choma Secondary School.

Then she returned to Penn State with a scholarship to pay the bills, and completed the course work for her doctorate in a short time: two calendar years. Dorothy was honored to be selected to pioneer a new way of taking comprehensive doctoral examinations at Penn State. After an intense summer of 18-hour days, she completed her dissertation, and in 1971, was awarded a Ph.D. in child development and family relationships.

A Domestic Faculty Appointment

Dorothy easily found a professional position after graduate school. Penn State, Messiah College, and a school in the Midwest each offered her a job. She was not ready to leave Penn State, so the day after she defended her dissertation she joined the faculty there. After one year, Kenneth Hoover, a chair of the Division of Natural Sciences at Messiah College, invited her to join his division's faculty. He gave her "a vision of what a department chair could be," and in 1972 Dorothy decided to accept the challenge of heading the Department of Home Economics at Messiah College.

Not considering herself a domestic person—she doesn't like to cook or sew—the idea of chairing this department seemed humorous to Dorothy. Affirming this self-assessment, her sister Karen remembers sharing a meal Dorothy had prepared during the time she was studying at Penn State. Later, Dorothy called to ask if the family was ill. After they left, she realized that she had forgotten to remove the plastic film from a casserole dish, and they had eaten corn with plastic melted into it. Fortunately, everyone was fine.

Even though she was not a natural homemaker, Dorothy brought comprehensive educational training to her new position. She began the Early Childhood Education Laboratory School, a day-care which gives Messiah College students who are majoring in early childhood education hands-on experience. After five years of chairing the Department of Home Economics, Dorothy accepted a newly defined position as chair of the Department of Behavioral Studies.

Taking the Helm at Critical Moments

Dorothy had served in that role for two years when she began the "worst year" of her professional life in the fall of 1979. Unlike other transitions in her life, Dorothy had no time to prepare herself for this challenge. The dean of students left suddenly, and Academic Dean David Brandt asked Dorothy to serve as acting dean of students. Dean Brandt remembers that prior to Dorothy's leadership the student life office had been loosely run with little control. He had confidence both that Dorothy understood student life and that she could effectively manage an office.

As she took on this new role, Dorothy intentionally became a visible presence on campus: she moved her office near the dining room, ate with students, and set out to act redemptively rather than punitively. Dean Brandt notes that she developed a system for dealing with student offenses. When Jay Barnes, the newly hired dean of students, began his work in the fall of 1980, she was ready to pass on to him a strong office.

"Mop up and move on" is one way Dorothy describes her professional career. She had "mopped up" the dean of students' office and was ready to "move on" to a sabbatical researching stress in missionaries. Using the Birkman Personality Test, which identifies stress responses, Dorothy studied workers from Brethren in Christ missions, Mennonite Central Committee (MCC), and Wycliffe Bible Translators. Her research took her to interview missionaries in Canada, Japan, Australia, Zambia, Zimbabwe, Bolivia, and Brazil. She also led seminars in Hong Kong and Thailand. During that year, Dorothy paid for her own travel, and other expenses, with the mission agencies picking her up at airports and providing room and board. The result of all this work was an article, "Sources of Missionary Stress," published in the *Journal of Psychology and Theology* in 1983, which has been reprinted several times and has served as the basis for several master's theses.

Upon her return in 1981 to Messiah College following her sabbatical, the pattern of the Lord opening doors to new professional positions continued when she was asked to be the assistant dean for faculty growth and development. During the previous year, merit pay, which bases salary increases on faculty members' performance, had been awarded to some faculty members, resulting in hurt and faculty distrust of the administration. The Messiah College Board of Trustees called for an evaluation system which would be the basis for merit pay, and yet realized that it was not fair to evaluate the faculty without offering opportunities for development.

As she did as acting dean of students, Dorothy would need to "establish order and build bridges." She began with conversations at the departmental level about what it meant to teach at Messiah College. After a year of discussion, she led the effort to establish a paradigm for faculty evaluation which is still in use today. Academic Dean David Brandt remembers how much Dorothy's work in faculty development improved the quality of teaching at Messiah College. He says, "She salvaged some faculty members. She is a great mentor who takes people from where they are to where they want to be."

Dorothy also focused on improving the way faculty members advise students. With colleague Donna Dentler she developed advisee guidebooks which the National Student Advising Association recognized in the "best printed material" category. David Brandt evaluates the work of Dorothy and Donna as a great contribution toward Messiah College's quality education. Dorothy soon took on additional responsibilities as the full-time associate dean for faculty development. Once again, Dorothy had "mopped up and moved on."

Important Relationships

When she first came to Messiah College, Dorothy was able to purchase a house on campus, which she has used to nurture and maintain personal connections with a wide range of people. She has always had students living with her, and several of these have become family. Bob Vanderhof, one of the students who lived in her house, still calls Dorothy "Mom." When his daughter came to Messiah as a student, Dorothy met with her weekly for Bible study.

Fellistus Munakombwe, a student from Zambia, lived with Dorothy all four years of college, and they developed a strong, warm mutual regard. Fellistus even persuaded Dorothy to join her in spending Christmas Eve in sleeping bags on the living room floor awaiting Santa's arrival. Although there was one difficult student, whom she does not name, Dorothy asserts that it is "easy to get set in one's ways, and kids keep the rough edges knocked off. They have added richness to my life."

While Dorothy's professional life seems to have evolved naturally, with only the expected stresses that come with increasing responsibility, she met with difficult personal tragedy when her mother was killed in a truck accident in 1985. Her sister Karen Sellers recalls that Dorothy is tempered like their mother; they were the ones in the family always "running here and there, *schushlich*," as the Pennsylvania Dutch would say. Mary Jane Davis observes that although Dorothy's mother appeared plain and rural, Dorothy saw in her a "flamboyant heart; she liked nice things and was proud of Dorothy. She was not that old when she died, and it was really hard on Dorothy." A lovely backyard garden at Dorothy's house is named "Leah D^3 Garden" in honor of her mother and three other people. Here Dorothy enjoys entertaining and has hosted several meals for her mother's brothers and sisters.

Even as Dorothy coped with personal loss, she continued to enjoy her work at Messiah College. Dorothy had good mentors. When she was acting dean of students and assistant dean for faculty growth and development, she and David Brandt developed an easy rapport. He loved ideas. They had complementary strengths. He remembers his collaboration with Dorothy as a partnership that worked well. While she was associate dean, Dick Gross, the president of Gordon College, served as a mentor. He told her she should not work all the time, but take time for herself. Dorothy took this advice to heart, and for a number of years Thursday morning was Dorothy's time at home for personal tasks and projects. Then came the difficult fall of 1993.

Dorothy's Career in the Mature Years

After a two-week retreat in Tahiti, Dorothy returned to Messiah College to answer the call to become acting dean of the college. Dorothy agreed to accept the assignment if the faculty would give her a vote of confidence. The response was an overwhelming 85 percent in support of her. So Dorothy served as acting dean for the last year of D. Ray Hostetter's presidency.

Dorothy remembers her first few years as dean as a time of intense spiritual growth. She had many difficulties with which to deal, and, as she continued her regular Bible study, numbers of times the scriptures related directly to the issues with which she was dealing. "It was exciting." She wondered, "Lord, what are you going to tell me next?" Her prayer became, "Lord, I can't, but you can. Let's go!"

In August 1994, Rodney Sawatsky became the new president of Messiah College and Dorothy continued as acting dean. She eventually was appointed academic dean and then vice president for academic affairs. Of her many contributions to Messiah College, Dorothy is probably most pleased with playing a key role in increasing faculty diversity. With this goal in mind, she and other colleagues at the college added 20 new faculty members, increasing gender diversity of the faculty by 60 percent, ethnic diversity by 20 percent, and age diversity by 50 percent (with the addition of younger faculty members).

Reflecting on her career, Dorothy expands on the idea of "mop up and move on." Much of her work has been done "at the vortex of institutional change." When she left both Macha Girls' School and Choma Secondary School, national teachers assumed leadership of the institution. Her doctoral comprehensive examinations opened a new way of doing such exams. As acting dean of students at Messiah College, she organized that office before the new dean arrived. Serving as assistant dean, she helped move the faculty from distrust to trust, and as academic dean she helped move the campus from fragmentation to cohesiveness. She learned to "conceptualize and implement new programs and then turn them over to someone else and keep my hands off." Dorothy summarizes her work: "Build on the past. Work on the difficult present. Empower someone else for the future."

At times as an administrator at Messiah College, Dorothy carried out team decisions which were not her choice. It was hard to end the Elderhostel program she had begun many years before, the Department of Home Economics where her Messiah College career began, the STEPS program she had started for underprivileged high school students at Messiah's Philadelphia campus, and the Adult Degree Completion program which had begun under her leadership. These were not directions Dorothy chose, but as an administrator she carried out team decisions.

Singleness, Relationships, and Vocation

Through all of the challenges and opportunities of her life, Dorothy has remained single. She has never, however, felt called to singleness. In fact, she was engaged to be married when she first went to Africa. Dorothy has had other special male friends over the years. She explains, "I did not say 'I'll never marry,' but I also think it's just as binding to say 'I have to marry.' If there's a man around that I could help serve the Lord more effectively and he could help me be more effective, I'd be very interested. All my life I've tried to walk through the open doors and be where the Lord wants me to be, so I've been busy doing what I needed to do. . . . "

Her good friend Mary Holland observes, tapping the table for emphasis, that over the years many men have loved Dorothy, and she has loved them and enjoyed their company. Nevertheless, she has followed her calling, and, when marriage would hinder her calling, she has said "no" to marriage.

Dorothy understands that it is difficult to feel whole as a single person in contemporary society. Weddings are hard; she still doesn't enjoy going to them by herself. Churches can be lonely places for singles; sitting alone can be uncomfortable. It often takes initiative to find someone with whom to do things. Yet Dorothy recognizes that the ideal person does not exist, and there are always trade-offs.

Nevertheless, over her lifetime, it has been difficult at times to understand why the Lord has seemed to say that others may marry but has never provided someone for her. That she has grappled with these issues is evident in the number of articles Dorothy has written on singleness over the years.[2]

In her life as a single person, Dorothy has nurtured close family connections. All of her siblings are married and live in Lebanon County, closer to Dorothy at Messiah College than any other place she has resided. When she's not traveling, she calls one or more of her siblings every Sunday afternoon "to chat and keep in touch." While teaching child development, she used her nieces and nephews as live illustrations in class, and niece Crystal lived with Dorothy for three years when she was a student at Messiah College. During summers, Dorothy hosted family picnics. On one occasion, the entertainment was tubing on the Yellow Breeches Creek for all 15 to 20 relatives including her father, who was in his seventies at the time.

Family members, including brother David and his wife, Pauline, have joined her on several trips. Dorothy's mother liked to travel, and, not long before her death, Dorothy took her parents on a trip to the South. Her three sisters all have October birthdays, and every year they look forward to Dorothy's surprise celebration. Her treats have included an ethnic meal, a bed and breakfast overnight, a massage and manicure, and a theatrical production.

Dorothy's role in the family has also been spiritual in nature. She read scripture in both a niece's and a nephew's wedding and performed the homily in her brother David's wedding. When the family was gathered around her father's deathbed, Dorothy prayed as he passed from this life into the next. Her sister Karen says, "Dorothy does a lot for the family."

She nurtures relationships with friends too. Mary Jane Davis remembers that when she began her ministry at the Grantham Church, Dorothy invited her to become a prayer partner. For 17 years they met weekly to share and pray in an accountability relationship which has evolved into an intimate friendship. When Megan, the daughter of Mary Jane, was serving with Mennonite Central Committee in Thailand, Dorothy took Mary Jane and her other daughter, Lynsey, to visit Megan. Her first overseas travel, Mary Jane laughingly recalls the experience as "a whirlwind trip." Mary Holland, who ministers to her family and church as a volunteer, has been Dorothy's daily walking partner for the last six years. Both of these women value Dorothy's caring affirmation of their very different roles.

Dorothy's recreational travel frequently has centered around friendship and missions interests as well. Knowing it is difficult for single missionaries to find travel partners, Dorothy has had the practice of inviting a woman missionary to join her for a vacation, subsidizing the cost as a gift to her companion.

Throughout her life, Dorothy has continued the practice of daily Bible study and prayer that she began as a new Christian in high school. Fellistus Munakombwe reports with awe that Dorothy gets up every morning, even Saturdays, at six o'clock to study and pray, not because she needs something, but because of the love God has given her. Mary Holland notes that, during their walks together, Dorothy frequently makes natural, spontaneous references to God based on her quiet time, and that Dorothy's Bible studies are organized and intentional, focused on unlocking the meaning of the passage rather than reflective journaling. Her former pastor Kenneth Hoke adds that she has notebooks filled with observations from her personal Bible studies and is knowledgeable when she speaks on an issue.

Commitment to Church

Dorothy takes her church affiliations seriously. Kenneth Hoke observes that if she is in town on Sundays, she is at the Carlisle Brethren in Christ Church, listening actively to the sermon and sometimes giving written feedback to the pastor on the way out. She has served her congregation as a board member, long-range planner, teacher, and small-group member. Over 20 years ago, she helped begin a nursery school in the church that continues to the present day.

Dorothy is willing to challenge and give constructive advice if it is needed. Ken Hoke gratefully admits to being sensitized to use inclusive language. Mary Jane Davis says that, although Dorothy is not a licensed minister, she has been a leader in the Brethren in Christ denomination. She has preached in many churches and even at General Conference. Younger women in the church look to her as a role model, and she affirms and encourages those who choose to serve.

Dorothy intentionally affiliated with the Brethren in Christ denomination. She appreciated that, as a young missionary, she did not have the burden of raising her own financial support.

Later, Brethren in Christ Missions provided helpful assistance during her year of research on missionary stress. She found, however, that on the mission field the executive board was much too dominated by males. Dorothy appreciates that the Brethren in Christ Church does not deliberately limit women; yet, she is disappointed that more progress has not been made in placing women in ministry positions.

As she reflects on her life, Dorothy offers advice to "anyone"—"male, female, married, single, whatever culture." She says, "The fact that God loves us and calls us to be his, that's a tremendous privilege. My advice would be don't wait for the future; live each moment to the full, not out of legalistic compulsion but out of sheer love for Christ, doing what you see the need to do at that time. Not saying, 'I'll do it tomorrow,' nor saying, 'Does this get me where I want to go?' You do need to be goal oriented, but I think you also need to be sensitive to the opportunities of the moment. I think you do not dwell on the mistakes of the past. Hopefully, you learn from them. And you don't live in the future, saying, 'Hopefully, next year this will happen or I'm going to wait until this happens.' You learn from the past, live in the present, and make plans for the future. Or I would say, 'You commit the future to the Lord.'"

Retirement: Living in Expectancy and Obedience

Having lived in high gear all of her life, moving quickly from one task to another, Dorothy faces a new challenge since her retirement in May 1998. She prayed for one year of rest before moving on to new responsibilities, but, after that year, no doors opened for her. Although she loves what she is doing each day, nothing big has emerged, and she wonders, "What am I supposed to do?" The answer seems to be to focus on "being," and to keep doing what she is doing. Her days are filled. She has taken two Brethren in Christ core courses and some Spanish classes at Messiah College. She has time for entertaining and has begun square dance classes. There is a stack of books to be read. Yet the big assignment has not materialized. Perhaps retirement is to be a time of service to boards. Currently, Dorothy is on at least seven boards and works on several committees, as well. Whatever direction her retirement eventually takes, Dorothy is certain she wants to do something more substantive than playing golf and tennis during the day and cards in the evening. So she lives in expectation, her future committed to the Lord, ready to enter the next door God opens.

Keeping the Family Together

Elsie Detweiler Underkoffler Hahn

by Pauline Nigh Hogan*

Elsie Detweiler was not an extraordinary woman. Her story is not unlike that of many other women who simply do their best, with faith and courage, to face the uncertainties life brings. But Elsie lived in a time of great change within the Brethren in Christ Church, and because of her particular circumstances, her story became intertwined with the history of the church in Canada. Moreover, as her children grew up and began to scatter across the continent, she kept her family together with frequent letters, filled with lively observations and frank opinions about church and community life. These letters testify to the heritage she passed on—no material wealth, but wisdom and compassion and a deep conviction that what is of true value is love of family and one's neighbors.

Happiness and Sorrow in Pennsylvania

Elsie grew up in the heartland of Mennonite and Brethren in Christ territory in Pennsylvania, with three sisters—Ruth, Mary Lizzie, and Emma. A brother, Jacob, died at the age of four. With their parents, Isaac and Annie (Heckler), they attended Souderton Mennonite Church. Isaac was a laborer who worked in a local cigar factory.

*Pauline Hogan is a Ph.D. student in Religious Studies at McMaster University in Hamilton, Ontario, and is active at the Falls View Brethren in Christ Church in music ministry and teaching junior high school students. She is the granddaughter of Elsie Hahn.

While still only a teenager, Elsie fell in love with a handsome local lad named Watson Underkoffler. She was 17 at her wedding in 1898; her groom was only 18.

The young couple started their life together with high hopes, but their marriage seemed to be dogged by tragedy. They rejoiced in the birth of their first child, Paul, and then wept together when he succumbed to fever and convulsions before he was two. A daughter was born, whom they named Beulah. This child, too, they lost to childhood illness. Years later, Elsie wrote about her feelings during these sorrowful days: "I know all about the heartaches the empty crib brings and the clothes and toys that must be put away. . . . When my first little boy died I felt as if everything was gone out of my life. But yet we cannot stop; we must keep on. Then when my next baby died I broke up housekeeping and went to work in the factory. It was too lonesome and quiet." [1]

Work in the cigar factory provided distraction for Elsie, as well as ammunition for warning tales later on. Learning that cheaper quality cigars were stuffed with the bits that were swept off the floor was enough to convince young listeners never to try smoking one.

But soon another child was born, and Elsie happily returned to mothering a little boy again. The couple bought a house, and little Willard survived the dangers of infancy. He was a healthy three-year-old and Elsie was seven months pregnant when her husband Watson died suddenly. At 26, with no savings and two small children to provide for, she was dependent on relatives who took her into their home. Eventually she found work as a telephone operator.

Perhaps it was at this point in her life when Elsie began attending the Indian Creek Brethren in Christ Church. We don't know exactly when she made this decision, but we do know that by 1914, along with her son, Willard, and her daughter, Hazel (born in 1907, two months after her father's death), Elsie Underkoffler was living and working at the Messiah Children's Home in Grantham, Pennsylvania, as a staff person. By this time she was a member of the Brethren in Christ Church. Elsie formed what would become a lifelong friendship with Roxy Anger, a young woman who had come from the Bertie congregation in

Ontario, Canada, to work at the Home. Her friendship would prove to be instrumental in a dramatic change in Elsie's life.

From Pennsylvania to Saskatchewan

The setting for this change was the new province of Saskatchewan, in Canada, still very much in its pioneering, often difficult years. In the early years of the twentieth century, a spirit of migration was stirring among the adventurous people of the eastern United States and Canada. Canada was opening up the West for settlers, and land was available for homesteading at nominal cost to anyone with a pioneering spirit.

The first group of Brethren in Christ arrived in Saskatchewan in 1907, under the leadership of Isaac Baker, and chose homesteading land near what is now Kindersley. Isaac and his wife, Leah, are considered the founders of the town; they established some of the first commercial enterprises there. In the next few years, several more families arrived, most, it seemed, from the Stayner area, and many of them related. Among the pioneers were Henry Hahn and his wife, Susanna, Isaac's sister. Henry and Susanna had a large family, many of them already adults, and several accompanied their parents west. Their daughter Lena and her husband, Archie Carmichael, followed her parents to Saskatchewan in 1910.

It was an accomplished group. Archie Carmichael was a schoolteacher and an elder (minister) in the church. Later he became the first schoolteacher in Kindersley, and then the town's first secretary-treasurer when it was incorporated. Eventually he was elected Member of Parliament for Kindersley, which forced him to leave the Brethren in Christ Church because the denomination was opposed to participation in politics. Fred Hahn, one of Henry's sons, became the youngest Brethren in Christ bishop in Canada at the age of 24.[2]

Yet life on the prairie was hard. Both Lena Carmichael and her mother, Susanna, died soon after arriving in the West. Archie needed a mother for his five little ones. In his travels he met Roxy Anger, whom he married in 1915. From Kindersley, Roxy began writing to Elsie, in Grantham, Pennsylvania, about the healthy air and the plentiful jobs available in the Canadian West.

Pennsylvania must have seemed a gloomier place after the energetic and forceful Roxy left. Elsie faced severe financial difficulties; she was forced to allow Willard to leave her and work as a hired hand for a local farmer. In addition, both she and her daughter, Hazel, were diagnosed with incipient tuberculosis. The doctors advised a move west. Elsie considered going to Kansas, where there was another lively Brethren in Christ colony. Roxy's letters were the decisive factor in Elsie's choice of Saskatchewan.

A Second Marriage

She arrived there in 1917, and found work with several families, including the widowed Henry Hahn. In addition to the farmhouse on his homestead, Henry had built a house in town beside that of son-in-law Archie Carmichael, the new husband of Elsie's close friend Roxy. The town and the church soon began to notice that Brother Hahn seemed very taken with Sister Underkoffler. Their friendship became a favorite topic around dinner tables, especially since Henry Hahn was now 67 years old, and Elsie was only 36, younger than many of Henry's children. It was no secret that some of those children were appalled at their father's interest in the young widow. Elsie's daughter, Hazel, secretly thought that if Henry's children hadn't been so openly opposed, her mother, who had a recognized stubborn streak, might have been more reluctant to accept his courting.

In 1919 Elsie agreed to marry Henry. Henry loved children; it was said that his wife never lost a bite of supper because he always fed the babies. Yet he could be strict when the children got older, and young Willard Underkoffler found it too hard to accept him as a new father. Although only 15, he persuaded his mother to allow him to return to Pennsylvania to live with his relatives there. It was a decision Elsie always regretted.

Except for the absence of Willard, Elsie and Hazel found their lives markedly improved in the new family situation. Henry had been a successful farmer, and although he retired into town after his marriage, he continued to plant a huge garden behind the house. He was a gifted gardener, even teaching lessons in gardening at the nearby school. Elsie shared his interest, and she continued to be an avid gardener the rest of her life, enjoying the beauty of the flowers she coaxed out of the prairie soil, and canning multitudes of quarts of vegetables and meat each year.

The family grew with the birth of four more children—Doreen, Roxena (named after Elsie's friend), Harry, and Enid. Elsie's talents in quilting and cooking earned admiration in the community, and the Hahns were often asked to board teachers and to host visiting preachers and missionaries. One year during the influenza epidemic, Elsie was asked to help cook in the schoolhouse, which had been turned into a hospital for victims of the epidemic. As she walked through the empty halls of the old school with her daughter Enid many years later, she said she could still remember the cries of the dying.[3]

Life for the Hahn family revolved around the church. The original meeting place, which had been in a tent and then in a sod hut, was finally replaced by a building on land donated by Isaac Baker. In 1919, however, divisive arguments over sanctification split the Kindersley church. Eventually a group led by Baker withdrew from the Brethren in Christ, but since the meetinghouse stood on his land, the building remained his property.[4] The rest of the Brethren in Christ congregation built a new church, which they called Clearview, outside of town.

Travel to church in the country for Sunday services meant, for town families, battling the snowdrifts in the winter and the incredible, gooey mud in the spring. Prayer meetings were held in various homes, however, and people who lived in town often met in the Hahns' home. In addition to their own events, the Brethren in Christ participated in activities such as Vacation Bible School and young people's meetings with the Free Methodist Church. Often joint prayer meetings were held, and any visiting missionary or evangelist could be assured of attendants from all the churches. Church activities themselves, therefore, could provide a busy social life. In addition, there were visits to make, quilting bees to attend, and any number of the kind of cooperative community events that prairie towns seemed to specialize in.

Hardship and Survival

Life was busy, productive, and comfortable for Elsie until 1931. By then the "dirty thirties" had begun, and the picture of life in the West was no longer so rosy as it had been a few years earlier. Drought threatened crops, wheat prices fell, and jobs became scarce in Kindersley. In the early springtime, Henry died. He was 81; Elsie was now 50. Hazel had become a schoolteacher, and was married in 1930.[5] Elsie still had four children at home to support, the oldest 13, the youngest only 4.

Is it any wonder that Elsie sounded as if she were battling depression when she wrote to Willard and his wife shortly after her husband's death? "I guess you wonder why mother does not write. But this is the first time I could really bring myself to write. Somehow since daddy has gone things do not go so easy. Everything is changed so much, I mean in loneliness and so alone. I do not take the same interest. But I am trying to make it go. . . . I am glad he does not know how lonesome he left me."[6]

Elsie had been hoping for a visit from Willard and his wife. Her comments reflect the devastation of the West in those years: "If there is a good crop Stan [Hazel's man] may need help for harvest. That [way] you could make your expenses. But the outlook is poor for any crop. We did not have enough rain around here to settle the dust. . . . The dust is so thick on the summer fallow down across the road in back of our barn that it looks like a high dark wall. . . . I've never seen such high winds before. The wheat looks yellow already. There is famine promised for the West. And it may come."

Despite her dispiritedness, Elsie's determination shows through. Yet there is a hint that she feared she might be forced to take desperate measures to survive, that she might not be able to keep all her children with her, as she had failed to do before: "Sometimes I think I must wake up and find everything like before. Last night I dreamed about daddy; I cried out in my sleep so loud that I wakened myself. I am going to keep the family together just as long as I can no matter how poor I have to live. As long as we don't starve I will not part them. I made that mistake once. I will never do it again if I can help it."

Even in her grief, Elsie's humor peeks through: "I will have to stop as the children have quit playing upstairs and have come down to be amused. . . . Goodbye to collected thoughts, the gang is all here."

As she had before, in facing widowhood Elsie again showed an indomitable will to provide for her family. This time she succeeded in keeping them all together. Her stratagems were manifold. She received a small widow's allowance from the government. The Brethren in Christ Church also provided a widow's allowance of $10 a month. Henry's older children, who had eventually become staunch friends of their father's second wife, helped when they could. Elsie also drew upon all her talents to earn what money she could. She made and sold quilts, traded her vegetables and eggs for other foodstuffs, boarded teachers, and employed her considerable economizing skills to stretch every bit of food. Someone said that "Mrs. Hahn knew a hundred ways to cook an onion." All the children had little jobs, which included carding wool for quilt batting, weeding the garden, and catching gophers to redeem their tails for pocket money.[7]

Elsie continued to give, as well as to receive. A member of the denomination's Board of Benevolence, which administered the allowances for church widows, told his family about the remarkable widow in Kindersley who received $10 each month and faithfully sent back a dollar every month as a tithe.[8] Her children remember that, throughout the years of the Great Depression, men riding the rails looking for work would come knocking on their back door. The men always received a filling meal, although Elsie cautiously made them eat it on the porch.[9] In town, neighbors often called on "Aunt Elsie" for her home remedies.[10] As well as making quilts to sell, Elsie continued to participate in the sewing circles that provided quilts and clothing for missions and relief. Elsie was able to keep the good-sized family house, and she continued to share it with visiting speakers, boarders, and friends who needed to stay overnight in town for any reason. In one letter she comments, "Roxy gives me lectures for having too much company, same as ever." [11]

Amazingly, the childhood memories of the family are not ones of deprivation, but of laughter, activities together and with the church, and a house always full of visitors. Her son Harry tells about taking her to prayer meeting one night on his sleigh. At one slippery corner, the sleigh tipped and Elsie was tumbled into a snowbank. Harry began to laugh, and Elsie couldn't help joining in. She got up, dusted off her bonnet, laughing all the while, and they continued to church. Once there, every time one of them caught the eye of the other during the service, they started giggling again.

Elsie drew upon her faith for the courage to keep going, and to make her children's lives loving and laughter-filled. She wrote to one of her daughters, many years later, when facing medical problems: "When I think how I got through when you were all small, I should not have to be afraid to trust Him now." [12] She did get through, and raised her children to think of themselves not as deprived, but as gifted, with talents to share.

Continuing Interest in Church and Family

Elsie's children were always very involved in the activities of the church. When the opportunity came, they wanted to attend the church's educational institutions as well. When they were old enough to earn the money to do so, two of her girls left home for this purpose. Doreen attended both Messiah College and Upland College; Roxena went east to Ontario Bible School (now Niagara Christian Collegiate, the denomination's high school). While they were at school, and later when they got married and settled in Ontario and California, Elsie used frequent letters to keep in touch and to remind them of her constant love.

Her letters to her girls were full of practical advice. "You better take the money I sent you for your skates and buy [a wash boiler]," she wrote to Willard and his wife, Violet. "A wash boiler is one of the things a housewife can hardly do without especially if [she] has a baby." [13] "Little babies bring lots of love and work and sleepless nights sometimes to try a man's patience." [14] She also shared spiritual wisdom: "Don't try and push your leadings on those who don't want it. . . . It takes *wisdom* to win souls." [15]

Her letters were also packed with bits of news about the community and the church. She frequently mentioned the guests she had for Sunday dinner, sometimes as many as 14 people. She commented on the weddings the church ladies were catering, and the number of quilts they were preparing to send to missions. She mentioned news of the wider church: "The last people that were here and told me about you were Mr. and Mrs. Morris Sider. He said he was going to teach at O.B.S. this coming term. . . . Mrs. Sider has a very sweet face. . . . Last Sunday was Robert Sider's farewell at Delisle. His brother and party came from North Star to be there." [16]

The family connections between East and West were very important to people in the Saskatchewan church, who sometimes felt a little isolated. Visitors from the East would be expected to bring news of one's relatives, and those who didn't have such news were deep disappointments: "News seemed so scarce from Stevensville and every one who came out here seemed to be from Sherkston church or Markham or anywhere but from Bertie, so I did not get much news out of any of them." [17]

The widow of a pioneer who participated in the migration to the West, Elsie lived long enough to see the church-planting movement, a new style of starting churches, develop among the Brethren in Christ. She acutely pointed out the central concern: "I see by 1960 they want to start work on a church in Saskatoon. . . . I hope there will be tithers enough to meet the needs." [18]

For all her wisdom, Elsie's letters are cherished as much for their touches of characteristic humor. About her boarder, who complained about all the people who came to the door while Elsie was visiting her daughter Hazel in the country, she wrote, "Mrs. Cameron says all the people that come. . . . and claim to be my friends make her nervous. . . . So I gave her a list this time when I left." [19] About a baby shower, she commented, "Tonight the women went to the [Free Methodist] parsonage after church and gave Mrs. Byggdin enough money to buy a baby carriage. I thought it would have been better had they waited till she had something to put in the carriage."[20] About old friends who had a new baby, she observed: "Joan and Pete's [names changed] baby is sweet too, even if she does look like Pete." [21] On changes in the church, she wrote: "Did anyone tell you there is an electric organ in our church? Naaman Climenhaga bought it. Since his girls are home he is getting quite modern."[22]

Always there are reminders in Elsie's letters that she longed to have her children gathered around her. She had worked so hard to keep them together. Once she plaintively commented: "It seems strange that I should have such a scattered family." Yet she continued to use her letters to give the encouragement and love she could not give in person. Her most usual salutation was, "My dear children." Her comments to a granddaughter are revealing: "I am sure you have lots of work being a mother to three wee folks. But when they come for a kiss we forget all about the work they make!" [23]

During the last few years of her life, Elsie moved into a seniors' lodge in Kindersley. She continued to be active in the church sewing circle and in bake sales at the lodge until shortly before her death in November 1959. Afterwards, Doreen wrote to her sister Roxena, who was unable to come west for the funeral, about the treasures their mother had kept with her as mementos of the happy days of the past: "Her wool carders, two pieces of homemade soap, the baby bonnet. . . . she had crocheted when I was a baby, letters from the orphanage girls, written to her when she was Sr. Underkoffler." Then, doubtlessly expressing the feelings of everyone in Elsie's family, Doreen concluded, "How I shall miss her letters!"

A Worthy Life

Elsie Detweiler Underkoffler Hahn was not an extraordinary woman. Yet she kept her family together as a single mother during a time when it was difficult for many families to survive. She steadfastly supported her church through many new and probably bewildering changes. She was a bulwark of community life during the Depression. She was like many other women, whose stories never get told, who taught their children to persevere, to use their talents, to trust in the Lord, and to laugh. Her story is a memorial to them all.

Living with Creative Tensions

Nancy Ruth Heisey

by Rebecca L. Ebersole *

Travel has syncopated the life of Nancy Heisey from an early age.[1] Her first memories include her father's breathless rhythm of church-related trips. In fact, in 1952, when her mother, Velma Climenhaga Heisey, gave birth to Nancy, her father was on a train traveling back home to Pennsylvania.

When Nancy was six, she began a ritual before her father's trips. At that time, J. Wilmer Heisey served as superintendent of the Navajo Mission and the family lived at this Brethren in Christ outpost located in a sparsely populated region of New Mexico. Before he left on trips, Nancy would press a piece of paper into his hand with Genesis 28:15 written on it. She had discovered the story of Jacob's vision of a ladder going into heaven at Bethel which contains this promise from the Lord to Jacob: "Behold, I am with you and will keep you in all places, wherever you go." This promise was Nancy's gift to her father. From a very early age, she showed both a precocious spirit and a growing understanding of her family's deep dedication to the church.

In addition to a strong commitment to learning and the church, many other themes run through her life: a keen experience of being a minority at the Navajo Mission and a corresponding respect for other cultures, a rootlessness born of her family's mission work and a related passion for traveling, an enduring love of family, strong ties to both the Brethren in Christ and

---

*Rebecca L. Ebersole met Nancy Heisey through the interviewing process for this biography. Rebecca is the writer and editor for the Messiah College Publications Office.

Mennonite traditions, and a passion for writing, research, and teaching. The beginnings of many of these themes can be traced back to her family of origin.

The Roots of Service

Nancy's father experienced a profound loss when he was 16 months, too young to understand it: his father died of pneumonia. In the following years, his mother raised Wilmer and his two siblings, selling eggs and milk to support the family. He remembers a sort of epiphany in his life when his mother said to him one day, "Wilmer, I hope that your life is in useful service to the Lord." These words echo through his life and Nancy's as well.

Nancy's parents met and eventually courted while helping to establish a high school among a tribe, referred to as a "head-hunting" tribe by its enemies, in the Philippines. Sent to that location by Mennonite Central Committee, Velma, an R.N., and Wilmer, a teacher, were deeply influenced by the years they spent in the Philippines. They developed respect and love for the people among whom they lived which would continue to influence their relationships with people of different cultures. They admired the tribe's profound practice of peacemaking. In tribe members' eyes, a stranger was an enemy until proven a friend, so the tribe developed rituals to transform strangers into friends.

On Being the Stranger: Nancy's Early Childhood in the Minority

When Nancy was only six weeks old, her parents moved their growing family to the Navajo Mission. In this mission school, Nancy—tall, blond, and fair-skinned—was conspicuous among her short, dark-skinned classmates, who frequently picked on her. She, her older brother, Paul, and younger sister, Mary Jane (M.J.), were the only "Anglos" at the school, which gave her an experience of being in the minority. Nancy says, "There's something about that feeling of not quite fitting in, wherever you go, that I think I was very shaped by [that experience]." In this way, her time at the mission school made her very aware of differences. She adds, "I think that's why I've continued to want to make space for people who are different."

Short and dark-haired, her sister, M.J., blended in more with her classmates. She remembers Nancy as the most emotional of the siblings, noting that Nancy would more easily cry and that she was always falling in love with one man or another. Men fulfilling alternate military service at the mission frequently caught her eye.

During her childhood, people expected much of Nancy because she was taller than most people her age. One time when her mother was away, eight-year-old Nancy cooked dinner for her father and other guests as well. She also had high expectations of herself. A precocious student, she competed with her older brother, Paul, who had the exasperating skill of being able to read something once and immediately commit it to memory.

The whole family's life was full of curiosity about the world and a thirst for learning. M.J. recalls that her father was so enthusiastic about the book *Dr. Zhivago* that he made sure all of the children read it. Expressing an artistic spirit within this intellectually rich environment, Nancy painted and sang while at the mission. Music has been such a driving passion in Nancy's life that she later told her sister that if she were not in church work, she would be a folk singer.

In addition to musical and literary influences in Nancy's life, her mother also subtly and profoundly shaped her daughter's formative years. She offered meals and lodging to a constant flow of church members who were traveling between east- and west-coast church destinations. Velma also instilled in Nancy a desire for order and introduced her to domestic arts—how to make exquisite pies and how to manage a household. She taught Nancy other important lessons, such as her philosophy that "the way the Christian faith makes sense is how you live it out in a practical way." At times Nancy did not fully understand her parents' decisions. Later in life, Nancy asked her mother if she knew how hard it was for the children at the mission school. Her mother said yes, but that she and Wilmer believed that they were called to serve God at the mission. In her view, the difficulty for the children was part of the family's sacrifice of serving at the Navajo mission.

When guests visited the mission, Nancy—who had a natural affinity for public speaking—frequently served as a tour guide.

She befriended park rangers, learned their speeches, and escorted visitors around nearby Chaco Canyon. On the mission, Nancy also found positive role models, including Mary Olive Lady, her piano teacher and also a teacher at the mission. Nancy says, "She epitomized what a Christian woman in the church should be. At that time there weren't a lot of women who were visible in the church." In her work at the mission and later in Zambia, Mary Olive modeled for Nancy a deep respect for the people with whom she worked.

After the social challenges of the early grades, Nancy blossomed in the Bloomfield High School, a public school. She says, "[At the mission school], it was extremely difficult to be the only white girl in my class. When I went to public school it was a lot easier. I wasn't so different." She experienced the freedom of being herself, according to her father, and just took off "whoosh—just like that in the first year."

Even though life at the Navajo Mission had challenged all of the children in some ways, when their parents announced that they would transplant their family to Pennsylvania, Paul, Nancy, and M.J. were opposed to the move. Nancy had made friends, tasted what teenage years could be like, enjoyed the freedom from religious expectations the family experienced in the isolated setting, and reveled in the colors, the place, and the climate of New Mexico. She remembers weeping uncontrollably in the car, the day the family left for Lancaster County, Pennsylvania.

Upon their arrival, the stench of a neighbor's chicken house, stifling humidity, and 100-degree temperatures greeted the family at their new home. They moved with no dishes and no furniture. Nancy remembers eating one of their first meals with just three plates and sharing silverware. Within a few weeks, however, her family had purchased these basic household items.

After the move, Nancy began her sophomore year at Donegal High School in Mount Joy. She moved freely in social circles, joined the band, and flirted with the idea of dancing. At one particular party, she longed to dance. Although her parents had not prohibited her from dancing, she knew that the Brethren in Christ Church frowned on it. In the end, she could not bring herself to join her friends. Frustrated, she came back from the party and said to her parents, "I couldn't do it. It's all your fault. You made me this way!"

The World Opens Up: Nancy As a Young Adult

On the tails of the Vietnam War, Nancy entered Messiah College in Grantham, Pennsylvania. An excellent student—History and English Professor E. Morris Sider remembers her as one of his best—she studied English as her major, honed her linguistic abilities in French, and spent her junior year studying in France.

In addition to providing rich cross-cultural experiences, her time in France also yielded two significant personal developments. Nancy sparked a friendship with an American Lutheran pastor which culminated in their engagement during her senior year of college. While in France, Nancy also submitted the winning design to a contest to develop a symbol for the Brethren in Christ Church. Her entry combined a dove, a cross, and a basin and towel.

In an article describing the symbol in the *Evangelical Visitor*, she writes, "To help us understand the things in life that are too complex to comprehend with the senses, we create symbols."[2] She included the cross, "for without Christ's death to break down the sin barriers between us and God, we would never have been able to break down the walls to call each other sister and brother." In her symbol, the basin and the towel represent service—as Christ's life and words emphasize. The dove symbolizes both nonresistance and following the Holy Spirit. When believers internalize and seek to understand these symbols, Nancy writes, "Then the greatest thing of all will happen—we will go forth as living symbols to a world still in search of the invisible meaning."

This symbol seemed to deepen her commitment to the church and all that it represented. In the wake of this intense reflection on her heritage, Nancy broke her engagement to the Lutheran pastor. She and her fiancé's disparate understandings of the role of church in individual lives and in the world contributed to this decision. The breakup and its aftershocks proved very difficult both for Nancy and her parents.

While Nancy appreciated many of the strengths of her heritage, she also struggled with aspects of it. She stumbled over the tradition's strong emphasis on spiritual experience, a version of John Wesley's "the heart strangely warmed." She sensed that her denomination held up one emotional experience of God as a model, and she could not get that experience right. She says, "I tried and tried and tried. We had revival meetings and spiritual life meetings, and campus life meetings—I tried them all." Her great-aunt Anna Zercher helped Nancy, then in college, as she was pursuing this illusive experience. Anna, who epitomized for Nancy what it meant to be Brethren in Christ, said, "This is not about experience. This is about living the way God wants you to live."

Finding Her Mission in the Global Church

After graduating from Messiah College, Nancy joined Mennonite Central Committee and taught school in a town called Mukedi in Zaire (now the Democratic Republic of the Congo) for two and one-half years. In addition to teaching classes in a French-speaking school, she also enjoyed the rousing and intricate singing of her students.

Shortly after her return, she wrote an article, "In Zaire Questions and Friendships Grow," for the *Evangelical Visitor,* the Brethren in Christ Church magazine. The article begins with this stark proclamation: "'Don't kid yourself!' my student Luange stood up and shouted, looking straight at me. 'You won't find a real, sincere, profound friendship between black and white anywhere in the world.'" Even though her student was only reciting his lines in play practice, Nancy ponders the meaning of his words in this article and examines the challenges and opportunities of cross-cultural friendships formed with Zairians.

In the article, she also addresses the struggle of teaching within a school system which relied almost solely on memorization and her feeling of helplessness at times when conflicts erupted in the church. She concludes by writing, "When I look back on time spent in Zaire, I remember with the greatest joy the friendships I made. But I wonder, is friendship enough?"[3] This pattern of deep friendships with people of various cultures and a deliberate blend of reflection and active service forms the tapestry of much of her professional and personal life.

In a similar way, throughout her life Nancy has consulted her father at key points about church service. In her emotional and intense personality, Nancy takes after her father, says sister M.J. Nancy agrees: "We're temperamentally alike. We're both curious about the world, take relationships very seriously, and respect other cultures." According to Nancy, some people have criticized her father for not being clear with others in his attempts to be a careful and sensitive communicator. She still remembers realizing their similarity, such as when a colleague at MCC told her to be direct and to say what she meant. Their professional lives have also followed similar paths with both pursuing service and working at MCC.

After she began working for MCC, Nancy sometimes felt that people in the Brethren in Christ Church suspected that she was "going over to the Mennonites" and leaving her tradition. Her father also dealt with this tension. She continued to accept Brethren in Christ speaking engagements; joined the Brethren in Christ Historical Society, serving as an executive member for several years; and strove to maintain connections to the church.

Nurturing both Brethren in Christ and Mennonite Church affiliations, Nancy continued to grow and develop in her service to the global church. After teaching in Zaire, she returned to MCC and joined the Information Services Department. After ten months, she accepted an invitation to join the Africa Department. She says, "That's where my heart was; I was really excited to have that opportunity." Many of her future leadership opportunities would arise from similar invitations. She eventually became co-director of the department, the first woman in a senior program administrator position at MCC.

Ray Brubacher, who appointed Nancy as assistant administrator, says that at first a few people wondered if this young woman was a token appointment. He says, "They soon became convinced that she was in the position because of her abilities." She directed the Teachers Abroad Program. In the 1970s this program had been declining as more people entered the burgeoning economic development field. Nancy kept the integrity of the program and encouraged the teachers already in the program. Ray sees Nancy as a courageous person who is willing to be the first person to go up against a barrier. At times, he says, this may involve personal pain for Nancy, but she's willing to wade into difficult situations.

Embarking on Another Adventure: Marriage and Family

While Nancy worked at MCC, her heart also warmed to Paul Longacre, a man who had recommended her for her position in the Africa Department. Paul's wife, Doris Janzen Longacre, who authored the *More with Less Cookbook*, a collection of recipes and insights which encourages global stewardship, had recently died of cancer. Nancy had known Doris and grieved with the other MCC employees after her death.

In time, Nancy and Paul deepened their friendship. Longtime friend and pastor Urbane Peachey caught the twinkling of potential between them. He says, "Once, while walking just behind Paul in the office, I caught a rather spectacular smile [from Nancy] signaled to Paul, and I knew there was hidden romance in the air." When asked what first attracted him to Nancy, Paul said playfully that he walked past Nancy's desk every day and she would wink at him. Almost on cue, Nancy responded, "I did not!" More seriously, he said that Nancy is intelligent and creative, and much more talented then he even knew when he first met her.

Through her years at MCC, Nancy remembers Paul as a friendly person who genuinely liked people. Dedicated to simple living, she resonated with the "more with less" image of his family and his commitment to the church. She also says, "Paul was a very handsome man. I noticed that long ago."

With his two girls in tow, they embarked on a unique and complex courtship. Their dates often consisted of miniature golf or hikes with his girls, who were 12 and 14 at the time. The family was still reeling from Doris's death. In this whirl of emotion and activity, Nancy remembers their courtship as a stressful time. From the beginning, Paul made his intentions clear: that he wanted to remarry and was not just dating for fun. Still affected by her broken engagement, Nancy also was committed to making this relationship work. She says, "I had a strong sense that if I was going to get into [another relationship], I was going to have to be really willing to work at it."

In 1981, Nancy, 29, and Paul, 44, married, and Nancy Longacre became the stepmother of Paul's two teenage daughters, Cara and Marta. She says, "It's been a real adventure. I think I knew in some very general way that marriage is difficult and that a second marriage for Paul would bring all kinds of extra issues along with it. But it was a lot harder than I thought it would be."

Like most families who experience the trauma of death and the complexity of remarriage, the newly blended family struggled to adjust to their life together. They lived in the same house that Doris and the family had inhabited, which brought unique challenges. The girls were coping with their mother's death and also trying to push away in independence during the teenage years. To maintain some continuity in the girls' life, the Longacres continued to attend Akron Mennonite, their home church. Nancy retained her membership at Cross Roads Brethren in Christ Church and eventually became a member at Akron Mennonite Church as well.

Each member of the family brought expectations to the household—but what was Nancy's role in the family? And what did it mean to be a stepmother? Nancy also was closer to the girls' age than their mother had been, which further blurred role definitions. At the same time, Nancy respected their mother's importance and place in their life. She asked the girls to decide what to call her. They decided to simply refer to her as Nancy.

Doris's presence and fame within Mennonite circles permeated other aspects of Nancy's married life. Embracing simple living, Nancy says, "I was as 'More with Less' as you can get." But when she joined the family, she found that at times they were weary of living in the shadow of Doris's cookbook. A member of the family could not discreetly buy a bag of potato chips from the grocery store without someone saying, "Why are you buying potato chips? Aren't you related to the 'More with Less' lady?" Doris's reputation also brought another challenge. People often mistook Nancy Longacre for the author of the cookbook. This confusion eventually led Nancy to legally change her last name back to Heisey to distinguish herself from Paul's first wife.

Sometimes Nancy immersed herself in work to escape the intense family adjustment pressures. She says, "I kind of withdrew into work and my other relationships. . . . There may have been times that [the girls] felt I was ignoring them or staying away. I sometimes did that because I let my work fill my life."

Despite the challenges, several positive factors sustained the family and eventually saw them through the transition. Nancy formed connections with the girls through teaching them domestic skills such as baking bread and concocting her special salad dressing. She also helped the girls grow in their writing abilities by carefully reading their school papers. Cara says, "Looking back, I don't know what we would have done without Nancy and her family."

During those years, the girls formed warm relationships with Nancy's parents and siblings. Sharing experiences also helped the family to get to know each other better. In addition to other activities, they took a trip to New Mexico to visit the Navajo Mission at which Nancy spent her childhood.

In a similar way, shared commitments pulled Paul and Nancy through difficult times. They both share a global perspective and a deep commitment to the church and to simple living. Their families of origin also had much in common, including the same Anabaptist understanding of the world, an emphasis on service, commitment to church, and consistency in belief and action. In addition, Nancy says, "[Our families] had a broad understanding of the church. Neither family felt like it was our job to go around ruling people out of the kingdom. And I think that's something that Paul and I share: a sense of the wideness of God's mercy."

Early on they developed a flexibility in their marriage which enabled each to pursue vocational goals. Nancy sees this as both a strength and a weakness—the flexibility allowed each person enriching opportunities, but the independence may also have delayed their congealing as a couple. As part of this flexible pattern, in 1985 Nancy spent a year in Burkina Faso as the interim director for MCC's program there. After she spent the first six months alone, Paul and Marta joined her (Cara was already in college). Marta learned to know Nancy better during that time. She says, "I thought of it as one big adventure. [My father and I] were in awe of Nancy: she communicated in French, led us through the city, and was in charge of MCC workers for the whole country." When Cara visited the family there, she realized "how much African blood is in her [Nancy] and how well she adapts to living with so little."

Seminary and a Two-Year World Tour

Upon her return, she and Paul sold their house and moved to Elkhart, Indiana, where Paul completed a master of divinity degree and Nancy took seminary classes. Even though they were in the heartland of many Mennonite churches, they drove a distance to attend the Nappanee Brethren in Christ Church, where Nancy sang in the choir.

For an independent study course, Nancy wrote a long article, "Of Two Minds: Ambivalence in the Language of the Brethren in Christ Missionaries," which was later published in two parts in *Brethren in Christ History and Life.*[4] In this article, she explores how the language of the missionaries reveals two attitudes: on the one hand, paternalism toward nationals—the missionaries, particularly in Africa, described nationals with words like "heathens" and saw evangelism as a civilizing influence in cultures which seemed strange at times to them—and on the other hand, missionaries saw the nationals as equal in Christ and intimately connected with them as children of God.

Her articles provoked passionate responses: the journal published one by a former missionary and another by the bishop of the Canadian Conference of the Brethren in Christ Church. Nancy later wrote that the bishop "clearly understood that the issue is not one of criticizing the past, but of considering the language and attitudes underlying our responses to the missionary call of the present."[5]

Nancy amended her views on these missionary efforts in a 2001 article, "Nancy Heisey's vision for world mission," by Valerie Weaver-Zercher.[6] In this article, Nancy says, "[I began to realize] the incredible commitment that [Brethren in Christ missionaries] made when they went off to Rhodesia in 1898. . . . The fact that they were prepared to do that on behalf of the good news really boggles your mind. . . . That kind of commitment is, in fact, what we are called to." In response to mistakes missionaries made, Nancy notes in the article, "Sure, they made lots of mistakes, but *so do we.* I often think that the next two generations are going to look at the things we do and say, 'Wow, what mistakes they made!' "

After taking seminary courses and studying attitudes of missionaries, Nancy and Paul embarked on a journey that took them on a study tour of the global church and deepened their relationship with one another. Several Mennonite mission agencies sent them around the world to 45 countries on a two-year listening tour to find out what national Mennonite churches were thinking and what they wanted from the mission agencies. Together, they wrote a report on their visits with the churches which was published in a series of articles in the *Gospel Herald*, a Mennonite magazine. In this collaboration, they started to see themselves as a couple, solidifying their relationship as true partners.

Upon their return, Nancy was invited to become the associate executive secretary of Mennonite Central Committee International. As she tried to juggle marriage, family, other domestic responsibilities, and career, she worked mainly with men who were in marriages with more traditional roles, ones in which their wives handled most of the family and household responsibilities. One of these colleagues, Ray Brubacher, remembers Nancy saying emphatically, "What I need is a wife!"

Throughout her life, as she moved in spheres of influence comprised mostly of men, she experienced both affirmation and discouraging moments. Overall, she says, "I didn't find it extremely painful." She has been invited to most of her positions of leadership and has not had to fight for a place. As she worked at MCC, she found her colleagues to be affirming of her. The challenges, however, express themselves in more subtle ways. Through repeated occurrences, she has noticed that sometimes she is not heard because she is a woman. She will propose an idea that will float away unnoticed. A day later, a man will suggest the same idea and others will rally around it. In our society, she says, a lot of men are not sensitive to this. She has learned to be assertive in these settings through practice.

She also notes a subtle challenge—that women's higher voices do not project as loudly as men's do. Early in her professional life, she attended a meeting at which members sang together.

Men's voices boomed all around her. Nancy's voice could not even be heard. She remembers thinking, "I wonder if they ever think of who they are drowning out."

During her tenure in the MCC executive office, a family tragedy struck which rocked Nancy's relationship with the Brethren in Christ Church. A youth pastor of the Brethren in Christ Church had sexually abused a cousin. She says that when the cousin brought the abuse to the attention of church leaders, they mishandled the situation. Nancy points to this as the biggest challenge in her relationship with the Brethren in Christ Church. She acknowledges that many churches struggle to deal with sexual abuse, "But for me this is a hurt that I experienced within the context of the Brethren in Christ Church. It's been hard for me." The cousin eventually committed suicide—an excruciating loss for his family.

As Nancy pondered her relationship with the Brethren in Christ Church, her sister, M.J., was a steadfast companion and confidant. A member of the Society of Friends and a doctoral student in history at the time, M.J. and Nancy discussed M.J.'s dissertation, which dealt with the Brethren in Christ Church. Nancy says, "Her work was really important in my acknowledging again what a big part of my identity [the Brethren in Christ Church] is."

Back to a First Love: Scholarship and Teaching

As she defined her denominational affiliation, she also considered her life's direction. From her first taste of instructing students in Zaire, Nancy had sustained the desire to be a teacher. In 1992, when she turned 40, she decided, "If I'm going to do this, I better get with it." With this goal in mind, she left MCC and completed her master of divinity degree at Eastern Mennonite Seminary. She then commuted to Temple University, where she eventually earned a master's degree and a Ph.D. in religion.

Away for the first time from a cohesive Christian work environment, she thought, "Here I am going to this big state university, and probably no one's even a Christian there; how am I ever going to find fellowship?" To her delight, she formed especially meaningful relationships with two other women. Patricia Martinez, a Roman Catholic woman from Malaysia, became one of Nancy's faith partners during graduate school. Patricia's liberation-oriented theology stemmed from extreme political oppression in Malaysia. Nancy also formed a friendship with Deborah Spink, a United Church of Christ minister who was "rooted in her faith and solidly committed to the work of Christ and the church." Nancy says, "These two wonderful women from vastly different traditions became so important in my life. They helped stretch out all my boundaries."

Her dissertation reflects an enduring connection with the people of Africa and to the global church. Nancy knew she wanted to focus on a topic connected with Africa and to study with the professor who taught early Christianity. She considers it unfair that many Africans have only heard that Christianity came to Africa from Europe, Canada, and the United States. She says, "They do not know that there is an ancient story of Christianity in Africa. From the very earliest times, there were Christian believers in Africa." With these concerns in mind, she chose to study Origen, a 2nd and 3rd century Egyptian theologian. A Roman Catholic publishing house in Nairobi, Kenya, published her dissertation, "Origen the Egyptian: A Literary and Historical Consideration of the Egyptian Background in Origen's Writings on Martyrdom." Excited by this endorsement from an African publishing company, Nancy says, this "affirmed that what I was talking about was of interest to Africans."

Early in her graduate school experience, Nancy became secretary of theological education for Mennonite World Conference, an organization that promotes fellowship, communication, and empowerment of the global Mennonite and Brethren in Christ churches. In her work, she carries a special concern for women in theology, especially African women involved in theological education.

New Beginnings and Turmoil

Soon Eastern Mennonite University (EMU) began courting Nancy. In 1998, she and Paul moved to Harrisonburg, Virginia, and she accepted the position at EMU of instructor of biblical studies and church history. Her Temple University advisor warned her that working at a church college would always put a crimp in her scholarship. She looks at E. Morris Sider, professor emeritus at Messiah College, as a guide through this process.

Through his experience and her own, she has realized how difficult it is to be a scholar in the church and how many tradeoffs have to be made.

Despite these tensions, Nancy finds teaching to be profoundly rewarding. Her favorite aspect of teaching is when she sees students responding in a way that signals they are understanding the topic. She is also gratified "even if they don't like the author we are studying, but they can say why." Affirming Nancy's teaching, one student recently wrote on an exam, "I feel like the New Testament has come alive to me."

In the midst of normal transition stress and a full-time teaching load, a health crisis commanded Nancy and Paul's attention. Nancy says, "When we moved down here, it seemed like everything just fell apart." A doctor diagnosed her with breast cancer, and she had to have a mastectomy; six months later she had to have a hysterectomy because doctors thought she had ovarian cancer. The beleaguered couple wondered, "Did we make a wrong move here?" During those hard months, their church congregations—both Akron and Harrisonburg Mennonite—sustained them.

Their family also rallied around them. Paul and his daughters, having lost a first wife and mother to breast cancer, knew the stark realities of the disease. Cara accompanied Nancy when she went for her biopsy and cared for her after her hysterectomy. She says, "It was special for me to be able to be with her in that way." Because surgery removed her non invasive cancer, she can now say that her cancer is a past event. Nancy comments, "As scary as it was, I'm very grateful I've now been given the freedom not to worry all the time."

Nancy Blazes Another Trail

As she taught at EMU and advanced to the status of associate professor, Nancy also continued her work with Mennonite World Conference (MWC). In 2000, her name was added to the ballot for president-elect of this assembly. She shrugged off the possibility of being elected; after all, the conference had always selected a man for the position. The current president and vice president were also in the running, but she assumed that allowing her name on the ballot would simply encourage people to think about women in leadership.

Colleague Ray Brubacher remembers a powerful experience that questioned Nancy's assumptions. The president of the Congo Evangelical Mennonite Church told him that he had experienced a vision from God that the next president would be the sister [on the ballot—Nancy]. After Ray told Nancy, she looked startled because "she knows the power of prayer in Africa." During the week between her nomination and the election, Nancy prayed candidly during her daily morning walk, "Please don't let them vote for me."

At the July 2000 General Council meeting in Guatemala City, she was elected as president-elect. After the election, the president of the Congo Evangelical Mennonite Church flashed a wide grin to Ray Brubacher. As the closing prayer ended, a swarm of people surrounded Nancy, blessing her and expressing their support. She says, "I got a strong sense of affirmation . . . that my life and experiences had given me the gifts that might be needed."

For the press release following the election, Nancy wanted to list her dual membership in the Brethren in Christ and Mennonite Churches, but first checked with Kenneth Hoke, the general secretary of the Brethren in Christ denomination. Without hesitation, he said simply, "that's fine." Nancy says, "For him to acknowledge that without question was just the kind of belonging that I would have longed for at other points, but not felt."

When she becomes president of MWC in 2003, Nancy wants to facilitate the widest possible involvement in the conference. She wants to make space for many people to speak. One of the big questions she will challenge MWC to address is, "How do we in our very different contexts live faithfully? This will look very different [from place to place]."

Maturing Relationships and Evolving Identities

Amid her busy professional life, Nancy enjoys a close relationship with her husband, stepdaughters, granddaughters, and extended families. In the later years of their marriage, Nancy says, she and Paul have learned to have fun together, attending concerts and performances, and laughing together. She appreciates his rootedness, which he expresses through a bond with his family's farm in Pennsylvania, through agricultural activities, and through hunting. He's a world traveler, yes, but also a farmer at heart. Through trials, they have learned to take each other seriously when one says, "This is a problem," something that they struggled with earlier in their marriage.

Nancy enjoys an intimate friendship with her sister, M.J., who says, "If I would ever lose her, it would be like losing half of myself." She appreciates Nancy's great devotion to people, her discipline and commitment, her sense of community, and her dedication to the church. She says that some people may not know the side of Nancy that is spontaneous, that "mouths off," that is funny and relaxed. When asked about Nancy's vulnerabilities, M.J. reveals that at times Nancy pushes herself too hard, to the point of exhaustion. She also notes that some people may not know that despite seeming very successful, Nancy grapples with insecurity. In certain settings, she may overcompensate and appear to others to be too self-assured.

In addition to her relationship with her sister, Nancy has also appreciated a deepening relationship with her stepdaughters. On Mother's Day of 2001, Nancy and her stepdaughters participated in a meaningful event in Philadelphia—a fund-raising walk to support breast cancer research. Nancy reports that it was a very moving experience. Many of the people wear names of survivors or women who have died of breast cancer. One daughter wore Nancy's name, another wore Doris Longacre's name, and Nancy wore the name of Marta's mother-in-law. At one point, all three of them burst into tears. "You recognized your vulnerability, what you've lost, your relationships, and what you have to be thankful for," Nancy says. "It's something that we belong together in, and our stories have come together."

The family dealt with another cancer-related scare during the summer of 2001. Diagnosed with chronic lymphocytic leukemia several years earlier, Paul developed a high fever, which doctors had told them is dangerous for his condition. He later became very sick and had to be rushed to the emergency room. Nancy calls this a "very sobering experience." Their oncologist later confided to Paul, "You were very close to the edge." Nancy says that she and Paul have had enough experience to know that life has its limits. In fact, in the months following his serious illness, she's reflected on their age difference and realized that there's a good chance that eventually she will have to spend many years without him. "It's hard, but also adds richness to life. The moments we have together with our children and grandchildren are precious."

Nancy and Paul share many special moments with Cara, Marta, and their families. Nancy finds joy in her two granddaughters, Ruby and Anika. She says, "For me this experience has a particular significance because I didn't share my own daughters' infancy. Now sharing their daughters' infancy is such a privilege." As soon as her second granddaughter, Anika, was born, she and Paul rushed into the hospital after midnight to see her. Anika entered the world just five days after the terrorist attacks of September 11, 2001. In the wake of such tragedy and such hope in birth, Nancy remembered the words of Bengali poet Rabindranath Tagore: "Every child comes with a promise that God has not given up on the world." And Nancy thought, "This is why we work for peace. This is why we strive to live as Jesus lived."

She continues this work for peace informed by her two religious heritages: Mennonite and Brethren in Christ. Thinking over her nontraditional journey with the Brethren in Christ Church, she says, "It shaped who I am. I wouldn't be who I am without my Brethren in Christ family, church roots, and experience on the mission. . . . " She also adds, "One of the things I'm really excited about is seeing some of the new thinking coming out of Brethren in Christ leadership." When she looks at the Brethren in Christ core values, she says, "Yes, that's me. I can say 'yes' to that."

Reflecting on a life marked by professional achievement, service to the church, and important relationships, Nancy Heisey sits at her dining room table as the scent of Vietnamese cooking wafts up from a woman living in an apartment unit in their house. She's just breezed in from meeting with a prospective college student. Her coon hound barks outside, alerting Paul and Nancy that it is time for a walk. African tablecloths and artifacts decorate their simple home. She crochets a green blanket for her second grandchild. Perhaps this scene represents the creative tensions of her life—travel and rootedness, family and professional life, individuality and family, church and personal piety, president of MWC and grandmother, and making space for others and for herself.

In all of the complexity of life, Nancy Heisey remains open with her joys, her struggles, and her questions. To her sister, M.J., "Nancy never presents herself as someone who holds herself as a model, but as someone who is struggling along with doubts and questions about the church, but ultimately as someone who has committed her life to the church."

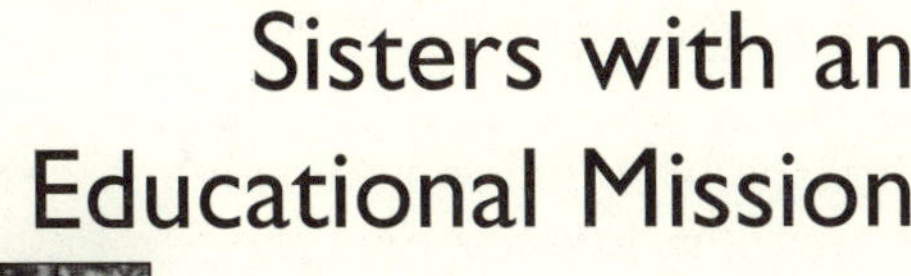

Sisters with an Educational Mission

Clara Engle Hoffman and Mary Engle Hoffman

by Wilma I. Musser*

When Messiah College was still in its infancy, two nurturing women came to help the school mature into a thriving institution of higher learning. These two pioneers in Brethren in Christ education—Clara and Mary Hoffman—were biological sisters who together gave 79 years of scholarly, devoted service to the school, often at the expense of personal fulfillment.[1]

Early Educational and Religious Experiences

Clara Hoffman was born on April 5, 1872, the second child of Mary (Engle) and Samuel S. Hoffman. Mary, the fourth child, arrived October 21, 1876. Poignant memories from their childhood years on the family farm in Lancaster County, Pennsylvania, included a developing love for nature and the out-of-doors, and happy educational experiences at the local country school.[2]

Shortly before Clara entered junior high school, the Hoffman family relocated several miles from their home in Marietta to the town of Mount Joy. The new location moved the sisters closer to educational opportunities, but they had to cope with other limiting circumstances. First, their father Samuel died suddenly at

---

*Wilma I. (Wenger) Musser first learned to know Clara and Mary Hoffman as a Messiah student in 1939–1940, and, after marriage, as their neighbor. Her husband, Arthur Musser, pastored the Grantham congregation for nine years and officiated at both of the Hoffman sisters' funerals. Wilma, a pastor's wife for forty-two years and former teacher, is a freelance writer whose articles have appeared in *Brethren in Christ History and Life* and other publications.

the age of 43, leaving a wife and seven children ranging in age from 22 to infancy. Two years later, a younger sister also passed away. Clara and Mary were both interested in more schooling, but these family conditions required them to finance their own education.

Clara, after graduating from the Mount Joy high school, successfully passed the county teaching examination and proceeded to teach in rural, one-room schools in various parts of the county (in one location, she taught 50 pupils at once). During the summer months, she attended the Normal School (a state-operated college for training teachers) at Millersville, Pennsylvania, graduating in 1896. She notes in a biography of her life that, in keeping with her love of nature, she particularly enjoyed the study of botany as a Millersville student.

In order to finance her education, Clara lived frugally. She told her students in later years that she owned two blouses, one grey skirt, and one Sunday dress while attending college. This economizing in early life prepared her to live contentedly on a meager salary.

Her efforts to support herself and continue her education were successful, and she eventually received a master's degree. But she decided to take several business courses from the Pennsylvania Business College in Lancaster rather than pursue the teaching profession. In 1900, she completed the shorthand and typewriting course, receiving high recommendations from the principal of the school. For the next ten years, she worked as a stenographer in several local business offices. Several letters of recommendation among her personal papers testify to her capable and efficient labor.

During her office employment, Clara had a conversion experience while attending evangelistic meetings in Mount Joy. She subsequently joined the Mount Joy Church of God in 1903.[3] But this experience was followed by a greater commitment to religious life after she joined the faculty at the newly opened Messiah Bible School in Grantham.

Her business skills and commercial training had garnered the attention of the school administration, and they offered her a position teaching typing and stenography. She arrived on campus after several rounds of negotiations, pleasantly startled by the school's appearance: "I came to Grantham in January 1912. When I stepped from the evening train, I was surprised to see electric lights lighting the path from the station to the main building. My first thought was, 'I'll be in the country with city conveniences.'"[4]

Her favorable impressions of the school, and her commitment to her position there, were strengthened when she joined the Brethren in Christ Church during one of the school's yearly Bible conferences, in 1913. She had an experience of consecrating herself to God (she termed it sanctification) and baptism, which preceded her membership decision. In an expression of commitment after her conversion, she penned her testimony; the words were later adapted in 1932 to form the lyrics for the first school song, "Alma Mater."

As a new church member, she donned plain clothing—a symbol of her separation from the world. A woman who made some of Clara's new clothing recalls that it was difficult for Clara to leave her friends at the Church of God and to begin wearing the church "uniform."[5] Her struggle to adopt church practice, however, did not prevent her from conforming to membership standards. From the time she joined the Brethren in Christ Church until the time of her death, she retained the style of her plain clothing. The plainness of her appearance is easily recalled by former students, especially when, in later years, the church's relaxing dress standards made her quaint attire more conspicuous. Her dress of a solid, dark color always included a cape (extra panel of material sewn over the bodice) and full, gathered skirt. The skirt, reaching to her ankles, revealed a glimpse of black stockings and black shoes. On her head she wore a large, white covering; narrow ribbons from the sides of the covering were tied under her chin in a neat, little bow. One student, reflecting on the appearance of "Sister Clara" and "Sister Mary" (the approved title for female faculty members),[6] thought the sisters resembled nuns.

Mary's path to membership in the Brethren in Christ Church (and thus, plain dress) and a teaching position at the Grantham school took a different route. She, like Clara, taught in rural Lancaster County schools after graduating from the Mount Joy high school and attending the Millersville Normal School for teachers. She had almost completed her third year of teaching in a Mount Joy grade school when she had a conversion experience. She joined the Brethren in Christ Church and became convinced that she should dress plainly. Her conviction caused some conflict with board members and parents at her school, and she resigned before the end of the school year.

After employment in several similar positions where patrons were more accepting of her appearance, the Messiah Orphanage, still in Harrisburg, hired Mary in 1906 as a school teacher for the orphanage students. For $200 a year, Mary taught the orphanage children (and an additional 24 students from the community) for five and one-half hours a day, ten months a year. She supplemented her work with the children by teaching classes for older students at Messiah Bible School, also still located in Harrisburg. She survived on a meager income. None of the workers—including Mary—received full compensation, and some received no pay, prompting one church member to comment that they were paid "one half of what the market price of their services would demand." [7]

When the orphanage moved to the Grantham campus of the relocated Messiah Bible School in 1914, Mary came along. With the exception of a brief period of teaching at a Brethren in Christ primary school in California from 1920–1922, she remained in Grantham as a teacher for the Bible school, even after the orphanage moved to another location in 1925.

During her years of teaching she continued her education, and finally received a degree from the Millersville Normal School in 1918. She also obtained a bachelor of arts degree from Pennsylvania State University, and took courses on occasion from that institution and Columbia University.

In an age when the Brethren in Christ denomination did not encourage higher education for women, the Hoffman sisters, with their advanced education and practical skills, were pioneers in this field. They were becoming the kind of women Mary praised in a 1911 article, entering "every field of labor formerly occupied by men and . . . proving themselves capable of doing satisfactory work in these places." [8]

Teaching at Messiah

Although the educational journeys of the sisters took them on divergent paths, they reunited again as teachers at Messiah. Living together in Hill View (former home of the school's first president) for over 30 years, they remained closely tied to each other and to the school for the rest of their lives. It is, therefore, virtually impossible to speak of one of them without mentioning the other. Their commitment to higher learning, and their experiences with frugal living, made them a perfect fit for a school that survived on the sacrifices of its educators and administrators. They were, college historian E. Morris Sider quips, "institutions within an institution...[and] as much a part of the campus as the buildings and trees themselves."[9]

As sisters, they shared the same last name, the same home, and the same dedication to the school and their students. But their personalities and interaction with the students emphasized their individual differences. Clara, known as a strict disciplinarian, had piercing black eyes that "looked right through you" (according to students) and commanded respect. Her prim and proper mannerisms prompted one male student to label her "extremely Victorian."

She was also highly organized and methodical. A woman who worked in the Hoffman home as a young girl remembers Clara being very particular—wanting to have chores done right and insisting on having them done her way. These characteristics served her well at the school in her roles as teacher of business and commercial subjects, preceptress or dean of women (1912–1926), and librarian (1916–1942).

Clara often spoke about the importance of reading, pointing out distinguished individuals whose lives and cultures were enriched through the intimacy of books. And she often donated books from her personal library to enhance Messiah's collection, so it was fitting that she should serve as the college's first librarian. Asked in 1913 to catalog and classify several shelves of books in a small room of the Old Main administration building, she took a summer library science course at Pennsylvania State College to learn proper procedures for the task. She served as official librarian until 1942, and continued to support the work of the library as assistant librarian and, later, librarian emeritus, until her death. Under Clara's supervision, the library continued to grow (moving three times in 45 years) from a few shelves to almost an entire wing of Old Main. Although she did not live to see the nucleus of Messiah College's present library building, dedicated in 1958, she was able to participate in the groundbreaking and cornerstone-laying.[10]

Clara served the college in areas apart from her official duties, and her service showed that beneath the austere exterior lay a kind heart. She often gave extra help to students at no charge. When she observed that two students in her shorthand class had previous training, she formed an advanced class for them. During the flu epidemic of 1917–1918, she nursed many students to health in the absence of a school nurse. She also offered her support to staff members. One school cook, for example, consulted Clara for advice and approval when students complained about the choice of food.[11]

She received little financial remuneration for her services to the school. In earlier years, the school relied heavily on the sacrifices of its employees, financial and otherwise, and Clara was no exception. Her early contracts are not available, but she received $20 a month for the 1943–1944 school year when she became assistant librarian, and her salary remained the same for the next ten years during her tenure as librarian emeritus. In 1953–1954 she served without salary "in recognition of present Social Security benefits." [12]

Mary also received small compensation for her service. For a teaching load in 1942–1943 that included four hours each of English I, English II, Problems of Democracy, and History Survey, she received $78.50 a month for nine months of the year.

Although she served the school with the same sacrificial spirit as her sister Clara, remembrances of Mary conjure up more lighthearted images. A 1935 article in the student newspaper describes her with "snow-white hair, merry, twinkling eyes, a smiling face, and the love of God dwelling in her."[13] A former student and faculty member comments, "Sister Mary was the personification of patience and cheerfulness—always optimistic, and putting the best construction on conditions and circumstances." [14]

Her smiling optimism was sorely needed since her naïve, gentle nature made her the victim of many classroom pranks. Many students remember stories of classroom misbehavior and Mary's subsequent inability to maintain good order. An oft-repeated antic involved setting an alarm clock to go off during class. When the alarm rang before the class officially ended—sounding remarkably like the closing bell—all the students stood up and marched out of the room. On one occasion, three alarm clocks were set to go off at the same time from different locations in the room. Every so often, when the clamor overwhelmed her, soft-spoken Mary would ask Clarence Musser, the professor next door, to help settle the class. In later years, Mary occasionally dozed in class when students were reading aloud. Taking advantage of her temporary lapse in concentration, the assigned reader skipped paragraphs or pages.

Repentance, when it came, was often short-lived. Mary laughed at the jokes played on her, but her gentle rebukes did not put a stop to them. It was common knowledge that she was the recipient of many apologies after student revivals brought conviction to her classroom pranksters. Characteristically, she granted forgiveness without holding grudges or retaining bad memories. One student, many years after his graduation, felt the need to apologize for the way he had acted in class. Mary replied with a kind smile and the words "You were a good boy."

Whatever her faults in exercising discipline, Mary attempted to make her classes interesting by taking frequent field trips. Since the Brethren in Christ emphasized separation of church and state and non-participation in government affairs, the destinations of her field trips were unusual. On one trip, students attended a local courthouse session and visited offices of the recorder of deeds and register of wills. A history class attended a civil court case, then visited the legislature and the museum in Harrisburg. They also toured a local prison and a Catholic cathedral. Unexpected surprises occurred in the classroom too. An English class feasted on coffee, Welsh rarebit, and cookies after Mary assigned oral reports on how to prepare these items.

Students appreciated Mary's teaching skills, remembering her as knowledgeable and well prepared. In addition to reading, she instructed her students in speaking and writing. One student, later a pastor and church leader, claims she taught him how to read scripture and use notes when preaching. Perhaps from a desire to instill modesty in her students, Mary marked a grade of "A" in a very small letter at the top corner of a paper. Other letter grades were written boldly across the center of the first page.

Although teaching was Mary's primary responsibility, the administration added the job of museum curator to her workload in 1943. The "museum"—housed at various campus locations in empty rooms—consisted of a collection of stuffed and mounted animals and birds. Artifacts, mostly from Brethren in Christ missionaries in Africa and India, joined the collection at a later date. Under Mary's care, and with Clara's assistance, the collection "became the nucleus for the present college and denominational archives." [15]

Contributions to College and Community

Aside from their official positions as employees of the college, the Hoffman sisters contributed to campus life in other ways. Both women loved nature and the outdoors, stemming from their childhood days on the family farm. They were widely recognized on campus as nature experts.

A former Grantham resident loved to play with her sisters in the stream that ran through the campus. Many times the girls brought flowers or plants found by the stream to Mary for identification. Clara often accompanied the nature study teacher, Edna Booser, on field excursions. After a number of trips, Clara could identify as many birds as Miss Booser, and soon became an avid bird-watcher. Her familiarity caused one student to note that she "spoke freely of these little feathery friends as intimately as she would of an associate and [seemed] to know them as well." [16]

Mary shared Clara's appreciation and knowledge of birds. In a November 1934 article for the student paper, she described and identified 17 different bird varieties seen on campus. The Hoffman house—with a bird bath, bird houses, and bird feeders—was a safe haven for feathered creatures. One oriole, which settled in the same location every year, received bits of string each year to help construct its nest. During one unusually cold winter, the sisters kept a flock alive by feeding them regularly from the porch of their home.

Both sisters turned their love of nature toward the improvement of school grounds. Clara, a frequent commentator on campus appearance, noticed the absence of trees in the early years.[17] She and another faculty member, Dean Asa Climenhaga, wrote the names of various trees on slips of paper and tied the slips to stones. Clara and Asa took turns throwing the stones on an open area of campus (the former outdoor amphitheater). Where the stone landed, they planted the name of the tree tied to the stone to give the random appearance of a natural woods. Mary, for her part, always planted flowers along the campus walks. One variety—a beautiful blue flower named Nigella—she called by its common name, "love in a mist."

Although lovers of nature, being in the company of people also pleased the Hoffman sisters. Clara and Mary were not socialites, but they were prim and proper, knowing and observing the rules of polite society. Modest and retiring themselves, they craved for their students the social graces that would make them accepted and admired.

Clara, in particular, took pains to train her students in proper etiquette. She frequently gave chapel talks on the subject. She delivered one such impressive talk, complete with a demonstration, just before the girls entertained the boys at a school banquet. An early school brochure containing instructions on how to ascend and descend a stairway, the proper way to sneeze, and how to handle silverware, among other things, "breathes the spirit of Clara Hoffman," according to Morris Sider.[18]

Both sisters regularly gave informal teas on campus for the entire student body. They also entertained students privately in their home, providing luxuries like fudge and popcorn for enjoyment. Mary, after field trips, often brought her classes to the house for ice cream. One visitor remembered their hospitality with pleasure: "I was entertained not as a mere student paying a troublesome call, but as an honored guest."[19] In conversation, they sought to inform themselves about topics that interested their visitors. One neighbor recalled with amazement Mary's knowledge about his occupation with the railroad and her ability to ask him intelligent questions about his work.

Social Limitations

The social lives of the Hoffman sisters, because of their devotion to each other and to the school, did not extend far beyond the campus or the Grantham community. In truth, their commitment to the school often overshadowed their personal development. Mary, in particular, suffered from the restrictions of her sheltered life. When Clara developed arthritis, trips and vacations for the sisters became infrequent. Mary told one acquaintance that she switched bedrooms every year just to experience a change in atmosphere. And it was rumored that she refused romantic involvement with a school colleague because Clara was unhappy with the idea. A former student, reflecting on Mary's "catnaps" in the classroom, said that she was probably weary from caring for Clara and their younger sister, Ruth, who lived with her older sisters and suffered from emotional and mental problems.

Clara, confined to a wheelchair for 25 years, endured the restrictions and pain of her arthritis without complaining, in spite of unusual treatments. One summer, she went weekly to a doctor in Harrisburg to be stung by bees. Professor Enos Hess—one-time president of the school and a bee-owner—often brought bees to her house, at her request, to sting her. What medical relief she hoped to receive from the stings is not known, but apparently the cure could be as painful as the disease.

Clara's physical limitations made movement from place to place difficult. She relied on Mary to push her around the campus grounds. In the days before elevators, a pulley attached to a platform in back of the main school building allowed Clara to be pulled up to the floor of the library and her office. Once in the library, she maneuvered around the room using a homemade wheelchair (a kitchen chair fitted with wheels).[20] Every now and then, she had to resort to more uncomfortable forms of transportation. A neighbor man carried her up a flight of stairs on one occasion. Humorously, he remarked, "Sister Clara, I don't know the last time you had your arms around a man, but you must put your arms around my neck so I can carry you!"[21]

Final Years

Unfortunately, few can remember the last days of the Hoffman sisters. Clara died at home on February 23, 1958, at the age of 85. At her funeral, faculty presented the following tribute, descriptive of her devotion to the school: "A tireless and methodical worker, thorough in scholarship, gracious and cultured in social relationships, ingenious and inventive in making a little go a long way . . . and always keeping in touch with the world, Sister Clara set a high example for both colleagues and students."[22]

The following year, Mary passed away on October 12, 1959, nine days before her eighty-third birthday. After breaking her hip in the winter of 1958, poor blood circulation gave way to gangrene, and her left leg was amputated. Although the amputation appeared successful, complications set in after surgery and Mary died soon afterwards. The faculty tribute to Mary is also descriptive of her contribution to the school: "A heart of sympathetic understanding, interested in other people . . . radiant personality, love for truth . . . compassion and devotion to her sister and patient in her own suffering."[23]

The above tributes reveal the personality and character traits of two sisters who shared a unique relationship with each other and the school they served. Their influence and efforts on behalf of their beloved institution—often at great personal sacrifice—ensured its ability to grow and adapt to changing needs. The college community they helped nurture to life still benefits from their contributions.

Pioneer Woman in Medical Missions

R. Virginia Kauffman

by Frances L. Harmon*

Virginia Kauffman likes flowers. As a child, she loved to grow and to arrange them for the enjoyment of herself, family, and friends. It seemed only natural that early in her life in southern California she planned to become a florist and spend her life doing what she most enjoyed.

Little did Virginia realize that although flowers would be an important part of her future life, it would not be her major profession. God had other plans for her—to be a missionary doctor. Growing flowers would be only a pleasant and relaxing hobby, not as a florist in southern California, but as the first Brethren in Christ woman medical doctor in South Africa. Eventually she spent 23 years in medical missionary work, much of it as a pioneer in remote areas where neither the gospel nor medical service had reached.

Even with her extraordinary skills in medicine, she always thought of herself as a missionary first, a doctor second, and a florist third. "I was called to be a missionary," she insisted in later life. "Then the Lord led me into medicine as I was preparing to be a missionary. I would never have been a doctor if I had not been a missionary. I would have been a florist!"[1]

---

*Frances L. Harmon, before retirement, was an elementary and secondary school teacher in the Upland, California, area schools. Among her major appointments in education, she was a consultant to Houghton Mifflin Publishers on textbooks and a Carnegie Teaching Fellow chosen by Ernest Boyer, President of the Carnegie Foundation for the Advancement of Teaching. She has been friends with Virginia Kauffman for many years.

Following God's Plan

Virginia was born in Pasadena, California, December 27, 1919, the second child of John and Ella Mae Kauffman who were faithful members of the Pasadena Brethren in Christ Church. She accepted Christ when she was eight years old, and joined the church at eleven. She later served the congregation as its pianist for several years and sometimes played her accordion at services.

Money was scarce in 1937, during the Depression, when Virginia graduated from high school at Beulah College Academy. To earn money for college expenses, she worked a few years doing domestic service and grading lemons in a lemon packing house in Pasadena. During this time she taught herself cake decorating skills and trained to be a florist—two skills she used and enjoyed all her life.

Between high school and college, Virginia felt the strong call of God to work as a medical missionary. Assuming this meant that nursing was to be her profession, she planned to enter the nurses' training program at Los Angeles County Hospital. She met all that institution's requirements and had a date set to be measured for uniforms, the last step before entering the program there. Sensitive to God's direction in her life, she was puzzled when she sensed that this was not what God wanted her to do.

Perplexed, she nevertheless informed the hospital that her plans had changed and that she would be entering college in the fall. Assuming that God wanted her to take two years of college before enrolling in a different nursing school, in the fall of 1943 Virginia registered at Beulah (later Upland) College. She decided to complete two years of college work there, taking all the prerequisites for entrance to the School of Nursing at Huntington Memorial Hospital in Pasadena.

The two years spent at Beulah College transformed Virginia's life and career plans. Two teachers (Hannah Foote and Lucille Lady) independently asked her the same question: "Have you ever thought about becoming a doctor, Virginia?" The idea of becoming a doctor evoked a stimulating response within her. Others who knew her abilities encouraged her to pursue the idea. God, she felt, was revealing his plan for her.

The financial challenge this idea presented, however, seemed insurmountable. Learning of an existing fund to help prospective missionary doctors, Virginia wrote to the Brethren in Christ Foreign Mission Board, presenting her need and asking for financial help. The board approved her request for a loan, but advised her that if she did not go to the mission field after medical school, the loan must be paid back immediately—with interest, "for the way of the transgressor is hard." With this assurance of financial help, Virginia transferred to the University of California at Los Angeles (UCLA) in January 1946 to take the necessary pre-med subjects.

Getting accepted into medical school was the next great challenge. In her senior year at UCLA, Virginia applied to six schools. It was not easy to get into medical school: many men were applying because of the delay in their education during World War II. Most schools had quotas limiting the number of minorities and women accepted. Many of the pre-med students had family members already in medicine and were given high priority. Virginia was the only one in her family who had gone to college, let alone medical school. Most applications asked why the student wanted to become a doctor. She thought that her answer that she planned to be a missionary doctor would probably be a turn-off with many medical schools. Five of the schools to which she applied refused her admittance. Understandably, this was a great discouragement and a time of inner uncertainty.

The response from the sixth school to which she had applied came much later than the others, but it brought acceptance by Hahnemann Medical College in Philadelphia, Pennsylvania. Virginia felt that this acceptance was another strong evidence of God directing her life. Now, in 1948, when she was almost 29 years old, she began her studies toward a degree in medicine.

For three years Virginia rented a room in a house across the street from the Brethren in Christ mission in Philadelphia and ate her meals with the mission staff. She carried a packed lunch, rode the subway back and forth to the medical college, and worked evenings at the college library to help cover expenses.

Virginia found medical school much more demanding than anything she had previously experienced. She claimed a promise the Lord had given her from Isaiah 50:7: "For the Lord will help me; therefore shall I not be confounded; therefore I have set my face like flint, and I know that I shall not be ashamed." But in recognition of God's faithfulness to her, she noted: "Although I won no special academic honors, it was not difficult for me to do well in medical school."[2] In 1952 she graduated with an M.D. degree. She completed her year of medical internship at Huntington Memorial Hospital in Pasadena. She was the first woman intern at this institution. Later, the five months she spent as a resident at St. Luke's Hospital in Pasadena gave her additional experience in emergency work.

A Doctor's Work in Africa

The Brethren in Christ Foreign Mission Board decided that Virginia should be placed in Africa rather than India. Virginia's decision to become a missionary and the board's plans to send her to Africa pleased Virginia's mother, who had prayed over the years that one of her children would go into full-time service. She and all the other members of the Kauffman family were at the train depot in Colton, California, to say their goodbyes as Virginia began her journey. This was the last time Virginia saw her mother, who died only six months before Virginia completed her first term of six years on the African mission field.

Before leaving for Africa, Virginia was ordained as a deaconess. As a deaconess she would have the authority to conduct funerals and take charge of burials at the mission graveyard. Distances and climate made it vital that these services be available soon after a patient's death. Virginia would conduct numerous funerals while in Africa.

On January 6, 1954, Dr. Virginia Kauffman sailed out of New York, accompanied by four young missionary women. Her arrival in Africa made expansion of medical missions possible. At Mtshabezi in Southern Rhodesia (now Zimbabwe), she replaced Dr. Alvan Thuma, the first medical missionary of the Brethren in Christ in Africa. Dr. Thuma and his family had moved to Northern Rhodesia (now Zambia) to build a new hospital compound at Macha Mission.[3] Women doctors were still a rarity the world over. When Thuma learned his successor at Mtshabezi Hospital was to be a woman doctor, he decided to grow a beard, explaining his action by saying, with his typical wry sense of humor, that a person was now coming to the field who could do *everything* he could do except grow a beard. And he did just that.

He grew a large, bushy beard to welcome Virginia Kauffman as the new doctor and chief administrator of the Mtshabezi Mission hospital.[4]

In her 23 years as a missionary doctor in Africa, Virginia was noted for her efficiency and professionalism. She was the first woman to be appointed to the Executive Board, the top governing body of the Brethren in Christ Church in Africa. On this male-dominated board she served with dignity and decorum for 20 years, and was the only woman to serve on the board for most of those years. She was the only official missionary remaining on the board for her last few years there, during which time the missionaries were transferring responsibility to the African leaders. She also represented Brethren in Christ missions on the Medical Committee for the ecumenical Rhodesia Christian Conference, which made recommendations to the government regarding government grants and other needs.

Virginia was also a doctor to the missionaries, treating them with compassion and understanding at times of emotional or physical needs. She provided a complete and thorough physical examination for each missionary. A former missionary remembers with appreciation the spiritual support, medical help, and compassionate understanding his family received from her at critical times—such as the sudden death of a young daughter and the illness of another child with rheumatic fever.[5]

Despite her heavy workload, Virginia began new clinics to meet the needs of the greater community for many miles around. She gave child-care lectures and taught nutrition at the prenatal clinics. Well-baby clinics drew large numbers of mothers and babies, which in addition to attending to regular patients in the hospital, made for a heavy day of work. "This was a baby-clinic day and we had a record high this time, 147 babies," she once wrote to her family. "There were about 30 general patients I needed to see. . . . I examined more than 175 people today, and to deal with that many people in one day is really tiring. We have several very sick people here now and that takes extra work."[6] "I always sort of dread well-baby clinic day," she added, "although I like it too, but it is such a heavy day . . . such a screaming!"[7] In another letter she reported, "My eyes are really heavy and I am terribly tired this evening. . . . I'll get my bath and get ready for bed, then sit on my chair and knit a bit before I crawl in. I really like my chair."[8] Of her workload for one week, she wrote, "We have had a busy week here, not so much with general inpatients but in maternity and outpatients. On Thursday we had six deliveries in about nine hours. We have 22 waiting. . . . "[9]

Emergencies often interrupted regular sleeping hours or time blocked off for office work. In a letter in 1975, she related, "Just as I was ready to start addressing envelopes, I had to go to the hospital to sew a finger back on. It was still attached a bit but was just barely hanging on. Just about the first joint had been chopped with an axe. . . . On Tuesday afternoon a bus turned over about six miles from here. They brought casualties in here, six of them...one woman with a possible fractured pelvis . . . one woman had a fractured wrist. . . . " "If one read the right report the other morning, it would sound as though we might be in Spain," she wrote in the same letter with her characteristic sense of humor. "A new patient had come in during the evening before and the night nurse wrote in the book that Micah had a *fight with a bull.* He did tangle with one...had a laceration on the lower part of his abdomen. . . , a number of abrasions and a fractured wrist. . . . "[10] "Making a diagnosis is more of a challenge under the conditions here than where it is practically done for you with all tests available at home," she wrote in an article for the *Evangelical Visitor.* "Our status is more like the old time country doctor."[11]

She had many responsibilities. Not only was she the doctor, she was also the hospital administrator, the ambulance driver, a preacher, and, at times, the funeral director. In another article in the *Evangelical Visitor*, she elaborated on such activities. "One is called upon to do many things. A TB patient asked me to mend his trousers. . . . I put enough stitching on them to add quite a bit of strength. . . . Another time a boy brought his mother's hand-turning sewing machine in—for three miles on the back of his bike, probably pushed most of the way through sand, and asked if I could fix it. (Why shouldn't a doctor be able to doctor machines too?) I checked it all over, did some adjusting, and finally got it going well again."[12]

Her resourceful nature and ability to be cheerfully flexible was apparent the day that Virginia sent Twala, the mission's African driver, to take a patient to the hospital in Bulawayo for further treatment. Someone soon came on a bicycle to inform her that the driver had car trouble. She jumped on her bike and pedaled about three miles on the sand road. "When I fixed the car," she reported, "there were about a dozen men who had gathered around while our driver was waiting. When I got the car going they stood there with their mouths open and just said, 'ah, ah, ah!' They could not quite imagine a woman being able to do anything like that, I guess."[13]

In the midst of heavy workloads and pressing needs, Virginia found times of soul-refreshing relaxation in her gardens. She had a deep love and appreciation for nature and rejoiced that God had led her to a place where she could have plenty of flowers. "As I look out the window here [at Mtshabezi Mission] I see a couple of jacaranda blossoms just coming out," she wrote one September. "That means spring for sure. The trees will be a mass of color before long. Speaking of my flowers, I have so many that I have lots of them in the house, keep giving away, and still there are lots in the garden. I am really enjoying them."[14] A month earlier she had written to her family about her flowers. "I got my *roses* pruned in the early part of July. They are starting to sprout now. My *sweet peas* are really doing well. My *Iceland poppies* are very pretty now too, and I continue to have *carnations*. . . . *Larkspur* are starting now and a couple of *snaps* [snapdragons]. . . . I have *anemones* and there are a couple of buds coming on my *ranunculas*. The *calendulas* are a mass of yellow and orange now and there are some lovely big yellow *marigolds* too." [15]

Obviously flowers brought much joy into Virginia's life, and she loved to share them as a gracious part of her missionary service. She made beautiful floral arrangements for Sunday services at the church, for African weddings and funerals. She takes delight in the memory of one bouquet that served a triple purpose. She arranged a large spring-like bouquet for the Saturday morning church wedding of one of the African Bible Institute teachers. On Saturday afternoon it was a funeral bouquet for the service of a very old African Christian woman. Then on Sunday it was the usual worship service bouquet.

The Kauffman gardens became noteworthy. One time when missionaries from a Dutch Reformed mission were being taken on a tour of the various institutions of the Mtshabezi Mission, they asked to be allowed to view Virginia's flower garden.

The doctor's fruit and vegetable gardens were also a source of satisfaction to her, a respite from the daily pressures of the medical needs she attended to. The produce added variety to the meals of the mission staff. She started asparagus and strawberries from seed. She planted rows of corn and picked the ears by the dozen, freezing much of it for future use. Beets, squash, Swiss chard, lima beans, and mulberries provided diversity. Her pleasure in sharing these garden treasures is illustrated in a letter to her family in the United States: "In Bulawayo (for a meeting of the Executive Board), I stayed with Edna as usual. I took a basket of vegetables and fruit from my garden for her. I had tomatoes, lettuce, radishes, green beans, lima beans, onions, and strawberries. Also I took some Shasta daisies, carnations, and pansies for her."[16]

Always aware that the Lord had first called her to be a Christian missionary, Virginia used every opportunity to share the good news of the gospel. Each Sunday, in addition to her rounds at the hospital, she conducted a Christian service. She played her accordion to attract patients and their families into the services, and usually gave an invitation to personal salvation at the end.

By her care and encouragement, the Africans came to understand Virginia's genuine interest in them. An African girl who worked at Mtshabezi Hospital told one of the missionaries that Dr. Kauffman "was *really African*—because she understands the people and can talk to them."[17] Years later, Dr. Kauffman recalled with a smile, "After my first few years in [Southern] Rhodesia several of the church women starting calling me *'inyanga yetu'*—literally meaning '*our* witch doctor.' "

Venturing into the Gwaii Area

She showed her pioneering spirit by accepting, without complaint, a 1960 assignment to the Phumula Mission in the Gwaii area, which was situated in a very remote area on the edge of the Kalahari Desert in Southern Rhodesia. Here she oversaw the development of a small medical clinic into a busy hospital that served all the people in the area.

This was in a scrub-brush region with very flat land and sandy soil. Big mukwa trees provided some shade, but although there were some days of lovely weather, there were seasons of oppressive heat. Virginia remembers one year when there were six consecutive weeks of temperatures registering between 104–114 degrees. Even the mukwa trees lost their leaves in such heat.

The Brethren in Christ had leased 200 acres from the government to build a mission in this area, in response to a need to minister to African families who had moved to the region from the overpopulated Wanezi Mission area. The government had bored wells hundreds of feet deep to provide a year-round water supply. But roads were undeveloped, and no bridges crossed the rivers. The area was 125 miles from Bulawayo, the nearest city. When Virginia went to Phumula, only limited housing was available. Until a doctor's residence was constructed in 1967, she basically lived in one room and used an outhouse.[18] Patients slept in mud huts with thatched roofs until a hospital was built with separate wards for men, women and children, and maternity patients. To obtain government grants, a special TB ward was added.

Training at Hahnemann Medical College in Philadelphia had not particularly prepared her for the vast number of medical situations she was called upon to handle. But her intellectual capacity, her practical nature, and her deep sense of God's presence in her life combined to make her a doctor of excellence for the African people, whom she grew to love in the 14 years in which she served them.

Lois Kipe, a nurse who worked with Virginia at Phumula Hospital in the Gwaii area, describes the sense of identification established between Virginia and the African people. "I watched Virginia put in long hours, listening to the many people who came to her for help, diagnosing, and treatment. I followed her on rounds through the wards and heard her greeting not only the patients, but the family members who were with them, stopping to chat with those gathered on the verandahs who were waiting for treatment or with relatives. I saw her laugh with the people and cry with them. I watched her work with them, worship with them, and witness to them."[19]

The workload at the hospital was heavy, with busy days and nights often interrupted by the arrival of extremely ill patients. Virginia once wrote to her family: "Most of those coming in have malaria and are really sick. Last night there were ten who came. . . . Of those, six had a temperature of 103 degrees or over, two of them over 105 degrees. . . . One woman was brought in unconscious. Hers was cerebral malaria."[20] Another time she wrote of a woman with terminal cancer who had been brought to the hospital by bus at midnight. "When I talked to her . . . she said she was not ready to meet God but wanted to be. So she prayed and accepted the Lord."[21]

The government opened a medical clinic some distance away but had no local doctor to oversee it. Answering the clinic's request for help, Virginia served there once a month. She often saw as many as 85 to 90 patients on those busy days, then would bring back to the Phumula Mission Hospital several patients who needed extra surgical attention. When the government clinic began, Virginia and a nurse attended the opening ceremonies. "There were several hundred Africans including three chiefs and the head fellows of the Gwaii Council," she reported. "There were only eight whites there. We sat under the shade of a big canvas . . . up with the chiefs and the Council heads. I received recognition in several of the speeches because I am '*Their Doctor.*' "[22]

Jake Shenk, who was superintendent of Phumula Mission for part of Dr. Kauffman's two terms there, remembers her as being "very keen to see the bushmen people come to an understanding of the Lord. . . . She was instrumental in helping the first bushman who was baptized and accepted into the church to be married by Christian rites, attend Bible School and serve as an evangelist in the church. . . . She employed some of them to work as general hands at the hospital. . . . She showed her interest in their spiritual well-being by witnessing to them, encouraging them, and providing Christian literature to help them."[23]

Dr. Kauffman mastered the Ndebele language soon after arriving in Africa. Her ability with this language endeared her to the Africans and made communication with them meaningful from the beginning. Spiritual tracts in the native language were developed under her guidance, and two booklets were translated into Ndebele for use with child-care and nutrition lectures.[24] She wrote in the *Evangelical Visitor*: "Tracts printed in the native language are conveniently placed in the hospital and a Testament at each bed. It is not uncommon to walk into one of the wards [at Mtshabezi] and find them being read." [25]

She had many opportunities to touch the lives of the African people with the good news of the gospel. In the TB ward at the hospital, she started a New Christians Class for the long-term patients who had accepted the Lord. To readers of the *Evangelical Visitor*, she wrote: "One of the men in the class said . . . that this is so good he does not know why he never repented before!"[26]

She enjoyed visiting the African villages in the Gwaii area, always taking her accordion and singing Ndebele choruses. One of her favorites was "Emafwini nangu yehla" ("Lo in the Clouds He is Coming").

In a letter to her family, Virginia wrote of an interesting visit she and another missionary made to a village. "Yesterday we got into a 'beer drink' and had a congregation of about 45 for the service. They were in all stages of sobriety. . . . The big beer mug was passed around while I was speaking. . . . The more sober ones shook their heads when it was passed to them." After the missionaries left the beer drink, some 20 children followed them from one village to another. "We felt like the Pied Piper!" In the same letter she reflected on what could happen in a village service: "It seems that there are so many distractions when we are having a service. The people around here have quite a few goats, and so there were quite a few times that someone had to chase the goats that were getting into things. . . . When I was speaking a little kid came walking right over my lap. . . . Two goats got their heads in a tin can and then could not get them out. They went rolling on the ground. . . . A hawk came swooping down to get a little chick that was running around, but fortunately, it missed."[27]

Through associations such as these, Virginia gained understanding of the African culture and insight into the spiritual needs of the people. Her strong belief in God and his ability to change lives gave her strength in confronting instances of immorality. She bravely confronted men who were ruining their lives with liquor, such as a chief she treated for delirium tremors—a man she had also treated for gonorrhea after he visited prostitutes. Always she prayed with such people, and counseled and encouraged them to make a new start.

Life in Africa took courage. Superintendent Shenk recalls a time when Virginia and a nurse were returning on an undeveloped road to Phumula after a heavy rain. A bus was stuck in a wide expanse of water on the road by the river. Being unable to continue, the two women spent the night in the small pickup truck that was loaded with supplies for the hospital.[28] Virginia recalled that "people were shouting back and forth to each other a good bit of the night, and from the sound of it there must have been a thousand frogs all raising their voices in chorus. . . . We heard hyenas howling."

By 1972, Virginia was the only remaining career missionary physician in Africa Brethren in Christ missions. In an article for the *Evangelical Visitor*, she emphasized her personal concern for the future of the total medical mission effort and the urgency of the need for medical personnel. "*We need help*," she wrote. "This must come from God, not just through medical personnel, but through all of you. Those doctors and nurses reading this article: ask the Lord if He can use you to help fill in these gaps. If you are not in the medical profession: Pray, Pray, Pray!"[29]

The situation was clearly desperate. Macha was a teaching hospital for Zambian nurses. She felt it was necessary to have a doctor there (preferably one prepared to do surgery) because of the training program. If the need wasn't met, she feared that the Zambian government would put one of its own doctors there, many of whom were from communist countries. She foresaw the closure of the two hospitals in Zimbabwe unless help came. Because the government of that country did not have sufficient doctors to fill all the vacancies, the mission hospital would eventually close because of lack of personnel and funds.[30]

Although flowers were more difficult to grow in the desert conditions of the Gwaii area, Dr. Kauffman always planted annuals and enjoyed colorful varieties such as pansies, snapdragons, and carnations. Each spring, the "night of the Spider Lilies" was a time of great excitement. These lilies were wild flowers that all opened on the same evening, stayed open the entire night, then wilted the next morning when the sun came up.

Virginia appears to have maintained a spirit of good humor and contentment throughout her 23 years of service in Africa. Her rewards were in such things as seeing what a difference a belief in God made in the atmosphere of a village at the time of a death, in leading a witch doctor to God before his death, and in remembering the words of a little African boy whom she had dedicated to the Lord: "The doctor doesn't hurt people, she prays for them."[31]

Former Bishop Shenk sums up her presence. "She was a true servant of God and people. Her love, compassion, and commitment will always be remembered. They serve as a lasting example for others to follow."

Early in 1977 the war for independence in Zimbabwe escalated. Military action expanded, and life became much more tense for the missionaries. Concerned for the missionaries' physical safety, the Executive Board of the national church requested that missionaries leave their mission stations, particularly in the rural areas. Under these circumstances, Virginia returned to the United States.

Continuing Faithful Service at Home

Back in California, Virginia worked for nine years as attending physician at a plasma center in San Bernardino before retiring. She worshiped with the Alta Loma Brethren in Christ congregation, which was only a little over a year old at that time and met in a local school building. She has remained a faithful member there and has served on local committees and boards. She is noted for the numerous hand-knit afghans that she donates for the annual relief sale of Mennonite Central Committee.

Dr. Kauffman has never regretted her decision to faithfully follow the Lord's plan for her life. The fragrance of her spirit still speaks of God's love. Her love for flowers is currently exemplified by the beautiful flowers growing in the outdoor hanging baskets at her apartment at Upland Manor, a Brethren in Christ retirement home in Upland, California. The fragrance of the flowers fittingly resembles the fragrance of her work as a pioneer medical doctor in Africa.

Overcoming Obstacles, Fulfilling Needs

Virgie Felker Lehman Garman Kraybill

by Dorcas I. Steckbeck*

Some women serve the church quietly. Virgie Kraybill served the church forthrightly and with vigor. Although she never held highly visible leadership positions, Virgie was a woman of influence who faced the needs of her family and her community with an organized mind and a strong heart. Her story—combining survival as the sole parent of a large household, devotion to the church and its institutions, and a keen awareness of the needs surrounding her—is distinctive among Brethren in Christ women of her time period.[1]

Religious and Intellectual Awakening

Virgie Felker Lehman began her life in the rural setting of Lancaster County, Pennsylvania. She was born March 9, 1896, in the small village of Rheems to Jacob and Amanda (Felker) Lehman. Jacob came from a Brethren in Christ family; his wife's family was Mennonite, but had contacts with Brethren in Christ young people through Lancaster County youth gatherings. Both joined the Brethren in Christ Church at the time of their marriage in 1892.[2]

Not surprisingly, the religious practices of the Brethren in Christ Church influenced Virgie's life from her earliest years.[3] As

---

*Dorcas (Dori) I. Steckbeck is director of the Brethren in Christ Historical Library and Archives in Grantham, Pennsylvania, which includes the Archives of Messiah College. She is an active member of the Millersville Brethren in Christ Church. Dori first learned about Virgie Kraybill while working in the Archives.

a young girl, she began wearing the plain uniform of church members *before* conversion and baptism, contrary to church custom. When she learned to understand the meaning behind the practice, she explained in later years, wearing plain clothes became an important step of identification with the church and with her Christian faith.

In addition to her zeal for church practices, Virgie valued church doctrine and life. As an eager learner and a forthright young woman, she actively pursued instruction on spiritual matters. Unfortunately, limited doctrinal and theological instruction was available to her. Her parents often did not know how to explain the practices of the church. And her local congregation did not hold revival meetings—a popular source for spiritual counsel and encouragement. So Virgie, and some of her Brethren in Christ friends, frequently attended Sunday school classes and youth activities at a local Mennonite church. They also attended Mennonite revival meetings. During one of these gatherings, Virgie first learned about "freedom from guilt," as she termed it, from the testimony of another woman. This teaching comforted her, since she sometimes resented the strain of trying to live an obedient life according to church standards.

Her strong identification with the church created other difficulties. Her plain clothes, for example, left her feeling isolated and lonely, even though she grew up in an area well populated by conservative religious groups. In later years, she remembered being teased as a child when she ran on the school playground and her covering fell off. The feeling of isolation she encountered during her childhood seemed destined to continue when the Lehman family moved to Harrisburg, Pennsylvania's capital city, in September 1910. Upon arrival, 14-year-old Virgie pronounced herself to be "the only plain girl in the city."

Her first impression, however, did not reflect reality. As the location of the Messiah Rescue and Benevolent Home, the city contained a modest hub of denominational life and plain-clothed church members. The Rescue Home provided facilities and care for elderly adults and orphaned children, and was the meeting place for the Brethren in Christ congregation in the city, the Messiah Home Chapel. On her first evening, Virgie walked to the chapel to attend services. She found, much to her surprise, the service filled with "interesting, beautiful girls and handsome young men." Of greater import was the discovery that the young people came from the denomination's newly organized Messiah Bible School and Missionary Training Home, which had opened the week before on 12th Street, several blocks from the Lehman home.

This early encounter with students from the school sparked Virgie's interest. She persuaded her parents to allow her to enroll at the school and began taking classes in January 1911, finishing her first term in June of that year. The opportunity for religious training and education thrilled Virgie. She chose preparatory courses that would equip her for eventual service as a missionary. Her classes included public speaking—meeting in the Messiah Home Chapel, equipped with a high, domed ceiling, helped students practice the "art" of throwing their voices—penmanship, missionary enterprise, missionary principles and practices, music, and English.

Virgie's involvement with the school provided opportunities for learning and interaction that were not otherwise available to her in the conservative denomination. Always eager to expand her knowledge, she supplemented her course work with a variety of extracurricular activities. On Friday evenings, Virgie participated in the school literary society meetings. At these meetings, students gathered to engage in debates and to practice their public speaking skills by giving impromptu speeches. Virgie found the society meetings so interesting that she claimed she "wouldn't have missed them for anything." She was also involved in other student organizations: the Good Will Purity Association, which promoted moral purity, particularly sexual purity; the Young People's Christian Society, which focused on developing the spiritual life, public speaking skills, and witnessing; and the Missionary Circle, which supported foreign mission work.

The cause of missions, promoted through classes and activities at the school, captivated Virgie. And the knowledge and skills she acquired during her school years produced a devoted young woman eager to serve the church overseas. When she graduated in 1915, her address to her classmates included an impassioned plea for mission work: "Surely the need for medical missionaries is great enough, the appeal pathetic enough, the urgency of the situation intense enough; and is there not in our hands as a church strength enough to furnish the means, and in our schools students enough to furnish the men, that these millions may find relief and learn of better things? . . . I submit that it is more Christlike to go forth and minister to the greatest needs of the greatest number than it is to stay at home and be spent in meeting the wants of the comparatively few."[4]

Virgie's interest in missions was complemented by a continuing appetite for religious instruction. She especially enjoyed attending the annual Bible conferences. The conferences—a popular event hosted by the school—attracted Brethren in Christ evangelists from throughout the denomination. The speakers and the sermons remained so implanted in Virgie's mind that she clearly remembered them in later years with appreciation. She also recognized the important benefits the church received from its connection to the school: "As I look back over these many years . . . and know what the Bible conferences have meant to the church, and what the Bible school meant to the church, I can only say that it was a great, great blessing to the Pennsylvania church that the school came this way."

The advantageous location of the school, and thus the location of the conferences, was equally beneficial for Virgie. As a result of the spiritual training and fervor at the 1911 conference, she decided to join the church. Her religious enthusiasm had earlier resulted in a conversion experience in February of that year. She became an official member of the Messiah Home Chapel congregation and was baptized in the nearby Susquehanna River in June.

Virgie's religious instruction was not limited to the programs of the denomination. As a capital city, Harrisburg lured famous theologians and ministers to its city churches to give lectures. Virgie attended these lectures and eagerly absorbed doctrines that were not always compatible with Brethren in Christ doctrine. In one of her Bible courses, Professor John Climenhaga asked the class to write about the deity of Christ. Virgie's written response elicited a sharp retort from Climenhaga: "Virgie, where'd you get that? You didn't get that in Brethren in Christ sermons."

Despite the occasional discouraging comment, Virgie willingly attended these meetings with another student at the Bible school, John Garman. John was the son of prominent church members Henry and Katie (Simmons) Garman and an ordained assistant minister at the Messiah Home Chapel. The congregation was struggling with the issue of sanctification, so senior minister George Detweiler asked John to attend lectures given by non-Brethren in Christ theologians, hoping John would receive insight to help both ministers present balanced teaching on the issue.

In the early stages of Virgie's friendship with John, she found employment with his parents at the Messiah Home. Katie, the home's cook, was so busy on Sundays preparing dinner for the residents that she often arrived at church as the benediction was being pronounced. At Katie's request, Virgie, eager to meet new people, stayed to help clean up after the meal. That was the beginning of her employment with the Home and the starting point for her developing relationship with John Garman.

While students at the school, Virgie and John shared similar interests. Both were preparing for missionary service and were involved in school organizations. After Virgie started working at the Home, John drove or walked her home when she worked until late evening—an act of kindness insisted upon by Virgie's father and Katie Garman. Virgie never thought the companionship signified anything more than friendship. John, however, had different ideas. From the first moment he spent time with Virgie, he told her later, he decided she was "a girl that I'd like to go with someday if I could." Although he initially refrained from expressing his feelings, fearing it would complicate Virgie's working arrangement with his parents, eventually their friendship developed into a committed relationship. Their marriage on February 25, 1916, took place at the Messiah Home Chapel in the presence of a large number of guests.

A Love Lost and a Dream Unfulfilled

Although both Virgie and John dreamed of serving as missionaries in India, an unexpected setback changed their plans. Soon after their marriage, John contracted tuberculosis. At the recommendation of a doctor, the couple moved to California, since John's illness required life in a warmer climate. The Garmans lived here from 1916–1918 and made many acquaintances in the Brethren in Christ community at Upland. Virgie nurtured her interest in missions through her involvement with the Upland congregation's missionary society.

Although John's health eventually improved, other difficulties emerged. The couple's first child, Henry, died in 1917 at the age of six months from cerebral meningitis. When John had sufficiently recovered from his illness, they returned to Pennsylvania in 1918, only to face another crisis. An influenza epidemic was already raging through the state when they returned. Weakened by his struggle with tuberculosis, John quickly succumbed to the epidemic. He died on October 23, 1918, at the age of 24, leaving Virgie pregnant with their second child.

Church members provided comfort after her devastating loss. John R. Zook, a colorful Brethren in Christ evangelist, visited Virgie to offer his condolences and an unconventional perspective. "Now Virgie, don't take it too hard," he consoled. "John was a good man and a good student of the Bible. God needs ministers for the other planets. He just took [John] to be a minister on another planet."[5] When men landed on the moon in 1969, Virgie remembered Zook's comment and wondered if life *would* be found on other planets.

After John's death, Virgie put her dreams of missionary life aside and prepared to support herself and her unborn child. She accepted the position of head cook at the Messiah Bible School, now located in Grantham. The task—a challenging undertaking—was made more difficult by the school's financial limitations. Virgie revealed some of the hardships of her position in a 1975 interview: "There wasn't enough money to buy better kitchen equipment. The granite kettles were cracked so bad on the inside that I was afraid to cook in them because the enamel might crack off and get in the students' bodies. . . . Many times I tried to make pies for the students and worked until ten, eleven, even twelve o'clock at night doing so because we didn't have oven room and equipment. We were [often] late with our meals, 15 to 20 minutes, because we could not get the fires to burn."

In the midst of these difficulties, Virgie's world was brightened by the birth of her child. After John Detweiler Garman (named for his father and Virgie's former pastor, George

Detweiler) arrived on January 12, 1919, he was Virgie's constant companion in the kitchen, often under the watchful eye of student helpers.

Surviving as a Single Parent

Through her involvement with the school and as a new member of the Grantham community, Virgie became acquainted with another widower, Martin Kraybill. Martin was a farmer and entrepreneur, owning several farms and hydroelectric dams. His first wife, Cora Smith (daughter of S. R. Smith), had also died in the influenza epidemic of 1918.

After a brief period of courtship, Virgie and Martin married on September 4, 1920, at Martin's home. They immediately moved to a farm in Brandtsville, several miles from Grantham. Their marriage brought together a large family under one roof. In addition to John, Virgie's son from her first marriage, the household included Martin and Cora's four children—Elizabeth, Victor, Martin Ethan, and Cora Gladys—and their foster son, Austin Neff. Martin and Virgie eventually added four children of their own to the family—Spencer, Amanda, Homer, and Mary Helen.

At this stage of her life, Virgie continued to display the active mind, industrious nature, and genuine interest in meeting needs that would characterize her for the rest of her life. At a 1923 council meeting of Brethren in Christ congregations in the Grantham District, she and Martin asked the council to consider how its members could meet the needs of disadvantaged young women. "Since it has been suggested at various times that we, as a church, make some provision for the feeble-minded, and since nothing has been done as yet," they declared, "we wish to suggest that our body give this matter consideration with the further feature of looking after fallen and neglected girls, said effort to be launched at some future time." The suggestion, referred to the Pennsylvania State Council, was never acted upon.

Virgie and Martin's cooperation in this effort could not mask the difficulties of their marriage. Their partnership, evidently, did not have a satisfying start—Virgie told an acquaintance in later years that her first marriage was for love and her second marriage was for convenience. Without a good foundation to survive relational and financial strains, the marriage soon deteriorated.

In 1928, Martin asked to be relieved from church membership; some time after that he moved permanently to his brother's home in Denver, Colorado.[6]

Virgie, left alone, faced a difficult situation. Although the three oldest children from Martin's first marriage were supporting themselves, Virgie was still responsible for the support and care of the remaining children. After Martin's departure, she relocated the family to Grantham, taking up residence in a house across the railroad tracks from the school's administration building, Old Main. The move cemented her relationship with the school. Son Homer summarizes the connection: "[She] was close to the school in interests and this [move] brought her close to the school in location." Living in close proximity to the center of denominational activity proved invaluable for the family's welfare.

From the beginning of her experience as the sole parent in the Kraybill household, Virgie's message to her children was clear: "In order to stay together, we've got to work together." And work together they did. Virgie, by all accounts, was a good organizer, and she mobilized her family to meet the demands of life without a father during the Depression. She taught the children to save every penny and to use necessities carefully. Each child also had specific responsibilities and worked outside the home at every available opportunity. Their earnings were shared with the entire household. When questioned about her ability to support her family, Virgie cited earnings from Elizabeth and Austin as a source of income (Elizabeth provided $25 a month, Austin, $10 a week).

Every family member contributed to the survival of the family unit. The girls prepared meals and managed kitchens in community homes. The boys walked miles to a neighboring county before dawn to be ready to pick berries at their destination before the sun came up. Elizabeth, the oldest Kraybill child and a licensed nurse, visited her family on weekends. During her visits, she often loaded some of the children into her car, drove to the grocery store, and purchased bags of groceries for the coming week. All the children had after-school jobs. The school provided many employment opportunities for them, including cleaning buildings after Bible and summer youth conferences.

Virgie was equally busy supporting her large family. Her efficiency and her willingness to take on any task to provide income caused one family member to dub her "a lass of all trades." Her nursing and domestic skills, in particular, allowed her to function effectively in a variety of settings. Her children remember that "she had a knack for . . . figuring out the intelligent and calm way to face a situation." These skills did not go unnoticed by the community. On one occasion, Virgie realized a home birth she was assisting with had potentially serious complications. She insisted on having the mother taken to the hospital. After the safe delivery of the baby, the hospital doctor said Virgie's common sense probably saved the lives of the woman and the child. This experience characterized her ability to work under emergency conditions. She had, states son Homer, a "deep reserve of strength" which she could draw from to handle stressful circumstances.

Her strength and her skills opened doors for employment in the community. She performed household duties and provided practical nursing care in many homes in exchange for remuneration. Virgie's nursing engagements occasionally separated her from the family for a week or more to care for unwell community members. Sometimes an emergency call asking for help in preparing a meal or entertaining guests sent Virgie rushing to a neighboring home to fill in for an ill wife. On one such occasion, she cooked at a moment's notice for a local family, telling her children that she had an opportunity to earn 35–55 cents—enough money to buy meat for their Sunday meal.

When circumstances seemed especially dismal, her strong will kept her focused on the task of caring for her family. Homer remembers one occasion, when she suffered from a broken leg, that especially illustrates her perseverance and resolve: "[A local man] hired her to come and cut potatoes, and she . . . sat there in the cold, drafty barn, cutting seed potatoes to plant. . . . When [my aunt] came out and saw Mother doing this, she said, 'Virgie, this is nonsense! You don't need money this bad. It's not right that you are sitting here with a broken leg, cutting potatoes, trying to make a living.' But Mother was a strong woman physically and also spiritually, and she said, 'No, I can do this. What are we going to do for money if I don't?'" Homer concludes, "Many women would not have been able to bear . . . the things she went through: the separation from her husband and the resulting loss of relationships, and the strain of the Depression."

No one questioned Virgie's ability to survive the hardships of her life, but she still needed support from family and friends. Her mother frequently traveled from Harrisburg to Grantham to manage the Kraybill household when Virgie was away at nursing jobs. And the family always had enough food, in part because of the generosity of church and community members. Local grocer D. S. Keefer deferred payment on the family's grocery bill. Sometimes their credit would accumulate to $100 or more—a large amount during the Depression—but Keefer never asked for interest when the Kraybills paid their bill. To maintain a constant supply of milk, Virgie purchased and shared a cow with the Jesse Brechbill family (Jesse was business manager for the school). One family milked the cow in the morning, the other family milked in the evening. John Minter, one of the Grantham congregation's pastors and an instructor at the school, provided meat for the family whenever he butchered. Since meat was not always available, this act was a kindness the family deeply appreciated.

A New Mission Field: Meeting Needs from the Homeland

Virgie willingly imitated the kind deeds bestowed on her and her family. The fruits of her active mind and industrious spirit, in addition to supporting the Kraybill family, provided limited resources to help less fortunate members of her community. She was particularly adept at identifying areas of need that, Homer declares, "a lot of people would not have the innate ability to uncover."

Her desire to meet the needs of others was, in fact, so strong that she boldly entered situations where others trod carefully. "She never flinched when she saw a need," Homer remembers. Less fortunate members of the Grantham community were frequent targets of her generosity. Many tramps, following the railroad tracks that ran through the town, passed by the Kraybill home. Almost always, they stopped in for a meal and were never turned away. Families in the neighborhood also received food and care from Virgie when they were in need. In one large family, both parents had steady employment outside the home, but Virgie often invited the children to her home for meals because she sensed they were hungry. Neglected women, plagued by illness or recalcitrant husbands, also received household goods from Virgie's limited resources to care for their families.

Virgie boldly cared for the community in another arena as an active member of the Women's Christian Temperance Union. As a Union member, she crusaded against the use of alcohol through public and school presentations, even though her stance provoked verbal taunts from alcohol users in the community. And when her municipal township—Upper Allen—offered a local voting option that banned the sale of alcohol within its boundaries, she promptly went to the polls to vote in support of the option, risking disapproval from some Brethren in Christ members. (The Brethren in Christ, as a sign of separation from the world, did not encourage participation in politics and government at that time.) The option, offered with the encouragement of Virgie and other Union members, successfully passed. Upper Allen Township remains "dry" to this day.

Virgie's ministry extended beyond the community to the Messiah Bible School. Living next door to her alma mater furnished her with many opportunities to serve. This Virgie willingly did—eager to aid the institution that had provided her and her family with educational opportunities (all of her children attended the school) and financial support. She often voluntarily led work groups to clean Old Main and other buildings in preparation for church activities and General Conference.

Virgie's service ranged from the mundane to the unusual. The Kraybill family had a telephone, since Virgie needed to be reached quickly for emergency nursing jobs. Because of the school's limited finances and limited phone lines (neither the president nor the dean had a personal telephone), the Kraybill telephone number regularly became a contact number for school personnel. The family often received calls asking them to relay messages to individuals on campus. When offspring of faculty or staff were stranded at the Harrisburg train station in the middle of the night, the Kraybills were called and asked to notify the parents. Rousing sleeping parents at such a late hour called for creative tactics, such as throwing gravel against the windows of their houses.

Virgie's interest in the school extended from the institution to the individuals who carried out its mission. In earlier years, many faculty members arrived on campus with few possessions and prospects of a meager salary. Virgie and her son Homer provided a necessity that was, in some ways, more valuable than monetary assistance—plots of ground on their property for gardening. As early as the 1930s, professors and their families were gardening on the Kraybill's land. Morris and Leone Sider, both employed by the school, remember canning and freezing many quarts of vegetables from the Kraybill's garden during lean years. In addition to land for gardening, Virgie freely offered other forms of material aid to financially strained employees: used apparel in good condition, used furniture, appliances, and material for sewing children's clothing.

Virgie's service to Messiah was equally matched by her interest in the work of the church, especially mission work. Although her dream of becoming a missionary never materialized, she served the cause of missions from the homeland with vigor.

Virgie was particularly adept at mobilizing financial and material support for overseas projects.[7] During World War II, she heard that the Brethren in Christ Church in Africa lacked the funds needed to hold its annual conference. Virgie, remembering the benefits she received from attending General Conference each year, decided missionaries should also benefit from the opportunity to meet and fellowship together. Along with two women from the Grantham congregation, she wrote to the chairman of the Foreign Mission Board to determine the amount needed for holding a conference. The three women then contacted Brethren in Christ Sunday schools in Pennsylvania to ask for contributions. Their efforts raised $700 for the conference—an impressive sum in those years, and $300 more than was needed. Virgie and her friends sent $500 to the African church and $200 to the church in India. Both regions held annual conferences that year.

During the same period, Virgie heard Leora Yoder, a missionary in India, discuss the need for a jeep to aid travel over India's rough roads. In her customary way, Virgie assessed the importance of the need and persuaded the Grantham congregation's vacation Bible school and Sunday school to provide funds for the purchase. The resulting offerings raised over $1,100. Sending a "used" jeep considerably reduced customs charges, so a local man drove the jeep for a brief period of time to put miles on the odometer.

As with her service to the school, Virgie's interest in missions reached beyond programs to individuals. When informed that native men at the Wanezi Bible School in Zambia had only one suit of clothes (and had to stay clustered in rooms while the suits were laundered), Virgie responded to the need. "The people listen better when the preacher is dressed well," she claimed. She persuaded clothing stores to donate suits, then asked school students and men from the Grantham congregation to wear the suits at least once. The suits arrived at their destination used—and thus cheaper—after passing through customs.

Virgie was particularly interested in the welfare of missionary families. When the Walter Winger family, missionaries in Africa, returned to North America in 1936, Virgie realized they would not have many personal possessions. She played a key role in helping them to settle in Pennsylvania, remembers a Winger family member, by providing clothing and other practical items for their new life.[8] When she fulfilled a dream of visiting the African mission field in later years, missionaries remember her entering their homes and asking, "Do you have anything I can sew for you? What can I do to be of service?"

In her belief that missionaries were always in need of material provisions or financial support, Virgie sometimes overlooked the relatively adequate life of mission workers overseas. One missionary, newly returned from Africa, visited Virgie's Pennsylvania home and bluntly remarked, "Virgie, most of the missionaries live better than you do."

Beyond missions, Virgie served the church through her involvement with the local Grantham congregation. She readily ministered there in a variety of positions: Sunday school teacher, vacation Bible school worker, sewing circle member, and counselor and cook for the annual Grantham youth conferences. As a community-minded person, Virgie encouraged the congregation to interact with neighborhood families. She helped to initiate, for example, an annual Sunday school Fourth of July picnic and celebration, an important outreach event for the congregation in former years.

Virgie's ministry was not without difficulties. Her strong mind and earnest desire to serve could transform her strengths into weaknesses. She sometimes, for example, assumed church members and neighbors were as willing and able to serve as she herself was, thereby delegating responsibilities to unwilling participants. Morris Sider summarizes this aspect of her character: "I think her [strong mind] carried her through a lot of difficulties. She had to have that kind of personality. But for some people—people who didn't really understand her background—it was kind of [abrasive]." Although Virgie openly voiced her opinions, thus occasionally encountering misunderstandings, she remained loyal to and supportive of church and community efforts.

A Life of Service Comes to an End

While Virgie's physical strength began to decline at the end of her life, her mind remained active. With her keen memory of Brethren in Christ people, places, and events, she was a favorite resource for church historians and laypeople. Through interviews, she provided significant information for three major church histories: *Quest for Piety and Obedience: The Story of the Brethren in Christ; Messiah College: A History; and To Have a Home: The Centennial History of Messiah Village.*

Her active mind continued to nurture a concern for the needs of others. As a capable seamstress, Virgie purchased material from a local dress factory to make blankets, quilts, and clothes for missionaries and local acquaintances. She often asked, towards the end of her life, "Who's going to do this when I'm gone?"

As her life drew to a close, Virgie's connections to her family—a family that had worked hard to stay together—continued. Although she visited with her children in other parts of the country, the old Kraybill house in Grantham, where she lived with son Homer and his family, remained her place of residence. After several years at a local retirement facility and a brief period of hospitalization, she died on June 12, 1992.

Virgie's life was fittingly personified by her strong mind, her will to survive, and her capacity to serve. From her desire to serve her Lord, she left a simple legacy of ministering to the daily needs of those around her, and, in her forthright way, encouraging others to do the same. Her story reminds us that a woman of faith can overcome formidable obstacles to help fulfill the needs of her family and her world.

Daring to Be a Risk-Taker

Kathleen Ruth Shaver Leadley

by Erma Sider*

In the past, the call to pastoral ministry in the Brethren in Christ Church was expected to come to men. Today, we see God gifting and calling both men and women to the pastoral role. Often that call is fulfilled by college and seminary education following immediately after high school. Yet our God sometimes surprises us. Here in the story of Kathleen (Kathy) Leadley we see a woman who spent years raising a family but who, in the end, could not evade God's personal call to her or the risks that following this call might involve.

A Southern Ontario Childhood[1]

After Kathleen Ruth Shaver entered the world on September 18, 1948, her family home in St. Catharines, Ontario, was never quite the same again. The eldest of three siblings, two daughters and a son, Kathleen was a high-spirited and adventurous child. Her environment was stable, her physical needs cared for. She was taken to a mainline church and Sunday school where she sat in a row with her friends in her cute hat, white gloves, and black patent leather shoes.[2]

---

*Erma Sider is the editor of two cookbooks: *Celebration of Hospitality: A Brethren in Christ World Cookbook* and the *Heritage Cookbook*. She is active in volunteer work in the Fort Erie, Ontario, area, including tutoring refugees in English. Erma and Kathleen Leadley have been friends from the early 1980s when Kathleen and her husband began to attend the Riverside Brethren in Christ Church near Fort Erie, Ontario, where Erma and her husband are members. Erma and Kathleen have worked together on committees planning Women Alive conferences.

Kathleen's teenage years followed the normal course of a young person growing up in the 1950s in a small city in southern Ontario. Together with her best friend Ellen, she entered the new and scary world of high school. Ready to try anything new and wanting to fit in with the crowd, they experimented with various shades of hair dye, teased their hair "a mile high," and visited the local teen hangouts. Kathleen later described those turbulent years: "We tried desperately to be cool Hellcats with our madras blouses color coordinated with wool knee socks and penny loafers."[3]

In her early teens, Kathleen considered the relevance of church attendance to her life. As a young child she had heard stories about Jesus in Sunday school. She understood that he was a good man whom she should emulate, but she doesn't recall hearing the gospel of salvation. Feeling that on her own she could be good enough, she gave up church attendance.

High school was the place where Kathleen met Robert (Bob) Leadley, her future husband. Growing up in the same city with families of similar lifestyles, they began dating in their later teens. Bob's mother, Irene, recalls that from the first time Kathleen came home with Bob, all the family loved her. Though several years younger, Bob's sister found a true big sister in Kathleen. Seeing that Kathleen was exactly what she wanted in a spouse for her elder son, Bob's mother set out to win her affection for the whole family. When, after engagement, Kathleen signed up for a sewing course, Mrs. Leadley did too, although, as Kathleen learned later, she already knew how to sew. She simply wanted this special girl to know she was accepted and loved by the family.[4]

Expanding the Family

Soon Kathleen found herself back at the church of her childhood, this time with Bob at her side for their wedding. Married just before their twentieth birthdays, Kathleen now feels they grew up together as Bob continued a chartered accountant (C.A.) program of studies while working under his father-in-law's skillful eye in a C.A. firm. Later, Bob launched his own accountancy business. Meanwhile, Kathleen was working as a dental assistant for an orthodontist to help pay the bills. Their first home was an apartment in a novel setting, the renovated Nubone Corset Company in the nearby town of Port Dalhousie.

For the first seven years after marriage, church meant little to this spirited couple, except as the appropriate place to be seen for the occasional Christmas or Easter service. They were industrious people actively climbing the social and corporate ladder with their move to a home in the suburbs of St. Catharines and the purchase of a sports car and other appropriate accessories for such a lifestyle.

After the birth of their first child, Jessica, and learning the joy of mothering, Kathleen was pained to realize that there were many children around her in desperate need of love and security. This led Bob and Kathleen to care for more than a dozen deeply scarred foster children from dysfunctional homes. Eventually they adopted five of these children. In their youthfulness and perhaps naïveté, they hoped that they could provide what was lacking in these abused young lives. They labored and wept as they lived through one harrowing experience after another. These children have now left home, but keep in touch with the family through phone calls and e-mail messages. Each of them is making better choices today because of the years of influence in a stable family environment. And Kathleen and Bob note that, as with all of us, God is not finished with these young adults yet. Little did the Leadleys know how God would take those early, painful situations to prepare them both for future ministry.

In the meantime, they rejoiced over the birth of two more of their own children—Rachel and Robert (Rob) joined the family. Being younger than the adopted children, life was not always easy for their three children, growing up as they did with siblings who had no concept of right and wrong and no apparent conscience to guide them. Despite often chaotic situations, Kathleen and Bob were able to provide healthy parenting for their own children. To the observer, no child seemed included or loved more than another.

Grown now, Jessica, an elementary school teacher; Rachel, an accountant in her father's office; and Rob, a university student majoring in business administration, all have warm memories of, and sincere appreciation for, their childhood home. One of them describes Bob and Kathleen as being "the perfect description of what a parent should be." Family highlights were board games during winter snowstorms, baking Christmas cookies, creating Easter chocolates, reading contests, but especially annual camping weeks in Ontario's Algonquin Park, with plenty of hiking, swimming, and canoeing. Kathleen reported only half humorously when she wrote in the local paper, "Camping is about teamwork. . . . We still need every member posted at a corner to get [the dining tent] up the first time. . . . Building a strong camping team builds strong families."[5]

Christian Commitment

Church, earlier seen as unnecessary by Kathleen, began to take on new significance when their children were born. She convinced Bob that to be responsible parents they should take their family to church. The minister quickly shocked these 20-somethings into reality when, holding his Bible high, he proclaimed, "If you don't believe that this is the Word of God, then what are you doing here? You might as well be at home in bed!" which, as Kathleen later notes, was exactly where they wanted to be.

Soon Kathleen was checking things out by attending the charismatic prayer and praise meeting. She recalls the song "Come to the Water" being sung and how the "words jumped off the screen and literally became 3D [sic], and it was as if Jesus was inviting me to come to the water to experience him in spirit and in truth like the woman at the well." The following morning she followed through on the invitation and quietly in her own home invited God into her life.

Life now seemed complete. No longer did she need to search for life's meaning in transcendental meditation or by trying to be a good person, which, she notes, "I was never able to quite do naturally." One of her foster children told her, "All you ever do is sit around and read your Bible!" Bob quickly followed her in this life-changing course: he devoured the entire Bible in two to three weeks.

Their new joy and enthusiasm soon spilled over to longtime friends Jill and Mel Sauer while they vacationed together. They too became excited Christians and followed through by their public confession of faith and, later, pastoral ministry. Already good friends, Kathleen and Jill now shared something more lasting than only their love of humor and communication.

Soon into their new Christian life, the Leadleys began to realize that there was something much more for them than a lifestyle of getting ahead. Suffering a downturn in business at one point, they learned to portion their funds carefully, placing specific amounts into envelopes according to the bills, and eventually paying back all they owed. New friends Don and Pat Cornell recall how impressed they were when they saw the Leadleys "downsizing from a new home to a less pretentious home in the country, giving up the sports car for a more practical vehicle, moving 180 degrees from a very comfortable yuppie lifestyle and big ideas in financing to a simple way of life."

Before their move to the country, Kathleen and Bob were struck a terrible blow when, in 1978, she fell prey to Hodgkin's disease. She was gravely ill for six to eight months. While she was in the hospital, Bob's mother moved in with the family so that Bob could spend as much time as possible with Kathleen.

This illness brought the young couple face to face with death. With seven young children at the time, the future seemed menacing. Courageously facing up to the situation, Kathleen prepared a detailed notebook of household tasks for Bob in the event he would have to raise the children alone. Then came the day for surgery. Bob later recounted how he was so overcome with tension and the possible outcome that he couldn't pray. Others prayed, and even though there were many negative test results, God was in control and miraculously restored Kathleen to health. This is one of those life situations which she has not always been able to understand, but she now says, "Because of my belief in God who always makes sense, I have moved forward. God is good in spite of circumstances."

From the early years of their marriage, Bob and Kathleen worked hard to build a successful marriage of equality. After dinner they asked the children to wash the dishes while they retreated to their bedroom, with a cup of tea, for a time for listening and learning about the events of each other's day. Regular, early bedtimes for the children gave them long evenings together. Throughout the year they scheduled several getaway times, leaving the children with Bob's ever-willing parents.

Setting aside time for devotions together has not been easy for them, but early in their Christian lives they began praying together. This spiritual discipline has helped them through the hard times, especially in raising their family.

A major and continuing influence has been the denomination which Kathleen and Bob now call home. After their move to the countryside, the family was introduced to the Brethren in Christ Church. Here, first at the Bertie church and then at Riverside Chapel (now Riverside Community Church), she says they experienced "the brotherhood principle as expressed through the love and acceptance we received as newcomers." Pastor Gordon Gooderham shepherded her and Bob into an accelerated and disciplined walk with Christ through his strong biblical preaching. This modified their lifestyle and even the way they raised their family. They were impressed with people who actually got ready for church Saturday evening to avoid Sunday morning rush, and people who chatted together and had fun times at potluck dinners. They learned that being a Christian is an experience of making Christ Lord in the dailiness of life. And they resolved that he truly would be Lord in every area of their lives.

Pursuing Education

All along her journey, Kathleen credits Bob's strong support as providing a solid background for her to be a growing person. In the early days of their marriage when her self-confidence level was very low, Bob was the one who saw her potential, often pushing her to areas beyond her comfort zone. He constantly reinforced her talents by encouraging her to study. She took one personal interest course after another, but it was not until many years later that she found the courage to leave the safety of her home and head back to school for credit courses, long one of Bob's suggestions.

So it was with deep fear and trembling that Kathleen embarked on part-time studies at Brock University in St. Catharines, close enough to her home for easy commuting. Her organizational and time management skills so helpful in family life were invaluable now. Bob was behind her all the way, stepping in to take over more family responsibilities. Scrubbing the kitchen floor became an area of expertise, although he acknowledges he never became much of a cook.

Kathleen entered this new world, she says, "with all abandon," earning a bachelor of arts degree when she graduated "with distinction" from Brock in 1991. Her zest for learning not quenched, she enrolled, part-time again, at Ontario Theological Seminary (now Tyndale Seminary), Toronto, in a Master of Divinity program, majoring in pastoral ministry. An award won there in 1995 was given to her "on the basis of academic standing and the promise of Christian leadership."[6]

The milestone of achieving the Master of Divinity degree propelled Kathleen to the next level, in which she is currently involved. In 1998 she enrolled at Fuller Theological Seminary in the Doctor of Ministry program with a major in organizational development.

Accepting the Call to Ministry

While still young in her Christian walk and avidly studying the Bible, Kathleen developed an increasing desire to glorify God. Others saw potential in Kathleen, so that ministry opportunities began to open up. Early on she took her turn in leading the Riverside women's Bible study group. She became part of the leadership team for Sunday evening Kids Kamp, with her own set of unpredictable youngsters in tow. She and Bob opened their home for "Supper 8," corn roasts, horse rides, ball games, and singing around the campfire, all of which were important facets of Riverside Chapel, where Bob and Kathleen had now become members.

Apart from local church life, they became involved in the Koinonia movement for lay renewal. When women of the Niagara region expressed a desire for a women's day, Kathleen brought together a representative planning committee for a regional conference of Women Alive, an interdenominational ministry with a focus on helping women to live purposefully in Christ. The conference proved to be highly successful, certainly due in large part to Kathleen's emphasis on prayer coupled with her drive and competency. Little did she know then that later she would become intimately involved with this national organization. Such experiences encouraged Kathleen to think more seriously about God's call on her life.

In her response in *Brethren in Christ History and Life* to an article entitled "Women in Ministry," Kathleen describes her journey. "For a long time," she wrote, "I tried to deny the call of God because it seemed too unspiritual to say that I was called, not just to a ministry but to *the* ministry—called to preach."[7] She knew that women preachers were not accepted in many pulpits, including some Brethren in Christ pulpits, nor by many other groups. She tried to convince herself that she should take the counseling major in seminary. Indeed, when she was registering in the preaching class, a male student questioned her as to why she should take what limited space there was from the men. Yet the call of God came not to counseling but to preaching. After stifling this call for some years, she knew with certainty that it was more important to obey God and be faithful than to follow the cultural norm.

Church Planter

Over the years of her faith journey, as she became more confident and focused, Kathleen experienced a growing vision to see a Brethren in Christ Church planted in her home city of St. Catharines. Testing this as possibly God's will, she approached her bishop, Harvey Sider, who brought up the concept to Brethren in Christ pastors in the Niagara region. Their favorable reaction led to a decision to launch the project. Gordon Gooderham, her former Riverside pastor, became senior pastor, and Kathleen was the assistant pastor. With the passage of time, and while still in seminary, she became the pastor.

Growth at Orchard Creek Fellowship was gradual through diligent, prayerful effort. In a 1996 pastor's report to the conference bishop, Kathleen recorded, "We need together to pray for many people to come. . . . I am excited that this year we will have our first prayer vigil—prayer for our church, community and people ongoing for 24 hours. . . . This could be a pivotal time in our personal and corporate life together." [8]

The story of Stan and Melva Kizul characterizes Kathleen's ministry at Orchard Creek. Melva was raised in a church environment, but not finding meaning there, she attended various churches intermittently over the years. One day her brother challenged her: "Why don't you pray about a church?" She and her sister took up his challenge, and the next day a flier came in the mail inviting them to the Christmas service at Orchard Creek. Melva began to attend. Soon she wanted to learn more about a personal relationship with Jesus, so Kathleen began a Bible study. Before long, seeing Melva's hunger for the Word, Kathleen was able to lead her to the Lord. Two of her four children are Christians, and they, along with most of her grandchildren, are Orchard Creek attendees. Melva is now the leader of the Bible study, which is still going strong.

Coming from a family of divorce with an absent father, Melva later commented, "God knew that I would relate better to a woman pastor than to a man." However, her husband, Stan, wasn't so sure that he wanted to be part of a church pastored by a woman. He told his wife, "I'll go with you to church but I'm pretty sure I won't be impressed by your pastor. There is no real place in the pulpit for a woman." Seeing his wife change dramatically before his eyes, however, he thought he should check things out. Much to his surprise, soon he, too, became a Christian. Baptism followed. Both Stan and Melva were now fully involved in the life of the church, eventually holding positions on the church board, or wherever there was a need. Stan confesses, "I now believe that being a pastor is not relegated to gender."

In such ways Orchard Creek grew, often through people who were led to the Lord by Kathleen's passion to share the good news of the gospel. Even her cleaning lady came to Christ at Kathy's kitchen table and later brought her husband to church. Statistics indicate there has been gradual growth and some setbacks. During her early years in pastoring, she found confrontation difficult, but with time and experience she grew stronger. Through such experiences, Bob was always a listening post for her, keeping out of the way and remaining confident that she was up to the task of resolution.

Always serving only part time, she nevertheless threw herself wholeheartedly into both evangelism and caring for the often very needy people who found a home at Orchard Creek. When a young husband was killed in an accident, she was there to hold the widow's hand and provide comfort and counsel. Attendees from dysfunctional families did not threaten this pastor, with her years of such experience. In court she supported new immigrants, even when those same people took advantage of her. She drove people for job interviews. For nine years without any salary except a small honorarium, and with no money available in the church budget, she often cheerfully and generously used her own resources to meet the physical needs of people (gas, groceries, rent money, appliances). Too generously, the church board thought, eventually providing a contingency fund.

Kathleen believes in team leadership but, being a self-confessed control freak in her early days in the pastorate, she may have tended to micro-manage because, quite naturally, she wanted things to be "just right." Her forceful personality, vision, and management ability tended to overshadow capable people on the team and in the congregation, at least at first. Yet John Gibbins, her associate, later praised her positive development in giving others the opportunity to grow.

John describes the deep mutual respect between them. He felt no sense of control or competition, except on games nights, when, he notes, "This otherwise reserved and 'proper' lady would become an aggressive competitor, especially if it was 'us' [men] against 'them' [women]." John also valued his opportunity to "do" ministry with Kathleen and Bob, both of whom were constantly challenging him to grow. Forgetting an assignment was noted by gentle nudging, "and sometimes not so gently."

With Kathleen so involved in the public ministry of church planting, her family was certain to be affected. Bob was already an ordained minister in the Brethren in Christ Church, serving as the director of stewardship and finance for the Canadian Conference while continuing his accountancy practice. All the while giving Kathleen wholehearted support in her role, he voluntarily stepped back from "up front" duties in the local church so that she would be seen as the leader and not "tagging along with [him]." The children were recruited to help and, along with Bob, could be found in the nursery or setting up chairs for worship, usually assuming the less prominent tasks so that others could be involved in the more exciting ones. Bob now transferred his scrubbing skills to the church floors. As one of the children says, all of this gave them a vested interest in the church, although that same child also says, "I learned a lot, and perhaps more than I wanted to, about being the pastor of a church planting effort." All three children found in their parents good role models of how to live a life dedicated to Christ, which, according to one child, "is exactly what I hope to do with my children."

For his part, Bob says he enjoyed being the pastor's spouse and was never bothered that Kathleen was the leader and he the follower. He recalls a humorous experience at General Conference when he was asked if he was attending as a pastor's wife. He sees this servant role as an opportunity to model for the congregation that men don't always have to be in positions of power.

Ordination in 1993 was a felicitous moment in Kathleen's life. Years earlier she would have been the last to consider herself as a candidate. Kathleen's public ministry as a preacher and speaker has been described by her colleagues and administrators in various ways: "often presented the plan of salvation, publicly and privately, and led persons to faith in Jesus Christ"; "precise and concise use of words"; "excellent audience rapport"; "speaks firmly and with passion"; "articulates her message clearly and warmly"; and "scriptural and articulate." In her pastoral mid-term review in 1997 she scored high on "sermons practical and related to life today."[9]

A Broader Ministry

Writing was another area of ministry which opened to Kathleen. From time to time her name appeared in denominational publications such as the *Evangelical Visitor*, *Brethren in Christ History and Life*, and *Shalom!: A Journal for the Practice of Peace and Reconciliation*. She was invited to write the column "Viewpoint" in her local daily newspaper, the *St. Catharines Standard*. This became a positive outlet for her often humorous viewpoints on topics like family camping, working in a man's world, appreciation for her mother-in-law, and regrets over lost opportunities, all the while upholding positive personal and family values in the community where she was known.

During the 1990s, Kathleen discovered a place for her gifts on the broader Canadian Conference scene. She was a member of the Board for Church Development, helped to plan an Ontario pastors/spouses retreat, and served on the Sexual Ethics Committee, among other committee and speaking involvements.

When a place on the denominational Commission on Ministry and Doctrine became vacant, she was invited to serve. This automatically placed her on the Canadian division of the Commission, of which she became the chair. The pertinent, concise, and clear articulation she had used in presenting her own doctrinal questionnaire now came into play in her communication with pastors in the ministerial licensing stream. She holds a high view of scripture and adheres solidly to Brethren in Christ theology, expecting no less of candidates. In her response to an article on pluralism in *Brethren in Christ History and Life*, she writes: "We must never become lax in the credentialing process. Evidence of critical thinking, an openness to change, and sympathies toward our unique heritage are the qualities in a candidate that are of utmost importance."[10]

Other General Conference assignments included serving on the planning committee for the pastors/spouses international retreat in 1995 and as a member of the Editorial Board of the Brethren in Christ Historical Society. She was as equally at home ministering as pastor to Camp Kahquah children or adult camps as she was delivering messages to both the General Conference and the regional Canadian Conference in 1996. To the Canadian Conference body, her message was "Be Strong and Do the Work,"[11] a theme highly reflective of her own faith journey.

Being invited to speak at a General Conference communion service was a significant honor not accorded to many pastors. Her love for the Brethren in Christ denomination was rather humorously displayed as she described a seminary class where her professor expounded on feetwashing, thinking he was presenting something novel to the group. Kathleen was quick to point out that her church practices feetwashing regularly. In her sermon, she went on to talk about Christ's gospel of grace and her own struggle with knowing about grace but not always acting upon it.

One of the challenges women clergy in the Brethren in Christ Church have had to face is full acceptance on equal footing with male counterparts. While the denomination endorses credentialing for women and their employment in every area in the church, practically speaking, women face an uphill struggle in breaking through the "glass ceiling" of senior leadership roles. This denial can be seen as rejection by women.

Kathleen struggled with these issues. Early in her ministry as a licensed and then ordained pastor, Kathleen says she felt full acceptance (although later she began to wonder if perhaps the resistance had simply gone underground).[12] Her résumé indicates many opportunities for messages and leadership in both Canadian and General Conferences, opportunities that male clergy may not have received. On occasion, some of them criticized the bishop for giving an edge to Kathleen, offering her opportunities that did not come their way. She worked diligently and faithfully to fulfill obligations. Nominated several years in succession for the position of assistant moderator in the Canadian Conference, she was not accorded the honor. Small wonder she occasionally felt it necessary to confront her male colleagues with the fact that women, too, are pastors.

Kathleen made a smooth transition after ten years pastoring at Orchard Creek (1989–1999) to service with Women Alive. Her role as national director took her into many churches, including Brethren in Christ, speaking and helping local committees organize rallies. A former director comments, "Her affable nature and organizational skills as she works with local committees are valuable assets, while her peers find her a good listener, accepting their ideas even when she may have something more valuable to offer."[13] After concluding her time with Women Alive, she now makes herself available to the broader church, teaching and speaking in interdenominational and Brethren in Christ settings.

Living life intensely and energetically, Kathleen purposely looks for relaxation in creative expression. The results of her gardening efforts provide an appealing setting for a good book or gardening magazine. Recent efforts in folk art painting are helping to bring balance to her workaholic pace. She delights in meeting her old friends for lunch or bridging the miles between them with phone calls or e-mails.

And always she enjoys being with Bob for walks to the nearby library, an occasional movie, or other downtown spots. "Being with family," she notes, "is both fun and relaxing." Seeing their three biological children walking with the Lord brings Bob and

Kathleen "intense joy." All of these things energize her and lift the depression she occasionally struggles with.

A Risk-Taker

Reflecting on the life of Kathleen Ruth Leadley thus far, we could summarize it as a life of risk-taking, a term she herself has employed in describing her faith journey. In "Viewpoint" she writes of "pushing past our natural fear of the unknown believing that the light will overcome the darkness."[14] She titled a presentation at a Women Alive conference "Dare to be a Risk-Taker!" In it, she defined risk as "exposing oneself to the possibility of loss, injury or failure." She offered such wisdom, no doubt learned from poignant personal experience, as "Don't call it failure—call it research" and "Remember the more risks you take, the richer your life!"[15]

One doesn't need to search long to discover the risks Kathleen took, among them accepting abused children as her own, pursuing her education as a mature student, and risking disapproval in becoming a pastor. Not for her the easy, no-risk road. She herself says it best: "Do I really want to get to the end of my days and congratulate myself on having played it safe? Whew—I made it and never risked at all? Somehow, I don't think so."[16]

Dairy Farmer's Daughter to Business Visionary

Lillian Frey Lehman

by Tasha N. Books*

As the sun sinks behind rows of cornstalks, Lancaster County, Pennsylvania, seems the epitome of tranquility. When someone mentions the fertile hills of the region, the last thing that comes to mind is booming business. Yet, for one woman, this fruitful farmland became the birthplace of opportunity. With a particularly keen business sense and a vision for possibilities, Lillian Frey Lehman cultivated two prosperous businesses despite a lack of specialized education or training. Although Lillian came from entrepreneurial roots, she took the Frey family tradition a step further, becoming a competent and successful woman in what was considered, at the time, primarily a man's world.

The Roots

Lillian Frey was the fifth of seven children born to Armor Paul and Mary Ann (Charles) Frey of Lancaster County. Although both Armor and Mary were raised in Christian households, they had each turned away from the faith by the time they were married. Convicted of their need for a Savior, however, both accepted Christ when their children were still very young. Mary had attended the Mennonite Church, but she never became a member. Upon her conversion, she joined the Brethren in Christ Church along with Armor, who had grown up in that denomination.

*Tasha Books is a Messiah College student majoring in English. While she never had the opportunity to learn to know Lillian Lehman well, Tasha is Lillian's great-niece.

After his conversion, Armor felt that he could no longer raise tobacco on the farm which he had inherited from his father. Consequently, he began to look for another means of livelihood which would be lucrative enough to support his growing family. In the process, Armor experimented with numerous enterprises, from raising sheep to growing watermelons. "Dad was a pusher," recalls son Emerson.[1] "He was always trying this, trying that, until he found something that worked." Armor even used Mary's savings to buy a flock of pigeons for a business venture which eventually failed to become profitable. As he searched for a new occupation, the family struggled to survive on their meager means.

Even as a small child, Charles, Lillian's senior by two years, was aware of the hard times: "I know they were really lean years because I remember my mother saying that when the baker came today and she bought bread, she didn't know where she was going to get the money to buy bread the next time the baker came." Despite the gravity of their situation, Armor and Mary managed to create a relatively comfortable home life for their young family. "As kids, I don't think we ever really understood that we were that poor," recalls Emerson.

In 1931, during the Depression, Armor knew that he was not making enough money to provide for his family, so he began to bottle milk from his own cows to sell. Taking his milk door to door, he started a small business, tapping into an open market. With a renewed sense of direction, Armor took a chance with the family income to build a small dairy. Initially a tremendous risk, the dairy would ultimately blossom into a growing corporation, providing the Frey family with the financial stability that they sought. Today, although no longer family owned, Turkey Hill Dairy is a prominent milk and ice cream supplier, competing with a diversity of suppliers of these products throughout Pennsylvania and much of the Eastern Seaboard.

Coming of Age

It was into this family of Christian commitment, perseverance, and willingness to experiment in business that Lillian began her life on April 27, 1928. Even as a child, she demonstrated a certain tenacity, a determination to make her mark in what her younger sister, Eunice Steinbrecher, describes as "a very male dominated society": a place where women were not necessarily expected to think or give input beyond the domain of the home. Simply stated, "She was aggressive," says Charles. Both Lillian and Emerson studied piano when they were young. Emerson remembers Lillian leaving the dinner table, dirty dishes and all, to practice. As the family sat at the table finishing their meal, Emerson recalls Lillian's marked attitude of perseverance as she played: "She used to make mistakes and it used to drive us crazy because she'd keep on going. . . . If I'd made a mistake, I'd stop and fix it up. . . . I never got to be a pianist: she did!" Already, in her piano practice, Lillian demonstrated a certain determination which would later come into play as she ventured into the world of business.

Despite the sibling rivalry taking shape, Charles asserts that in the midst of their differences, "there was a glue being manufactured there that sort of kept us together after we grew up." Armor and Mary built a common denominator for their children as they stressed the importance of following Jesus. Sister Eunice reminisces on the influence of her parents in the lives of the Frey children: "We must have learned how to work . . . and we must have learned how to love God." In addition, she says, "I think we learned that church and . . . participating in the life of the church was very important. And we must have learned that the Brethren in Christ denomination was very important to us because we have, by and large, all of us . . . stayed very connected."

In 1940, only six months after Eunice was born, the Freys experienced a great tragedy. Lillian's older sister, Pauline, died of diphtheria at the age of eighteen. Although she was only twelve at the time, Lillian was now the oldest daughter in the family and took on added responsibilities in the home. Deeply affected by the death of her oldest daughter, her mother experienced a great sadness which, according to Eunice, she carried for the remainder of her life. Demonstrating a characteristic strength in the face of tragedy, Lillian did her best to help pick up the domestic pieces of the heartbroken family. On the first Christmas following Pauline's death, the family decided not to celebrate, but Lillian refused to let the holiday go by without festivities and almost single-handedly created Christmas in the Frey home. In many ways, claims Eunice, "[Lillian] was really . . . more of a mother to me than my own mother." She says, "From the time I was four years old until the time I probably graduated from high school, whatever excitement happened in my life, basically was generated from her." Throughout her life, Lillian remained the close mentor and friend of her younger sister.

Having attended Manor–Millersville High School, Lillian, like many Brethren in Christ young people at the time, headed to Messiah Academy to complete her formal education. During her time at Messiah, she met Joseph Lehman of Carlisle. Joe sang in the Victory Quartet with Lillian's brother Emerson. Eventually, he and Lillian courted and were married on Labor Day weekend of 1946. Lillian's oldest son, Roger, suggests that his mother and father "were from . . . two opposite backgrounds." Lillian had grown up in a large and business-savvy family while Joe and his only brother were raised in a single-parent home after the death of his father. Both, however, had grown up in the Brethren in Christ Church.

Soon after they married, the couple moved back to Joe's home area in Carlisle to assist his mother with the family farm. Although Joe's father had been a dairy farmer before he died, the remaining family focused their efforts on the poultry business, regularly taking chickens and eggs to market. Eunice remembers visiting her older sister in their beautiful two-story brick house with hardwood floors, situated across the yard from Joe's mother's home. In Eunice's eyes, her sister was living the luxurious life of a grown-up. But Lillian was not happy in Carlisle. In fact, she was so unsatisfied with her life situation, recalls sister-in-law Ann, that she would come back from market and cry. In addition to her dislike for life in Carlisle, Lillian apparently felt a very strong connection with Lancaster County and battled feelings of homesickness. Eventually, the Freys offered Joe a position at Turkey Hill, providing a way for Lillian to come home. After living in Carlisle for only two years, Lillian and Joe moved to Lancaster County.

Turkey Hill Years

The Lehmans built a new house just across the road from Turkey Hill Dairy. Although the original structure underwent some remodeling as room was needed for a growing family, Lillian lived in essentially the same house for the rest of her life. During the early years at Turkey Hill, the young couple worked hard to make the best of the little means that they had. Joe worked at the dairy, and both he and Lillian helped to milk the cows. Eunice describes Lillian's frugal style of homemaking in those early days: "The economics of the time forced her to be creative . . . You raised your own vegetables, you sewed your own clothes, you bought as much as you could on sale. You found your entertainment among your family and among your friends just doing things at home." Perhaps out of necessity, but complemented by a natural creativity, Lillian developed a marked adeptness when it came to domesticity. "She probably was a Martha Stewart before there was a Martha Stewart," remarks Eunice, recalling her sister's many domestic talents, which included sewing, cooking, and gardening.

Lillian gave birth to her first son, Roger, at Columbia Hospital on May 8, 1951. Three more sons would follow: Jeffrey in 1952, Gregg in 1955, and Todd in 1957. Raising four boys was not always easy, but Lillian found ways to be both a mother and a friend to her children. "Mother was always willing to let the boys get out and stretch," says Roger, who found out firsthand the risks which were involved with this philosophy. When he was only five years old, he and younger brother Jeff decided to climb a silo on Grandpa Armor Frey's farm. Jeff climbed to the top and back down again, but when Roger reached the top, he slipped, falling fifty feet. Miraculously, he sustained no serious injuries. "We don't look at medical miracles in the same way now as what they did then," says Roger, who notes that "most farm accidents took the life of those involved." When it came to the ups and downs of raising four boys full of energy, Roger points out that "Mother was a little more resilient than what Dad was." Lillian saw the importance of allowing her boys to explore even if it meant risking their personal welfare.

When the boys pushed the boundaries too far, Lillian became what Todd calls a "creative disciplinarian." When they were younger, the brothers recall that one of them refused to brush his teeth. As a result, while the rest of the family sat down at the dinner table, this son was required to run around the outside of the house, stopping every time he reached the glass doors in the dining room to say, "A big boy like me should remember to brush his teeth!"

As the boys grew older, their ignoring of the rules became more pronounced, but Lillian rarely found reason to raise her voice. Joe became the authoritative parent, stepping in when needed to keep things running as smoothly as possible. Roger recalls his father taking them for Jeep rides so that Lillian could have some time alone without distractions. Once, when the boys were smoking on the back porch, an activity of which they knew Lillian disapproved, she called each boy inside separately for questioning. When all returned outside, they discovered that Jeff was the only one who had confessed. Lillian, however, did nothing, and eventually the rest of the boys were driven to confess because of their known guilt.

Lillian stressed the importance of family. Seeking to strengthen the relationships between her children, she often said, "No matter what, you can always count on your brother." More than anything, Lillian wanted them to know Christ and to reach their full potential in life. Lillian believed in her children, and she wanted them to believe in themselves. Being a rather timid child and a picky eater, Gregg remembers that he could not muster the courage to face the scary cafeteria lady at school in order to buy his lunch; Lillian made it a point to come to his school at lunchtime, helping him to get through the line. "I had a great relationship with my mom," says Jeff, who attributes most of what he has learned about his faith to Lillian's example.

As an adult, he recalls a very intense experience which illustrates the close spiritual connection he had with his mother. After suffering with arthritis in his foot for an extended period, he found himself desperately praying for healing while in the shower one morning. Suddenly he felt a sensation rushing through his body and the pain leaving his foot. The arthritis never returned, and Jeff stresses how important it was to him to share the experience with his mother.

Her four boys were very important in her life. Much of what the boys saw of their parents' relationship centered around the family. Joe and Lillian worked together well as a team, understanding their strengths and weaknesses and allowing each other to fulfill the roles that fit best. "We almost never saw open disagreements," says Roger of his parents' relationship. "Some of that was because mother's way was obviously the clearer way to go and all five males saw that." Daughter-in-law Marian remembers that Lillian was not subservient, yet conscious of her responsibility as a wife and mother. Joe, a naturally quiet and reserved man, was very supportive of Lillian, allowing her to take the lead in numerous situations.

Many who knew Lillian well will affirm that her marriage was not all that she might have hoped it would be. Some believe she was the kind of woman who would have benefitted from having an extremely strong husband. But despite the obstacles, Lillian and Joe stayed together, determined to keep the family and their marriage intact.

Lillian and Joe did their best to create a home that was inviting to others. Lillian became the hostess, inviting friends and family members over for an afternoon or evening. Joe roasted corn on the grill between two burlap bags on many summer evenings. "They were just very easy to spend time with," remarks Marlin Thomas, a longtime friend of the Lehmans and founder of Willow Valley Resort. The Lehman household became a favorite hangout for the boys' friends. A swimming pool was built near the house which, suggests Roger, "ended up holding [the] family together" because the boys brought their friends over to the Lehman home rather than going elsewhere. In this way, Lillian was able to know personally the friends of her children, and she learned to know them well. When she got in the mood to do some hair cutting, her boys were not the only susceptible victims. "It didn't matter whether you belonged in the house or not, you got buzzed," remembers Roger.

Because they lived so close to Lillian's extended family, there were always plenty of cousins to play with on the cow pasture, more familiarly known as "The Range," which combined the backyards of multiple houses in addition to the Lehman home. "The Frey kids were a big enough conglomeration that we were our own force wherever we went," claims Roger.

Lillian attended Manor Brethren in Christ Church during her childhood and she remained an active member of that congregation for the rest of her life. A natural leader, she actively involved herself in the life of the church. When prayer time started up at 6:00 a.m. on Tuesday mornings, "Lillian . . . was right there and encouraging other people to come," says Marlin Thomas, who recalls that she was one of the first persons to introduce herself when he and his wife, Doris, started attending the church.

Although Lillian became involved in various aspects of church life, her heart remained strongly attached to music. She was the church organist for many years and, along with brother Emerson, did much to improve the music program of the church. "She and I always worked well together when it came to the music things. We didn't always agree in other areas, but whenever we were working with music, that's when we'd get along best," says Emerson of their shared passion. He adds, "She had a really excellent alto voice." Lillian did not hesitate to serve on various church committees. She was instrumental in the expansion of the new Christian educational wing, which, says Gregg, "changed Manor in a tremendous way."

New Roads

In every way, Lillian was a motivator of change. She tended to push away from the more conservative attitudes and patterns of the church. "She was very forward thinking in the types of music that she felt . . . they should be using in the church," says Gregg. "She was a rebel," says sister Eunice with a smile. "She challenged everything." Although she did not agree with everything that happened in the church, she was committed to her congregation and strove to be a positive influence for the adjustments she thought beneficial.

With this spirit, she challenged tradition whenever it did not make sense to her. Lillian was one of the first women in her congregation to remove her head covering. As Todd points out, "She was one who was willing to go out and say . . . it really doesn't matter what this covering means, it's just a symbol. . . . What really matters is what's in my heart and what's in my life." She had grown up challenging convention, and in her late thirties Lillian embarked on a new phase in her life which would, once again, turn the tables on societal expectations for women.

Like her father, Lillian began experimenting with new ways of bringing income to the family. According to her brother Charles,

Lillian "really . . . stepped out into the business world" when she contracted the building of two houses which she then sold. She and Joe also ran two laundromats, one in Lancaster and one in Columbia.

In 1967, Joe left Turkey Hill Dairy after experiencing some health problems. The Lehmans looked for something more substantial to support the family. Lillian "felt like the responsibility of their livelihood was starting to rest on her shoulders," recalls Charles. She sold her shares in the Turkey Hill Dairy and embarked on a new adventure, buying a small business called Shank's Extracts. Having learned about Shank's from the former owner and salesman, Paris Rohrer, the Lehmans were ready to buy when he decided to sell. Joe soon took the door-to-door sale of bottled extracts to a store operation, bringing sales up. Eventually, says Jeff, Shank's "became more of a private packer for the spice industry," reaching customers "from coast to coast."

As Shank's Extracts continued to grow, Lillian ventured into another business initiative, purchasing a furniture store which was about to go out of business. With a progressive vision for the store, Lillian worked to give it an ultramodern image. Calling it Interiors 2000, Lillian hoped to provide the surrounding community with something that they did not already have. "I think she was one that strove for excellence," says Marlin Thomas, "and Interiors 2000 was known as the premier store [for] design and furnishing and all the accessories . . . in the Lancaster area."

Jeff recalls that his mother had an almost uncanny business sense. Joe was a very hard worker, but he did not possess the leadership abilities which came naturally to Lillian. Although Joe worked mostly with Shank's and Lillian with Interiors 2000, "both places needed mother to keep them running," says Roger. "She was shrewd very much the same way that Grandpa Frey . . . was shrewd. They just knew how to structure a business deal so that it was fair for both sides of the bargaining team, but still was a very good, wise, sound business decision for them," says Eunice. Friend Doris Thomas recalls Lillian's keen sense of quality: "I can still remember how she'd shut the door [of her car]. She'd say with satisfaction, 'Hear that clunk?' "

Lillian's business successes seem to have come from a combination of her naturally good business sense and a particular talent for the types of endeavors that she chose. Both Shank's and Interiors 2000 were "a reflection of the things that [Lillian] enjoyed doing," says daughter-in-law Marilyn. "Mother always had a flair for interior design," says Roger, of Lillian's natural inclination toward the furniture business. Lillian did not hesitate to share her decorating abilities with church and community. She spearheaded the decoration of the new parsonage among other projects at Manor and, in 1977, helped to decorate the main building of the new Messiah Village facilities in Grantham, Pennsylvania.

Despite her heavy involvement in business, Lillian continued to remain active in the church. She experienced a significant spiritual turning point near the middle of her life. When Bishop Henry Ginder was the visiting evangelist at Manor, Lillian confessed an area of struggle. As a young pastor's wife, Lois Jean Peterman said that she was moved when this completely in charge woman acknowledged her struggle. With an open, repentant spirit, Lillian was "seeking God's forgiveness, wanting to totally follow him."

Joe and Lillian encouraged their children to pursue spiritual things through family routine. Church attendance and family devotions were a regular part of the Lehman family schedule. Lillian used to wake up her children on Sunday mornings by playing the piano on the other side of the wall from their bedroom. Tithing was important, remembers Gregg. From the very beginning "it was just a given that that's what we would do." As her boys grew older, Lillian taught Sunday school classes, partially, Jeff recalls, because she was the only one who could make her own children behave. Even during the services when both parents were occupied on the platform, Lillian kept the boys close to the front where she could keep an eye on them. When she no longer needed to monitor her boys so closely on Sunday mornings, Lillian especially enjoyed teaching adult Sunday school classes and later taught some elective classes on business. Lillian had a knack for relating to a variety of age groups, remembers Gregg, who recalls numerous lasting friendships that his mother developed with her students.

Her personal faith continued to be the top priority of her life. At one point of particular spiritual growth, Lillian came home from church and experienced a profound sense of God's presence. She walked down the hallway, raised her Bible in the air, and said aloud, "I know you're up there. I *know* you're up there."

As the family businesses became more successful, Lillian allowed herself to indulge in some of the luxuries which had not previously been available to her. She is well remembered for the little Mercedes that she drove, according to multiple testimonies, very fast. Todd recalls that Lillian would reward herself materially with the purchase of a nice coat or ring when business was going well. Joe and Lillian often took vacations with friends and family, which would have been unheard of in her family of origin, says Eunice: "Vacations were what city people did, not country people." Lillian "enjoyed business success," Todd recalls, "but only because it was the gravy on the top. Her happiness came in seeing us succeed."

In essence, Lillian's business endeavors were part of her plan to help her children succeed. Todd recalls that his mother purposely encouraged two sons to work in each business according to how well their personalities would complement each other. "I think she realized very well the potential that each [son] had," says Gregg. "Because she had the businesses, she was able to keep us together, and I think that was part of her goal in life." Gregg became involved with Interiors 2000 when he was in high school and never left. Although Todd left to attend Messiah College, he returned to work with Gregg. On the other hand, it was difficult for Lillian to watch her children going down a different path from the one she may have chosen for them. When Jeff decided to leave the home area to attend the University of Miami, Lillian was heartbroken by the idea. However, she allowed him to go despite her misgivings, and Jeff returned after a year to attend Messiah College.

In the late 1970s, due to Joe's deteriorating physical condition, Lillian knew she would have to sell Shank's if Jeff did not join her in the business. He agreed. When he asked how much he would get paid, she told him he could pay himself whatever he wanted as long as she got the same amount, thus creating a stimulus for expansion. It took longer to convince Roger to work with the family: "Usually the path that I was breaking was not the path that they . . . wanted to be traveling," he says of his parents. After working for IBM for eight years, however, Roger came back to work with Jeff at Shank's. "I have had the best of both worlds," Lillian told the Lancaster *Sunday News*. "I raised a family and then started in business [with my family]."[2] "I think this business thing came up through the family from generations back," suggests Emerson of the family business tradition.

A Relational Approach to Business and Faith

There can hardly be any dispute that Lillian was a people person. Her involvement in business and church life helped to create an extensive network of friendships over the years. Lillian even had a tendency to turn business acquaintances into friends. She was able to take potentially bad situations and work with disgruntled customers so that, in the end, they became good friends. According to Gregg, Lillian did not like confrontation, but found ways to work through a difficult business transaction by "being bigger than the other guy," a phrase she cited frequently. She often told customers that they did not need to yell at her. For Lillian, it was most important that all business deals be conducted ethically, remembers Jeff. "She was very concerned that it was a win–win [situation] for everybody," affirms Eunice.

Lillian's ability to build good relationships spread into the way she shared her faith with others. "She was concerned for people who did not know God," says Doris Thomas, remembering that Lillian often brought business associates to special services at Manor. "My mother was always interested in sharing her faith with others, but she did that in a very careful, but very deliberate [way]," remembers Todd. "Her approach was to be a friend first and then to share the importance of God in her life." Lillian saw a great need in the community and wanted the church to become more involved in outreach, recalls brother Charles. "She loved . . . people for who they were and was not afraid to be seen with a non-Christian person," says Gregg.

Not surprisingly, Lillian found it very easy to relate to men in general. "Mother spent her whole life learning how to deal with men," muses Roger. Lillian carried this talent into the business arena. Eunice recalls how much her sister enjoyed verbal sparring with the men in her life. "She was an attractive woman, and her aggressiveness . . . I think, made her more attractive," says brother Emerson, who claims that Lillian had certain advantages over men. As a woman, however, relating to the rest of the business world—primarily men—was sometimes difficult. Eunice recalls her sister's frustration with furniture representatives who came to Interiors 2000, assuming they could cheat her because she was a woman.

Conversely, because she did not always fit into the current conventional model of a woman, Lillian sometimes found it harder to relate to women. "Mother was working at a time when women weren't working outside the house, so there was tremendous pressure from other women," says Roger. Lillian did have to balance her life as a wife and mother with the time she invested in her businesses. Feeling a great responsibility for her family as well as the businesses, Lillian worked very hard to see both succeed. After making dinner for her family, she would often return to work in the evenings.

Lillian felt it was important to be at the store "because she felt people wanted to see the owner and buy from the owner," says Eunice. "She probably would have been considered a super mom," says Todd of Lillian, who often worked sixty or seventy hours a week in addition to caring for her family. "She was the kind of person who wanted to be everything for her family. . . . She was very driven in that respect." According to sister Eunice, Lillian's stressful lifestyle was not without cost. "There is no question in my mind that one of the reasons she developed cancer was because of the stress in her life."

Despite the stress, a well-developed sense of humor seemed to help Lillian remain upbeat and positive. She had the constant ability to keep things lighthearted, even when the boys were sick. Her humor also extended into church activities. Once, while standing at the front of the church for communion, Lillian spilled grape juice on her white blouse. Humiliating as the situation could have been, she was able to laugh at herself. "At times [her life] was just like everybody else's life, very ordinary . . . very much get up in the morning and go to work whether you feel like it or not," says Eunice. Lillian did what she could to keep life interesting. One time, just for a lark, she drove her Mercedes across a cornfield after realizing she had forgotten something at the store.

Trials and Enduring Faith

In 1980, Lillian experienced one of the biggest trials of her life. On the eve of July Fourth, the Lehmans were driving home after watching fireworks in Lititz when they were stopped in traffic because of a fire. To their horror, they soon learned that Interiors 2000 was the burning building. Although they were able to salvage some things from the ruin, the fire caused $250,000 in damages. "In a lot of families that would have been just enough to really put everybody under," says Gregg. He recalls the strength with which his mother faced the devastating situation as the family gathered at Jeff's house that night. "It was a night of pain, of course, but . . . not of sadness, but of thankfulness that we were all still alive," he remembers tearfully. Lillian helped her family to understand that what had happened was all in God's will and that it was not the end, but the beginning of a new phase in business, says Gregg. "We will take care of our customers," Lillian later told the *Lancaster New Era*. "We will definitely be in business as soon as we can find a new place."[3] "She was very strong-willed, and that was good and that was bad," says Eunice, "but it's what got her through many difficult situations."

For those who were closest to her, Lillian's death remains a powerful testimony to the way she lived. She was diagnosed with leukemia in June 1985 and died in November of that same year. Lillian did not fight to prolong her life, choosing to remain at home with her family until she died. Recalls brother Charles: "She was aggressive, but whatever was the end, she accepted." Her family remembers the peaceful nature of her death: "She felt that she had done what she could do for us," says Gregg of his mother, who lived to see all four of her sons married and the births of seven grandchildren. Roger recalls a special moment near the end when Joe took Lillian's hand and said, "You've been a wonderful mother." "That meant so much to her," says Roger.

Lillian was concerned for the spiritual health of others until the very end. She confidently left this world for a better one. "I think that was one of the first funerals that I've been at where there were so many uplifting songs," says Marlin Thomas of the service held at Manor. "That was her; she wanted it to be a time of praise and . . . a time when the unsaved people would receive a message." Roger adds, "I think that Mother's greatest joy was that she could say, in the end, she had fully loved the Lord."

A Dream Delayed

Janet Marie Witmer Peifer

by Kim W. Dalton*

"It's what women do. We bear the brunt and forgive and hope God will reward and fulfill the desires of our heart."[1] This is how, in retrospect, Janet Peifer has come to make sense of her calling to be a pastor and the long, sometimes difficult, and ultimately fulfilling journey to serve in church leadership as a woman.

One of her earliest memories is of playing church with her brother and sisters. Janet would write an order of worship and, from her pretend pulpit on the open staircase, she would direct the congregation and preach the sermon. She also remembers organizing a worship service. In addition, Janet, with two of her siblings and two neighbor girls, would walk to the bungalow of an elderly, bedridden neighbor and lead a church service for her.

From an early age, Janet committed her life to spiritual matters. She made a decision at age seven to commit her life to Christ. The very next day at her one-room schoolhouse, this shy, Mennonite-raised girl witnessed to a large group of her peers. Despite children's taunts in elementary school, Janet led daily Bible studies on the merry-go-round at recess. She continued to be active in her teen years in Christian ministry. Leading others to accept Christ as Savior brought her great joy as she worked in Vacation Bible School.

---

*Kim W. Dalton is a licensed psychologist in private practice in Harrisburg, Pennsylvania. The mother of three young boys, Kim is married to Glenn "Woody" Dalton, Jr., senior pastor of Harrisburg Brethren in Christ Church. She has known of Janet for many years, but established a friendship with Janet through the interviewing process for this biography.

A Mennonite Upbringing

Born on April 13, 1945, into a Lancaster County, Pennsylvania, Mennonite home, Janet Marie Witmer was the first of eight children. She had one brother and six sisters (Richard, Mary Ellen, Jeanie, Doris, Barbara, Betty, and Rose). Her family lived near Manheim, Pennsylvania, and operated a dairy farm. Janet's parents brought up their children to be involved members of their home church, Hernley Mennonite congregation in Manheim.

Her father, Paul Witmer, had long been a lay-leader in this church. During Janet's pre-adolescence, her father officially became an ordained Mennonite deacon by the drawing of lots within the congregation. He had no formal schooling, but was self-taught. He would arise at 4:30 a.m. each morning to study until 6:00, when he needed to milk the cows. Janet described her bi-vocational dad as "a very involved father and husband." Janet's mother, Mabel (Myers) Witmer, came from a large Mennonite family; she was one of ten children. Janet greatly admired her mother and witnessed the energy it took to care for eight children and fulfill responsibilities of being a preacher's wife, where entertaining was her expected role. Her mother also managed the family finances. She taught her children about the envelope in the desk drawer that was the "Lord's money." No matter how much the family could have used that money for other necessities, Janet's mother modeled the principle that no one could take anything from what was designated "the Lord's."

In 1963, Janet graduated from Lancaster Mennonite High School, but not before meeting and falling in love with Elvin Peifer. When asked what attracted him to Janet, Elvin replied, "I appreciated her gentle spirit. She's always been like that and has remained that way, easy to get along with." Janet attended nursing school for one year and received her Licensed Practical Nurse degree at Chambersburg Hospital in 1965.

That same year, in September, Janet and Elvin were married and two months later moved to Lakeland, Florida. These newlyweds served in a Mennonite Volunteer Service (VS) unit in Lakeland for two years, 1965–1967. Janet explained that she and her husband, Elvin, were both co-leaders of the VS unit at the young age of twenty. "It was kind of a joke because we were so young to be leaders. . . . But we did okay." Elvin worked in a local hospital as a carpenter. Janet managed the VS home of eight people (two married couples and four singles). She cooked, cleaned, and handled the finances, along with her other duties. Obviously, this loving, home atmosphere also included time for leisure and recreation. During this period, the Peifers celebrated the birth of their first child, Lori.

From Florida, the Peifer family moved to Quarryville, Pennsylvania, which had been Elvin's childhood home area. Their second child, Scott Douglas, was born September 24, 1970.

While Elvin settled into a new job, a salaried position with a construction company, the family searched for a church in which to set down roots. The Mennonite church in the area was very rigid regarding the roles in which women could minister. At that time, women were only allowed to teach Sunday school for children or other women. Serving in leadership of any other kind was a closed door to Janet. As a young mother and church member, she found contentment in her roles, but she and Elvin decided to leave their Mennonite home church when it became embroiled in controversial questions regarding interpretation of scriptures.

Because of this controversy and their positive years in Florida with another denomination, Janet and Elvin visited several churches and decided to join the Refton Brethren in Christ Church. They knew that their conservative parents initially would object to their children's leaving their Mennonite roots. Elvin and Janet's hope was eventually realized that their parents would accept and support the decision because of the similarities between the two denominations.

The Refton Years: Lay and Pastoral Leadership Roles

In the early 1970s, the Peifer family moved to Willow Street, near Lancaster, where they lived for 21 years. The family calls the period "the Refton years," referring to their intense involvement in the Refton Brethren in Christ Church.

.Janet gives glowing praise to Dale Allison, the senior pastor of the Refton congregation, for giving her the first opportunities to serve and use her pastoring gifts. She wrote in her journal, "The [Refton] church was so much like the Christian Missionary Alliance church we attended while in Florida, such a good spirit! . . . These seven years were a marvelous time! . . . [Dale] recognized my leadership skills and let me do everything under the sun, even preach! It was a horrible crash for me when he left. I was never as fully supported by any other Brethren in Christ pastor, bishop, or administrator."

Scott, the Peifers' son, reported that he and his family were more than just regular attendees at the Refton church. They were always among the first to arrive for every service and they helped to close the building after the service ended. He observed that his mother never just went to church to chat; she would invariably be available to others for in-depth talks. He said, "We'd walk in the door and my parents would be whisked away . . . no sneaking in and sneaking out." Wednesday nights were reserved for church activities. This was a family that was intimately acquainted with all aspects of the church, a family in which all members actively participated in ministry.

Over the span of their membership in the Refton congregation, Elvin and Janet served in a variety of ministries: deacon couple, informal joint counselors for other members, and on many committees and commissions. Scott remembers his father as the church's "computer guru, sound man, the head of the building committee, video-guy, treasurer, and board member." Between them, Lori and Scott list the following church involvements of their mother: choir director, pianist, intercessor, worship leader, lay-counselor and care-giver, deacon, administrator, Sunday school teacher, ministry coordinator, event coordinator, preacher, Vacation Bible School and Pioneer Girls leader, and pastor. Scott summarizes his description of his mother's church involvement by saying that "functionally, she was a senior pastor but was not validated or recognized as such title-wise," and that she knew her "flock" from an intensely personal connection born out of years of listening and giving of her time and self. These were qualities well recognized by many people.

Leadership Training Through Life Experience

Reactions to Janet's leadership roles ranged from direct affirmation to outright rejection. Janet had to weather comments such as, "If only men would be doing their job, women would not need to be in these positions." She did not know how to respond to questions that were posed by others who held to the notion that women should be prohibited from leadership roles. Even when she clearly functioned as the senior pastor when the church's senior pastor was on a three- month sabbatical, her designated title was "pastor of care and counseling." Not until 1984 was Janet introduced to solid biblical exegesis which affirmed all believers could serve as called and gifted by God without regard to gender.

When asked, "Who was the first person whom she had to convince of her calling?" Scott postulated that this person was his father. Scott observed that his father became increasingly affirming. He said that over time his father changed and became one of his wife's main supporters in her calling.

Elvin explains that his "conversion" of theology regarding the acceptance of women in church leadership roles was a gradual process. "I don't know when or why it was okay," he comments, "but I knew it was right for her to minister." He might have objected if his wife was seeking recognition or political power, but Janet showed that she was truly concerned and cared very deeply about what was happening in people's lives. Elvin says simply, "She's a natural" at pastoring.

Janet's father also had to be convinced to accept her calling. Scott says that his mother seemed "deeply bothered" that her own father, a pastor himself, did not support her calling. Certainly her father would have had no reservations for a first-born son to be called to pastoral leadership. But Janet was a first-born daughter. Scott and Lori voiced differing opinions regarding whether Grandpa Witmer has ever totally accepted his daughter's ministry. Lori describes her grandfather as a man who thinks deeply and, despite "long, long years of indoctrination," now accepts his daughter's role and calling.

Janet's children witnessed a steady growth in their mother's confidence, especially through the people who came to her for counseling. This was a natural type of recognition and affirmation, as Scott put it, "not from the top down, but from the people up." When she was finally able to go back to school, her confidence and credibility as a minister increased even more.

All family members agree that Janet's zeal for ministry carved out unexpected new roads in her life. Janet herself, as surprised as anyone by the transformations, wrote in 1987, "I'm not so naïve as to expect easy sailing, but I am free to be who I was meant to be and not some accident of nature that put male abilities inside a female frame. . . . Arriving at my position came after years of trying my best to live within the traditional female roles taught by my parents, teachers, and pastors. I struggled to fit into the mold but discovered invariably that I sensed God's power working through me more when I stepped outside the mold. By nature I never was rebellious, wanting rather to live up to the expectations of my family, husband, friends, and spiritual leaders. Some of them encouraged me to pursue my gifts and others encouraged me back into the mold. That two-way pull frequently sent me on a guilt–elation 'yo-yo' excursion."

After her mother's premature death from pancreatic cancer in 1982, Janet came to realize the extent to which her mother had positively influenced and shaped her calling and life direction. Janet's mother was 58 when first diagnosed with the disease, just after her youngest daughter's graduation from high school. She died four violent months later at the age of 59. At the funeral, friends of her mother told Janet something she would never forget: that her mother always knew Janet was different, special, and would do something great with her life.

Janet says that the trauma of facing her mother's death was a profound growth experience, forming her into a wounded healer. Up until that time, Janet had tried to avoid all funerals and even talking about death. She often sat with her mother, who spoke openly about her illness and impending death. This experience inspired Janet to study books about death. Seven months later, Janet had the opportunity, knowledge, and courage to sit with a very close friend as she died—an amazing about-face for someone who had spent 37 years of her life avoiding the subject of death.

In 1990, Janet began to lead workshops in her church dealing with grief and loss. She did this twice yearly for six years and has continued to offer support groups and workshops on grief, death, and dying as a routine part of her pastoral ministry. Looking back, Janet credits this period in her life as having taught and prepared her for her current position as director of pastoral care for residents and employees of Messiah Village and as associate pastor of Messiah Village Brethren in Christ Church—roles which bring with them continual exposure to death.

Triumphs and Trials in Parenting

The Peifer children, from their perspectives now as adults, describe their parents and childhood in near-idyllic terms. Neither child could remember having a single negative or critical word from their mother. Lori acknowledges that during her mother's back-to-school years, Janet had every reason to be cranky at times. Somehow she managed never to raise her voice to her children. Scott and Lori describe their mother as "quiet, steady, and supportive." When pressed to come up with any negatives, Lori offered weakly, "Well, maybe at times Mom was too passive when it came to getting the career recognition she deserved." Scott responded, "Maybe that she was better at Greek than I was." Both Lori and Scott agree that they never heard their parents argue.

"They're probably being a bit generous there," explains Elvin. While he remembers few marital conflicts, he says the years just prior to Janet's return to college were difficult ones for them. Elvin describes Janet's frustration as "impatience to begin her education." He did not personally feel this urgency. Janet, however, felt her life was slipping away too quickly. Elvin thought that her mother's death (when Janet was 37) added further urgency to her desire to pursue her calling, which intensified by age forty.

Janet journaled to release the stress of those difficult years prior to her return to school. In one entry, she wrote: "Now that I found myself outside the expected, traditional role for women, things at home went less smoothly than did my church roles. My husband was not as enthusiastic about my new discovery as I was, and understandably so. We had entered our marriage with the same expectations—I would be housekeeper, mother, and helper in the church and work as an LPN only when financially necessary. We never had any counseling on how to handle dual careers in marriage because in our tradition that was not one of the questions that needed either to be asked or answered. I began to question my own integrity and wondered where I had gone wrong—that I should enjoy anything so much more than mothering and housekeeping. But commitment to our marriage, no matter what, sustained us through the mixture of disagreements and happy times that filled the next years."

A family joke provides a hint of the couple's struggle to find marital unity in so startling a change in traditional gender roles. Janet tells Elvin, "If I had known that I was going to be a pastor, I never would have married you. Pastor Peifer sounds silly." Elvin responds, "If I had known that you were going to be a pastor, I never would have married you!" This in microcosm shows the goodwill, resilience, and humor of a couple who have worked to remain faithful to all their vows.

In her journal accounts regarding marriage, Janet describes how both she and Elvin have grown and changed. Instead of repetitive efforts to change each other, they came to understand and practice mutual submission. This has strengthened their marriage. Now both spouses work at affirming each other's unique gifts and calling. Elvin says that being a pastor's spouse is not a problem for him. He has kept busy in his own calling and ministry, while maintaining a quiet support of Janet's path.

Listening closely to Elvin, Lori, and Scott reveals some of the developmental difficulties that many families experience. Sibling rivalry existed. A hectic schedule pressured the family, especially when Janet became a college student while her children were still in high school. Despite a relationship increasingly characterized by mutual submission, Janet and Elvin divided family chores along traditional lines. Elvin did the outdoor, home maintenance, and construction jobs. Described as "very industrious" by his son, Elvin served his family well with his handy man talents. "If he wasn't working for his job, he was working at his desk at home on church or job stuff, or working around the house or outside," shares Scott. "My parents . . . rarely sat down," Lori remembers. "Lazy" was this family's version of a four-letter word.

As another example of the family's challenges, Elvin was the stricter parent against whom both children rebelled. Scott worked out his quiet rebellion in ways unknown to his parents, among them by racing his motorcycle at speeds up to 165 mph.

Lori rebelled in the more traditional way of moving far from home as early as possible and spending time away from church. Even in this family crisis, Janet drew upon her pastoral care skills. She did research about the area to which Lori planned to move, finding a Church of the Nazarene in Kansas City for Lori to attend. Lori explains, "She did not push me to live close to the family. If she had, I think I would have rebelled more. As it happened, she gently supported me." In a serendipitous experience, Lori met her future husband at that same Church of the Nazarene.

There were other obstacles, like food preparation, that the family faced as when Janet moved into her back-to-school years. Her daughter described Janet as "a good cook, not fancy, but a good cook." Janet would often have guests over for meals. On these occasions, she would quickly whip up a tasty meal. She did not enjoy cooking, however, and spent as little time as possible in the kitchen. When Lori requested tutoring in the culinary arts, her mother replied, "You'll figure it out when you have to." Elvin did not become transformed into "Mr. Mom" either. One evening, Scott left a note for his father with directions on how to make soup on the stove top. "To see when the soup is ready, stick your finger in it and see if it's hot." Scott did not think that this was unusual advice because he knew that his father was unfamiliar with the kitchen.

As they dealt with challenges, the family bonded together through recreation. They especially enjoyed boating and water-skiing together, and considered church activities to be recreational as well.

Internal Struggles

Even amidst a supportive family, Janet's journal entries from the early 1980s reveal how long and deeply she had to labor for her dream of becoming a pastor to be realized. In 1981, she wrote about her frustration over the delay of her goal. "In checking the cross reference of Jeremiah 1:5 with Isaiah 49 where God also told Isaiah that before he was born, God had his life planned, I continued reading to verse four which reads thus: 'But I said, I have labored to no purpose; I have spent my strength in vain and for nothing. Yet what is due me is in the Lord's hand, and my reward is with my God.' Amen, Isaiah! I couldn't have said it better myself. Only a person who had sensed God's call on his life, heard him say, 'I will display my glory through you,' and then been left sitting high and dry could have written those words. Since mid-summer when the invitations to speak and sing ceased, I have searched my life and asked the Lord for some word of confirmation that I am indeed where he wants me to be. I haven't been able to share my deep sense of frustration with anyone on earth. God has graciously sat with me, while I've cried and asked 'why?' . . . One consolation in the back of my mind was the promising possibility that maybe finally my formal education would be starting in January 1982. I should know by now that every time the path toward my education looks uncluttered, the Lord will allow yet another obstacle to come my way. . . . So there I was—no invitations to speak and no money for school. I was so sure the Lord was working through me in every speaking and singing engagement. People told me so. . . . "

In 1982, in another journal entry, Janet compared the waiting on her dream to an extraordinary delay between an appetizer and the main course of a meal. She had experienced "a period of glory" in which she tasted pastoral ministry. Then nothing opened up; no opportunities to serve as she felt called. Janet's logic interpreted this waiting as a way for God to keep her from becoming proud and to further prepare her. "All that logic, however, does nothing to make the waiting any easier . . . ," she wrote.

Her husband and children had only a vague understanding of the internal trials Janet endured. Lori shares that in retrospect she believes her mother "went through a period not of depression, but close." She saw some of her mother's tears and sadness, and knew there were internal struggles which her mother tried to keep to herself. When Lori was in high school, Janet shared her struggle more openly. Scott recalls that his mother shared her pain without anger and in a humble manner. He believes that Janet may have shared more with him than with his father because she did not want to appear to Elvin that she was complaining.

As the realization of her dream appeared to be no closer, Janet felt sensitive about aging. She wrote in her journal in

1983, "Having another birthday this week and seemingly no closer to my goals in life than last year, eats away at my soul and emotions. Today was a heavy day for me. Felt terribly tired but kept my chin up because I needed to be available for people. . . . Sometimes I just get so weary of helping to carry other people's burdens. Others have done it for me so often that I feel I have committed an unpardonable sin just by writing that sentence. . . . I read the scripture . . . today . . . if you have asked the Savior to use you as a witness to his grace, don't think it strange that he has sent a fiery trial to mold and prepare you for that noble endeavor. I do believe he is molding and shaping me . . . it frightens me a bit because I don't know if I'm at the beginning, the middle, or the end of my affliction. . . . I feel weary and heart- sick and constantly near tears. Thank God for my faith in him. In due time, I shall walk out into the sunshine of his love. Meanwhile knowing his love is here in the shadows, helps me to serve him by waiting. . . ."

Janet shed many tears before her return to school in 1984. Outwardly she looked busy and happy in ministry; inwardly, however, her desire to respond to God's calling by returning to school rang nonstop, like a clock's alarm. The alarm's pitch and power increased disturbingly after the premature death of her mother, but Janet tended to keep that part of her suffering to herself. Introverted by nature, Janet used writing as an emotional release valve.

Dream to Reality

The year 1984 was pivotal. She had first dreamed of becoming a pastor nearly 20 years earlier. After the agony of waiting, Janet stepped into the reality of formal studies to equip her for her call to pastoral ministry. "It was a birthing!" is how Janet describes her experience in 1984 at a Mennonite Conference on the topic of women in ministry. There, among other women who felt called by God into roles of leadership, Janet received both affirmation and confrontation. She was faced with questions, such as, "Are you willing to rock the boat?" by other women who knew the history of Anabaptist-related churches. The idea that a woman could serve as pastor and become licensed and ordained had only received official sanctioning at the Brethren in Christ's

General Conference in 1982, and was reaffirmed in 1992. As an aside, Janet confides, "I never even knew about the General Conference debates and ratification of licensing and ordination of women until 1987 when I was doing research for my master of divinity degree." She wonders aloud why none of her male colleagues in pastoral leadership, knowing that she served in lay pastor and intern pastor roles, ever spoke to her of the General Conference's discussion and decisions regarding women as pastors. Careful not to point fingers at specific churches or male pastors, Janet comments, "I have worked in some difficult situations with various people. . . . I was perceived as being vital for the ongoing ministry of the church, but never was considered for a senior pastor position because I was a woman."

After attending the Mennonite conference on women in leadership, Janet returned home more convinced than ever of her call. However, the obstacles of finances and of convincing her husband that the time of that calling was *now* still needed to be addressed. "It was my year to start!" explains Janet. So, at age 39, with two children in high school, she enrolled in her first college classes at Millersville University and Lancaster Bible College. Lori was a senior, Scott and Janet were "freshmen." The Peifers charged Janet's first semester classes on their credit card.

After one and a half years at Millersville, Janet transferred to Messiah College as a full-time student. In 1988, she and her son were both graduating seniors. She felt that her family members were her "biggest rooters!" Within one month of her mother's graduation, Lori was married; and, by the fall, Janet had begun her master of divinity graduate degree at Eastern Baptist, an American Baptist seminary in Philadelphia.

Pioneer Pastor

The late 1980s and 1990s were Janet's blossoming years. In 1990, she became licensed as a minister in the Brethren in Christ Church. She passed her written exam and answered standard questions posed by the bishop and the Board of Ministry and Doctrine to receive her four-year license in 1991. That summer Janet completed her Clinical Pastoral Education (CPE) at Philhaven, a psychiatric hospital. In August 1991, in addition to her half-time pastoral position at Refton Brethren in Christ

Church, Janet became a part-time associate pastor at Landis Homes Retirement Community, where she was able to combine her nursing experience, love of the elderly, and pastoral skills.

Don Good, the chaplain at Landis Homes Retirement Community, knew she was the right one for the job when Janet applied for a part-time position as chaplain. Pastor Good was impressed with her verbal eloquence—she was able to clearly express her mission and how she wanted to carry it out.

Good relates that Janet was instrumental in expanding the chaplain's role to include ministry to staff members. He describes Janet as a strong, natural leader who "did it so humbly." Despite some initial negative reactions from residents to her being a woman, Janet won them over gently, gradually, sometimes going to their rooms and explaining scriptures.

Janet wrote of her days at Landis Homes in her doctoral dissertation. "I was quite aware," she says, "that my presence as a clergy woman was a new experience for most of the residents and staff, and that reactions may have approached religious cultural shock. However, I had experienced acceptance of my ministry on other fronts in earlier days . . . and I believed that with patience and time, it could happen again. . . . Almost a year transpired before I preached my first sermon, even though I'd been preaching for several years in my parish church ministry. I could wait because I too had sat where the dissenters and those who felt troubled sat. Not fifteen years prior to this, when a new believer whom I was discipling told me I should be a pastor, I had said, 'but the Bible doesn't allow for that.' How could I be anything other than patient with these saints of God who had believed that for twice as long as I had?"

In February 1992, Janet began serving as Refton Brethren in Christ Church's pastor of care and counseling. In April, she received her master of divinity degree from Eastern Baptist Theological Seminary. Anticipating her ordination vows, Janet wrote, "They will have no less significance to me than my vows taken at believers baptism forty years ago and my marriage vows thirteen years later." She was ordained at Refton church in November 1992, one of the first six women to be ordained in the Brethren in Christ denomination.[2]

In February 1995, Janet began her self-designed doctoral program at Lancaster Theological Seminary to study what women bring to the pastoral care of older adults. To enhance those studies, she resigned her half-time position at Refton and accepted a full-time position at Landis Homes, continuing to serve there as the first woman chaplain until June 1997.

Developing warm friendships with the residents came easily for Janet. As a former nurse and spiritually sensitive servant, her "bedside manner" was superb. Pastor Good witnessed Janet's giftedness in prayer, public and private. "Her words were heart-cries that engulfed you and touched you."

Mentors: Midwives to the Dream

Webster's Collegiate Dictionary defines midwife as "one that helps to produce or bring forth something." In the labor process of giving birth to her dream of pastoral ministry, Janet had the aid of a number of spiritual midwives. Dale Allison ranks prominently in Janet's story as one who helped her achieve her dream. Before her return to school for higher degrees, Dale recognized and validated Janet's gifts and call to pastoral leadership. The years spent under Dale's nurturing eye gave Janet pastoral experience prior to her own intellectual and theological understanding of God's special call on her life.

Janet was in seminary when she heard that Dale was diagnosed as having a brain tumor. Admittedly, she felt anger at God. In hindsight, she realized that the anger came out of a long-held hope that one day she and her mentor might work together as true peers, pastoring a church. His death ended this part of Janet's dream.

Professors Al Long and E. Morris Sider were among Janet's midwives during her Messiah College years. Two residents at Landis Homes Retirement Community, Mary Honaman and Paul Miller, also became important mentors to Janet. Mary and Janet were close, perhaps because of Mary's initial contact with Janet on her first day of work there. "You just love these people and you'll be accepted," this Episcopal bishop's wife said.

Paul Miller was a leader in the Mennonite Church who had retired to Landis Homes. He supervised a portion of Janet's doctoral projects and made himself available to her for personal discussions regarding theology, faith, and the Christian walk. He agreed to be on her dissertation review committee and was to be the first one to read Janet's dissertation. One week before he was scheduled to read her dissertation, he died unexpectedly. The shock was so great that for a brief time Janet considered delaying her graduation.

Following the Dream

Elvin and Janet moved in 1996 to Boiling Springs, Pennsylvania, "to follow Janet's career," he relates. In 1997, Janet began her current employment at Messiah Village; one year later she was named director of pastoral care for residents and employees. She also serves as an associate pastor at the Messiah Village Brethren in Christ Church.

In May 1998, Janet published her doctoral dissertation entitled "Clergy women and Pastoral Presence Among the Elderly: In Advocacy of a Conscientious Response to the Aging Church and Community with Implications for the Calling of Licensed and Ordained Clergy Women to Pastoral Leadership in the Brethren in Christ Church." In the dissertation, Janet credited her predecessor, Martha Lady, with being a positive ten-year influence at Messiah Village. She modeled competence and compassion in pastoral ministry. Rev. Lady, as a woman in pastoral leadership, had broken new ground with Messiah Village's 750 residents. "And I, as her successor," says Janet, "would have no need to walk in uncharted territory as I did when I began my ministry at Landis Homes."

When asked to describe a typical day of work at Messiah Village, Janet good-naturedly explained that no such thing as "typical" exists. On any day, at any time, Janet's planned responsibilities must yield to unexpected situations. A resident's or employee's personal crisis, a specially called meeting, a death—any of these can alter the course of a work day for Janet.

As director of the department of pastoral care, Janet must be present at numerous meetings on a weekly basis. She leads various Bible studies and guides weekly staff meetings. Every other month, she plans a Service for Remembering, in which biographical sketches are shared to honor recently deceased residents. Janet is in charge of planning two ecumenical services a year for residents and employees to worship together during the weeks of Easter and Thanksgiving. Fridays are hospital visitation days. Monthly, Janet facilitates two Loss and Change support groups, one for residents, the other for employees. She preaches approximately six times a year at the Messiah Village church and, when asked, conducts funerals. Pastoral counseling with an individual resident or employee comprises yet another part of her ministry duties. She chairs the Ethics Committee monthly and she selects and distributes educational booklets, called "Care Notes," for those entrusted to her pastoral responsibility. She also mentors other women who sense a call to pastoral leadership.

Many of those interviewed praised the gifts Janet brings in ministering to those coping with loss or the death of a loved one. Ruth Zercher tells about her experience with Janet's pastoral care, given during the days and hours leading up to the death of her husband, Ray. While at Holy Spirit Hospital, Ruth became very upset when Ray had to be taken away for a procedure. Just as he was wheeled away, Janet appeared in the doorway—a pastoral presence, a comfort during deep distress. Ruth further describes Janet's care on the day of Ray's death in 1998. She came by the Zercher residence just to sit and listen, to quietly speak to Ray and Ruth, and to pray with them. "She has a calming effect," says Ruth. "It's hard to explain. Her bedside manner and prayers just seemed to be the things we needed." Ray died twenty minutes after Janet said goodbye. At the one-year anniversary of Ray's death, Janet checked in with Ruth and took her out to dinner.

"Being with Ray and Ruth was special," Janet recalls. "I felt so loved, accepted, and approved by them in my ministry as a clergy woman. I grieved that Ray, who was one of those model servant leaders and openly accepted women in ministry had to die when he had so much more to give. While with Ruth after Ray died, I felt blessed by her, which is often the case. I go to bless the dying and the grieving and, in turn, I am more blessed by them than anything I could have given."

As she helped Messiah Village residents and employees face loss, Janet also coped with a serious illness. In September 2000, she was diagnosed with breast cancer. She had surgery, radiation, and chemotherapy during the succeeding months. She says, "Having to hear the words, 'I'm sorry to say that your tumor was cancerous' has given me new empathy and understanding for those to whom I minister who hear similar words." She also lost all of her hair within two weeks of her first chemotherapy treatment. She says, "That experience makes me a better companion to other women who lose their hair due to medical treatment." Her cancer was caught in the early stages, and she can now say she is a "breast cancer survivor."

The hardest part of coping with her illness and related limitations occurred in January 2001 when she learned that her 34-year-old daughter, Lori, who lives in Detroit, had a serious form of cancer. "While she was extremely ill from chemotherapy and radiation, I was unable to be with her because I needed to be near home to get my own treatments," Janet says. "It was a terrible spiritual and emotional battle [for me] to accept her illness and the horrible treatment, surgery, and recovery she needed to face."

Despite the distance, the relationship between Janet and Lori grew deeper through supporting each other. Already enjoying a close friendship as mother and daughter, Janet and Lori noted that a new dimension in their relationship developed through their illnesses. Both now healthy cancer survivors, they frequently speak words of praise to God for their healing.

Moving Beyond Suffering

Even though Janet has experienced periods of suffering, she continues to show a positive outlook. This is evident in verbal exchange with her, in the reports of peers and colleagues, in family members' glowing descriptions, and in her own public and private writing. Hers is the kind born out of "a long obedience in the same direction" (from Eugene Peterson's book of the same title). Peterson's book expounds on the Psalms of Ascent and the Hebrews' pilgrimage to Jerusalem: though the journey is long and uphill, their faces stay pointed toward the Holy City as their feet move forward one step at a time.

Throughout her life, Janet's journey often has been an uphill climb. She has wrestled with the formidable forces of depression and despair and endured rejection and discrimination because of her gender. She is a 17-month survivor of breast cancer and has journeyed with Lori during her illness. Through the challenges, waiting, opportunities, and triumphs of life, however, Janet has held fast to the dream God has revealed to her, and she has continued to channel her struggles into positive ministry to others.

A Ministry That Transcends Boundaries

Sara Cabrera de Peraza

by Carol Geiger*

Habana, Cuba, 1997[1]

In the dream she is running through the corridors of a vast government building. She gasps for air as she demands more and more of her sagging limbs. Cousin Alexi, her companion in this desperate race, is now far ahead. All around her the piercing shriek of the siren warns that the doors and windows will be shut within the next few moments. If she is to be free, she must leave the building. In the distance she hears Alexi shouting—something about having found a door to the outside—urging her to run faster. The interior of the building echoes with the alarm's piercing and insistent clamor as it settles into deepening darkness. She can hear the doors slamming and locking, the windows crashing down on their sills. Heart hammering in her ears, she realizes she will not be able to escape. She is too slow and it is too dark.

She awakens to the anguished cry of her own voice and the aching rhythm of her heart in its fruitless attempt to propel her to freedom. She looks at the clock. It is much too early to get ready for work at the Cuban National Headquarters of the Salvation Army, where she serves as the receptionist. The apartment is oppressive, as though the walls were calling out to her, "Sara! Decide! Decide, before it is too late!" As she has done throughout her life, she begins to pray, "Lord, is this dream to show me I am supposed to leave my job and go and care for my

*Carol and her husband, Bob, are presently involved in a Brethren in Christ church-planting project in Lancaster, Pennsylvania. She first met Sara Peraza at an Atlantic Conference church-planting banquet.

ailing parents? And what about my four children if I leave? Help me to know what you want me to do." She lies back against the pillow, thinking of the many ways the Lord has led her in the past.[2]

Habana, Cuba, 1958

Sara Cabrera Coca de Peraza was born on either January 11, or February 11, 1958, depending on whether the official or unofficial version is referred to. As was the custom with many rural Cuban families, Sara was born at home. When her father made the trip to town to formally register the births of Sara and her older sister, Elizabeth, convenience was perhaps foremost in his mind. He opted to use the month of Elizabeth's birth for both girls when reporting, so Sara, although she was born on January 11, 1958, has an official birthdate of February 11, 1958.

Sara was the second of five children. Besides Sarah and her older sister, the Cabrera family included three younger siblings: David, Odalys, and Daniel. Her mother and father, Eunices and Francisco Cabrera, lived on a small piece of land in the mountains of Cuba. Sara remembers her mother speaking of the long hours Francisco worked on the mountainside cutting wood to be made into charcoal. He would leave the house for six days, returning home on Sundays to attend church.

When Sara was five, the family moved within the city limits of Habana, the capital, thanks to the generosity of the Perdomo family. The Perdomos, members of the Cuatro Caminos Brethren in Christ Church, were committed to helping the young Cabrera family have a better life. Now Francisco Cabrera was able to work as a dairy farmer, rising every day at 2:00 a.m. to milk the cows, and working the land to raise enough food to feed his family. The Cabreras also joined the Cuatro Caminos church. Under Pastor Juana Garcia's firm but loving guidance, the Cabreras raised each of their five children to love and serve Christ.

These were difficult times for Cuban Christians. Government regulations forbid them from speaking about God, except in church or in the privacy of individual homes. To openly declare one's faith in school or any other setting was to invite severe consequences. Christians were also limited in the kinds of work they were allowed to do. Any application for work or study included a section of questions about one's faith and practice, along with the name and address of the church one attended.

Habana, Cuba, 1973

At age 15, Sara followed in the footsteps of her older sister, Elizabeth, and was sent to a Bible school to prepare her for leadership in the church. Every 45 days the students were given a break and allowed to return to their homes for a visit. Longer vacations were dedicated to ministry. The students conducted weeklong daily vacation Bible schools, which might occupy a month or more of the summer recess. When she graduated in May 1975, Sara was prepared to serve the church as a Sunday school teacher or a youth group leader. However, the renewing of her acquaintance with a handsome young preacher sent her plans for ministry in a different direction.

Sara was twelve when she encountered José Peraza, nine years her senior. They first met when José visited the Cabrera farm with Elizabeth's boyfriend. Both men were training for the pastoral ministry, and their trips to the country to share with the family brought them a welcome respite from the ardors of study. José's mother had died when he was 15, and the joyful moments with the Cabreras seemed to assuage a loneliness deep in his heart. Sara recalls her early relationship with José as one of close friendship.

But soon young José began to see Sara as much more than a friend. When she was 17 and recently graduated from Bible school, the two announced their plans to marry. The Cuatro Caminos Brethren in Christ Church leadership did not look favorably upon this decision because they had contributed funds for Sara's studies and had plans for her to help in the ministry. Some of the leaders said that before he married, José should *quemar mas hojarasca* (which refers to the need for more experience and means literally 'to burn dead leaves after they've fallen from the trees').

The growing contention over the appropriateness of their relationship resulted in a shift of direction for Sara. She and José would marry and minister in a different church, the Full Gospel Church. The general lack of sectarianism in Cuba, fostered by the fires of persecution after the revolution, greatly diminished the stress of becoming part of a different denomination. The pastor of the Full Gospel Church was often a guest in the Cabrera home and knew the couple well. He agreed to marry them and, at his invitation, they lived for a few months in a tiny apartment attached to his church building.

For their part, Sara and José enjoyed their brief time of ministry in the church. But after six months, they were required to move, as their pastor friend had not received official permission to house a pastoral couple in his church. Little did the young wife realize that she was about to begin a series of ministerial beginnings and endings that would last more than eight years.

Pinar del Río and Habana, Cuba, 1976–1986

The Perazas were invited to work with another pastor in a different area of greater Habana. José would help in the ministry, and Sara would share with the pastor's wife in the household responsibilities. Upon arrival, the young couple discovered that their living arrangements consisted of an area of the parsonage living room, cordoned off by a sheet. This arrangement continued until the birth of their first child, José Emanuel (affectionately known as "Eme"). When José came home from the hospital on the day of Eme's birth, he found that his senior pastor, in consultation with the landlord, had removed the sheet, a sign that it was time to move on.

The family moved in with another Christian family in the province of Pinar del Río, a rural area far from where they had been living. Sara and baby Eme saw very little of José. The needs of the family obligated the young pastor to rise early in the morning to take a six-hour bus ride to his job in a nearby city where he worked in a nursing home, caring for the facility and its residents for a salary of 60 pesos ($3.00) a month. Time and financial constraints forced José to limit his family visits to weekends so that he could remain near his job during the week.

When baby Eme became severely ill with parasites from the unsanitary water supply, the Peraza's time of residency in Pinar del Río was cut short. Eme's infestation was so severe that he had to be hospitalized in Habana. The doctors informed Sara and José that Eme would not survive long if they returned to Pinar del Río.

Once again, the Cabrera farm in Habana became their safe haven. Sara's parents gave them an extra bedroom which had been vacated after several siblings moved out. Here, baby daughter Zabdi was born.

Sara and José had only recently moved their family into the Cabrera house when the Salvation Army called for their help in a local village. The Perazas went to live with the pastor and his family, to help with the ministry and to attend classes in the new Bible Institute that was planned for the area. Seven months later, the Bible Institute project was canceled. Their hopes dashed, the Perazas returned once again to the Cabrera farm. The promise of a home and ministry of their own had eluded them still another time. Their discouragement intensified when they learned that water from a leaky roof damaged a large number of the possessions they had left behind, including all of Sara's books from Bible school.

By this time, Sara was expecting a third child. As a result, Sara's parents gave her growing family a small structure near the parents' house that had been used as a rabbit hutch. It had a tin roof and an earthen floor. José filled in the walls. The building was so small that only a bed, a large crib, and a tiny cooking area fit inside. The Perazas used the same crib for two of the children (after the third baby arrived), laying their heads at opposite ends. Little Zabdi slept in her parents' bed. José and Sara joked about the need to enter their domicile with humility, since they had to bow low in order to get through the doorway. They also needed to watch diligently for large black scorpions, which were capable of killing a child.

Their poor living conditions contributed to feelings of great discouragement. After they came back to Habana, the family returned to the Cuatro Caminos Brethren in Christ Church. Sara remembers many occasions when only she and the children attended the service. Disillusioned and disheartened, José wrestled with the Lord and with his call. The sense of testing and doubt increased after their third child, Samuel, arrived. Samuel was delivered by emergency C-section because the umbilical cord was wrapped three times around his tiny neck. The baby struggled with an underdeveloped digestive tract, severe bouts of bronchitis, and a weak immune system. These required successive hospital admissions, culminating in a stay in intensive care when he was four and one-half years old. Subsequently, God touched Samuel, and he was never again sick enough to require a hospital stay. After recent disappointments, the knowledge that God answered her prayers for healing inspired Sara.

Pueblo Diezmero, Cuba, 1986

Eight years passed before the Perazas received another invitation to minister. When they accepted an opportunity to serve as the pastoral couple of an established Salvation Army church in Pueblo Diezmero, the Perazas encountered a new kind of challenge and sacrifice. Ministry in the church came with the stipulation that both Sara and José would complete the studies required for pastoral ordination with the Salvation Army. While they studied, José worked in the Salvation Army's Old Age Home from 6 a.m. to 8 p.m. For the first year he worked without pay; afterwards, he earned about $5.00 a month. Later, he received a monthly stipend of $15. Sara contributed to the family finances as well by selling oil, lard, and coffee—items that could be spared from the family's meager government food rations.

The Perazas finally made Pueblo Diezmero their new home in July 1986. The church and parsonage were set up as a duplex, each occupying part of the building space. It was a humble beginning, indeed. The church was located in a neighborhood hostile to evangelicals. Young people delighted in pelting the building with rocks and shouting to disturb the services being conducted inside. Sara was convinced that this was mostly due to the frequent blackouts from electricity rationing, which deprived the youths of their radios and televisions and sent them into the streets looking for something exciting to do. José was firm with his new neighbors; he visited the families, helped the poor, and spoke of the necessity of bringing up young people in tolerance and decency. He soon gained their respect and the vandalism ceased.

Perhaps even more daunting were the problems with the building itself. During the period immediately after the Cuban revolution in 1958, most church buildings were ransacked. Sara believed the many leaks in the 100-year-old church roof resulted from rocks thrown by the young people. Unfortunately, one of the worst leaks developed directly over José and Sara's bed.

Another challenge was the church's dwindling congregation. In 1986, the church had only four members. Many times during those first few weeks the Perazas served as both the pastoral family and the congregation. A fourth Peraza, baby Sarai, joined the family during this period, boosting attendance by one.

Sara and José continued to attend classes, completed the requirements for pastoral studies, and were ordained to the ministry. Sara was surprised by her own resourcefulness and God's grace as she juggled home, ministry, school, and the hours of bus rides in order to complete her studies. But eventually, the church began to grow. On days with more than one service, Sara practiced hospitality whenever possible, sharing food and fellowship with attendees who lived too far away to return home for meals.

Sara found her greatest delight in leading people into a relationship with Christ. Her method of evangelism was very relational. When she became aware of a need in the community, she used the opportunity to draw near to the family in crisis. Many times she had opportunities to pray and advise others, in this way pointing them to God. Sara was careful to take brothers and sisters from the congregation with her to evangelize, thereby training others as well. She found herself delighting in the Lord and in opportunities to minister in his name. Eventually, the Diezmero church grew to 50 members, with between 80 and 100 in attendance on any given Sunday.

Pueblo Diezmero, Cuba, 1993

In 1993, seven years after taking the assignment to pastor the Diezmero Salvation Army church, José received an invitation that would bring great change to the lives of the Perazas. The Salvation Army invited José to attend a month-long leadership training course in North America. José had earlier visited the United States in 1991, and had been resistant to staying longer than necessary, even though his relatives in the United States urged him to do so. This time, José did not dismiss the thought of visiting a truly free country; he knew of the Cuban asylum law, which states that a Cuban is guaranteed political protection by the United States if his or her foot touches U. S. soil. He decided to visit and remain in the U. S., even though it would mean a separation from his family of unknown duration—the asylum law does not grant the family permission to join the defector.

Pueblo Diezmero, Cuba, 1993

Sara stayed in the church she and José had pastored together, shouldering the burden of the ministry herself, rising to the challenge as best as she could. She was surrounded by people who questioned what happened, but who also loved and supported her. Her leaders in the Salvation Army were in favor of her continuing to lead the church, even though there were many things about the ministry that had previously been handled by José. They gave her status as a single pastor and granted her official recognition as the leader of the congregation.

She remembers consciously deciding to force her mind away from the uncertainty and insecurity of her situation and into improving the care of the congregation and her own family. She would trust the Lord to take her through the next steps, and she would wait to see what he would do. For more than a year, she discovered new resources of inner strength by living a life of simple faith and reliance on God. José kept in touch by letter and by phone, sending money whenever he could to improve the family's finances. "Please tell the children I did not abandon them," he wrote in his first letter. This was also a time of great challenge and uncertainty for him, as he struggled to find his way in a new place, away from family and familiar surroundings.

Pueblo Diezmero, Cuba, 1995

On New Year's Day, January 1, 1995, Sara had been working steadily that morning, as she had on the previous day. New Year's Eve celebrations had lasted well into the early hours of Sunday morning. After only a few hours of sleep, Sara began the day with a church service. Many parishioners planned to join Sara and her family for the noon meal because a special Sunday school meeting would be held that afternoon. Sara served the lunch, but found herself unable to eat anything. She had one of her excruciating headaches, but she had long since grown accustomed to them, frequent and ferocious as they were. She would lie down as she always did. Then she would be able to attend to the Sunday school meeting.

But this time her headache was a harbinger of a terrible new difficulty. She awoke at 1:00 p.m., but found her body strangely rigid and unresponsive. She had been lying face down on the bed and was unable to turn over. When this condition persisted into the next day, Sara's terrified family called their friend Maria Júlia Delanoval, who borrowed a car and rushed Sara to the hospital. Sara lay face down in the back seat of the car, unable to move, speaking only with difficulty, wondering what could possibly be wrong with her.

In the hospital, she was given benedryl, told she must have suffered damage to the spinal column, and was sent to another hospital containing more beds and a neurology department. At the Cuban Institute of Neurology, doctors pondered Sara's strange set of symptoms. Her body remained rigid, she was unable to move her hands, and her feet were unresponsive when pricked with a needle. Even more unusual, when she lay on her back, she experienced excruciating pain, to the point of severe muscular spasms if she remained in that position. Only lying face down ameliorated her symptoms. Doctors at the Institute were hard pressed to discover either the cause or the cure for Sara's illness. After days of intense efforts, they released her to Maria Júlia's care, explaining that Sara would face a long period of recuperation, if she recovered at all. Maria Júlia took Sara into her home. Meanwhile, Sara's mother went to the parsonage to care for the children.

Sara entered a period of utter physical dependence on Maria Júlia and complete spiritual dependence on the Lord. Maria Júlia comments, "Sara has always demonstrated great, great faith." Sara's times of prayer provided such excellent comfort and communion that she began to think of her illness as a source of great blessing. Her son, Samuel, remembers hearing her visitors comment that while they had come to minister to her, Sara was the one who cheered and comforted her guests.

Unable to diagnose Sara's illness, the doctors remained unsure of any medicine that would help. In the end they prescribed large doses of vitamins and iron to be given intravenously and by injection to build strength. Christians began calling on the Lord for healing and supporting Sara in prayer.

Sara gradually began to experience a slow but steady recovery. After three months, she regained the use of her hands, resting each time they began to shake uncontrollably. Maria Júlia was the only one who could understand Sara's garbled speech, even though Sara attempted to communicate with everyone who came to visit her.

Sara knew that, despite all obstacles, she must return to her home at the Diezmero church. Her mother, who had shared child-care responsibilities with church members, left to care for Sara's father, also desperately ill. Sara returned home and received round-the-clock attention from concerned parishioners and neighbors. At night, the children took turns sleeping with her, in case she should awaken and need something. Even little Sarai, who was only four, insisted on having a turn at caring for her mother.

Eventually, Sara was able to sit on her own and control her hands enough to feed herself. A few weeks later, it was time to learn to walk again. Each time she stood, the painful headaches returned, but Sara refused to give up. With each small step, her body responded with violent trembling. Stairways were a source of great fear, as Sara struggled to control her legs. She rarely approached them without help, even a year after her initial debilitating attack. Recovery often seemed painfully far away.

Throughout the ordeal, Sara focused her spiritual communion with the Lord on biblical personalities who had undergone times of great testing—characters like Paul, Moses, Elijah, and Job. Many of these heroes of the faith were brought to a state of absolute dependence on the Lord. God stood with them in their times of difficulty and despair. He brought them to a place of salvation again and again, despite the recriminations of others. Sara remembered these Bible characters when some of her friends were accusatory, telling her that her sins had driven her husband away and would now destroy her health. Some arrived with biblical passages or words of exhortation that left her feeling weak and under condemnation. Others came to pray for instantaneous, divine healing. When this failed to occur, they blamed Sara's lack of faith.

Like her favorite Bible characters, Sara also experienced God's provision of physical and spiritual comfort. One time a neighbor, who was unsaved and openly opposed the things of God, remained all night, caring for one of Sara's ill children. Another time, the Communist father of a church member contributed a large quantity of food when he heard that the Peraza children had nothing to eat. During this period, Sara's faith and trust in God, already tempered in the fires of adversity, were strengthened on a daily basis. Eventually, she came to the place where she could say, "If I can walk, but my spiritual life would lessen, I would rather remain the way I am."

Pueblo Diezmero and Habana, Cuba, 1996

One year after the beginning of her illness, Sara recovered her health sufficiently to take up the threads of her life once more. The Salvation Army had found a new pastor for the church and offered Sara a position as a receptionist working at the main headquarters in Habana. Along with the position, there would be an apartment for Sara and her four children. Sara eagerly accepted.

During this time, Sara continued to receive phone calls and letters from José. Still, communication between the United States and Cuba was very difficult. She knew he was desperately seeking work and that he was very concerned about the family's financial needs. Her son, Samuel, remembers the many who encouraged Sara to think about divorce. But she refused, stating repeatedly that what God joined together, no one can separate.

During her long illness, José called and sent as much money as he could. He often sent her long letters expressing his concerns for her well-being and explaining his efforts on his family's behalf. With her new job, Sara felt she and the children were at last in a more comfortable waiting position.

Habana, Cuba, 1997

She is praying while she serves the children breakfast and sends them off to work or to school. She senses that the dream about trying to escape a building is almost certainly related to what is happening in the office. Changes there have occurred with lightning speed and the balance in relationships is unhealthy. Sara feels the currents swirling around her. Her thoughts turn towards home, the little Cabrera farm. Suddenly she knows that the Lord is using the dream to tell her she is not to remain any longer in Habana, lest the doors and windows of opportunity close in around her. As she has done so many times before, she seeks refuge at the family farm, with the support of the Cuatro Caminos Brethren in Christ congregation. Her brother Daniel is visiting the United States. He has promised to bring news of José. Instead of waiting for him in Habana, Sara and the children will be meeting Uncle Daniel at the farm.

Epilogue: Trenton, New Jersey, 1998–2002

In his position as head of the Cuban Brethren in Christ Church, Daniel Cabrera must travel from time to time to the United States and Canada. On one of his first trips, Daniel was able to spend some time with his brother-in-law, José. Daniel suggested that José and the small group of Christians that he began pastoring should join the Brethren in Christ as a Hispanic congregation, an idea José was delighted to accept. The Brethren in Christ requested a visa for Sara and two of the Peraza children to join José in the United States (Eme and Samuel had married and were living on their own). They emigrated and the family was reunited in November 1998, after a separation of almost five and one-half years.

The Perazas are presently involved in planting a Brethren in Christ Spanish-speaking church in Trenton, New Jersey. Sara continues to be in good health as she works outside the home and relates to neighbors and people in need in this busy city. She says the greatest lesson she has learned through the trials of her life is an unshakable belief that God is in control of everything. "This is why I take things very calmly," she says. "God has already provided all we need before we even ask. I have seen him do this innumerable times." Sara likes to remind herself of the story of Paul and Silas singing praises while they were prisoners in jail. "If they didn't complain about their circumstances, why should I?" Sara declares emphatically. "I have learned never to see myself as a victim of suffering. Instead, I praise the Lord for using me as his instrument to bring him glory."

Sara's family and friends in both the United States and Cuba affirm her dedication to the Lord and his service. "My mom doesn't worry about herself," says Sarai. "She helps so many other people in whatever way she can. I miss her sometimes when she is doing things for the church, but I know she is making it possible that we can all praise the Lord together." Her husband comments, "There are people who give direction, and there are leaders. My wife was born to be a leader. She lays down her life for others."

The church planting offers Sara new avenues for ministry. "In a way, I am doing what I've always done," she explains. "I'm serving the Lord in this new church planting in whatever way I can." At the present time, she has many things to do—helping in the needed remodeling of the church meeting place, caring for new members, and reaching out to others. "She's just the same as she always was," comments daughter Zabdi. "She gives to both her family and the church."

According to son Samuel, Sara's ministry continues in Cuba, even though she is now a resident in the United States. "The fragrance of her love and sacrifice lingers here in Cuba in the hearts of many people," says Samuel, who is often stopped by strangers who recognize him as Sara's son. "They ask how she is and if I will let her know she is loved and remembered."

Sara's unshakable faith and spiritual commitment continue to minister to others and to define who she is in all circumstances.

A Brilliant Mind and a Generous Heart

Dorothy Evelyn Sherk

by Mary O. Fretz and
Sandi (Fretz) Hannigan*

Dorothy Sherk was a pioneer who blazed a leadership trail for women in the Canadian Brethren in Christ Church. She was the first woman in the Canadian Conference to earn an academic degree and the first to become principal of a high school. In her younger years, she undoubtedly held more board and committee positions than anyone in the Brethren in Christ Church. In this she modeled service for women who were to follow in similar roles. Additionally, she exemplified, as Ronald J. Sider has indicated, the Brethren in Christ ideal of being "solidly evangelical and socially concerned."[1]

Formative Influences

Dorothy was born on October 7, 1915, in Stevensville, Ontario, a village near Fort Erie, a few minutes from the Canadian–United States border. She was the oldest of nine living children in a family of four boys and five girls. Dorothy's father, Gordon, did some farming and other odd jobs to provide for his

*Mary Fretz was a teacher and consultant in Ontario public schools for many years. In retirement she is active in ministry to seniors. While a student at Niagara Christian Collegiate (near Fort Erie, Ontario), she was significantly influenced by Dorothy Sherk, who was then principal and a teacher at the school. They later served together on the school's trustee board. Sandi Hannigan is the Christian Education Coordinator of the Erb Street Mennonite Church in Waterloo, Ontario. She has written a biography of church leader E. J. Swalm for youth and is a writer for the Jubilee Sunday school curriculum. Dorothy is her mentor and former deacon in the Westheights Brethren in Christ Church in Kitchener, Ontario.

family; her mother, Lillie (Wintermute), cared for the children. Because Dorothy was the oldest, she learned at an early age to help with chores and to look after her younger siblings. This care and concern for others, planted early, continued to grow and flourish through her adult life.

From the time she was born, her parents took her to the Bertie Brethren in Christ Church. During the Easter season when she was five years old, she asked while sitting on a stool, "Mother, what is Easter all about?"

"Well," her mother replied, "this is the time when Jesus was crucified for our sins and rose again so that we can give our hearts to Jesus and he can live with us."

"Then I want to give my heart to Jesus." She climbed off the stool and went into the living room, where she knelt beside the couch and prayed, "Dear Jesus, come into my heart. Amen." Her mother thought it was just a cute childish caper, but Dorothy meant it with all her heart.

When Dorothy was seven, she wanted to be baptized and join the church. Some church leaders said she was too young, but Bishop Bert Sherk came to her defense, saying, "Let the *little* children come to him. For to such belongs the kingdom of heaven."

At the time of joining the church, Dorothy stood before the congregation with a number of adults and a few teenagers. She was asked to promise two things: never to attend the theater and never to hold anything against another person. If someone offended her, she promised to go to them and make it right.

"The theater part wasn't a big deal," Dorothy says. "But I guess I got into the church on a fib with the second promise. I knew I would be too afraid to ever go to someone who had something against me."

Her childish concept of God was partly based on fear. "Maybe I've sinned today and if I die, I'll go to hell," she would think as she was going to sleep. Her bedtime prayers seemed to go on continuously because she didn't want to sleep until she had confessed everything. Eventually she came to a better understanding of the grace and love of God.

Dorothy began attending public school when she was eight. "I guess my mother hated to part with me!" Dorothy says jokingly.[2] But Dorothy had already learned a great deal from her mother before beginning her formal education. Her mother was an avid reader; Dorothy inherited her mother's love of books.

"When I had to do a task like ironing, I would prop a book up so I could read while I ironed," Dorothy recalls. Before she reached her teenage years, she had read through the Bible, as well as *Pilgrim's Progress*, her favorite Sunday book, since that day was a time for her mind to dwell on the sacred. This practice gave to Dorothy not only a grasp of theology but also an appreciation of good literature and writing style. "I have an aversion to classics rewritten in basic English or reinterpreted by Hollywood," she claims.

Dorothy completed her elementary education in five years rather than the usual eight. This was perfect timing because a continuation school (high school) was being built in the field next to their house.

The Road Less Traveled

While it was not then common for teenage girls to go to high school, Dorothy's mother was very eager for her to attend. She was the driving force behind Dorothy's continuing education. Her mother admired a missionary by the name of Anna Engle, who was well educated and acted like a lady. This is what she wanted for her daughter.

Dorothy, too, had a love for learning. The idea of attending high school appealed to her. Some neighbors criticized her parents' decision: "You should be putting Dorothy out to work to help support the family," they commented. "As long as they don't have to support us," Dorothy's mother sniffed, "it's none of their business." It wasn't that school was considered evil by some neighbors, only a waste of time for girls, who probably would get married anyway.

Dorothy's father was also in favor of her going to high school. "Boys are strong and can do heavy work," argued her father. "But girls need a good education if they have to provide for themselves." Dorothy's father pulled the family through the Depression without going on welfare, a source of great satisfaction to an independent man such as Gordon.

"Because the school was next door to our house, I couldn't get away with anything!" chuckles Dorothy. "My mother could see whom I was socializing with at recess time."

After four years of high school, Dorothy decided she wanted to become a teacher. To be eligible to enroll in normal school (teacher's college), Dorothy attended grade 13 at Ridgeway High School, about four miles from her home. As a member of the Bertie Brethren in Christ Church, she wore the required head covering. While few teenage girls wore a head covering to school, this was not a large problem for Dorothy. "It was just expected, and I did it to toe the line," she says.

After graduating from high school, Dorothy set out for teacher's college in Hamilton, a city about 60 miles from Stevensville. This was a big step: it meant moving to a city, boarding with strangers, being exposed to other worldviews, and financing her education. She was able to finance the cost of $300 with help from her parents and a loan from her Ridgeway High School principal, Dr. Gerald Grant, who helped many aspiring Depression youth by making a rolling fund available to them.

After teacher's college, Dorothy was hired to teach in a one-room school near Stevensville. She paid her loans in her first year. Shirley Bitner was one of her many students from Brethren in Christ families. Dorothy's example and influence played a significant role in Shirley's future decision to become a missionary in India.

"When Miss Sherk started teaching me, I wasn't a Christian," Shirley observes. "She invited a small group of neighborhood girls to her boarding place during the evenings for Bible study. I had a growing desire to become a Christian and finally accepted Christ at a revival meeting at the Bertie Brethren in Christ Church, my home congregation. For a long time, Miss Sherk wrote me notes to encourage me on my spiritual journey."[3]

Struggles and Victories

Dorothy was looked at with suspicion by leaders of the Bertie congregation because they knew that at teacher's college she had been exposed to other belief systems. She was criticized because she quoted scripture rather than testifying from her heart. This suspicion was so strong that a church leader was sent to her

Bible study to see what she was teaching the young girls. He found no errors, but these were difficult years for Dorothy. "I was ready to leave the church," she says.

Dorothy continued to teach for five years at the elementary school. By 1938 she was receiving $900 a year, a good salary. Although she wasn't expected to give her salary to her parents, she often bought things for her siblings, like socks, which cost 15 cents a pair.

Most of Dorothy's peers were dating and getting married, but Dorothy continued to concentrate on her career in teaching and to indulge her passion for knowledge. "Many of the eligible men weren't interested in the things I was interested in, like philosophy and theology. I wanted more in life than to settle down, get married, and have babies. I wanted to know what the great thinkers of the world were thinking. I would rather pick up a book than pick up a baby."

At this time, Ontario Bible School was moved from Gormley (north of Toronto) to Fort Erie. Dorothy was invited to teach along with Peter J. Wiebe and Carlton O. Wittlinger. This was a difficult decision to make because it meant a significant financial sacrifice: her salary would be $10 a month in addition to free room and board, and at that time teachers in private schools were not eligible for the government pension plan. In the end she accepted the position.

"I prayed about it and I felt the Lord leading me to Ontario Bible School," Dorothy recalls. "I knew my family was doing fine financially. My father had left farming and had a good paying job at the Fleet factory in Fort Erie. So I accepted the invitation."

After she paid her school debt, Dorothy began taking summer courses at the University of Toronto, graduating in five years. While there, she also attended many different churches, both Protestant and Catholic, and thus was exposed to many great preachers who challenged her mind and warmed her spirit.

Since Dorothy embraces the idea that a faith that needs protecting is not a faith worth having, she was never afraid to confront non-Christian thought systems. Yet her faith was never seriously challenged. The hollowness of secularism and the incompleteness of most faith systems made her aware in a deeper way of what a treasure she had in the true gospel of Jesus Christ.

Dorothy's disillusionment with the church began to change with wider experience and increasing contact with church leaders. During revival meetings at Ontario Bible School, gentle men like Henry Ginder, E. J. Swalm, Luke Keefer, Sr., and the Hostetters (Chris, Henry, and John) came to speak. The legalistic teaching she had grown up with in the Bertie congregation was absent in their preaching. These men gave Dorothy a different perspective on the Brethren in Christ Church. She admired their godliness, which was evident in their surrender to the Holy Spirit and their lives of discipleship.

A Model for Women

Dorothy became one of the most highly educated and respected women in the Brethren in Christ Church, recognized not only for her academic achievement but also for her wisdom and commitment to the church. Her leadership enabled what is now Niagara Christian Collegiate to make a good start, which, in turn, preserved a generation of youth for the leadership of the Brethren in Christ Church, as well as for the Mennonite faith community.

Dorothy was also a role model for women in leadership. She spoke in most of the Brethren in Christ congregations in the Canadian Conference on behalf of Niagara Christian Collegiate. Under the encouragement of Bishop Roy Sider, Dorothy eventually served on many denominational boards and committees, including the Niagara Christian Collegiate Board of Trustees, the General Conference Program Committee, the Canadian Conference Board, and the General Conference Task Force for Restructuring. She was a resource person at youth conventions and Women in Leadership gatherings. She edited *The Pilgrimage of the Brethren in Christ* for the denomination's bicentennial in 1978 and wrote numerous articles for the *Evangelical Visitor*. She was also an active member of the Sherkston Brethren in Christ Church.

Since she had not been conditioned either at home, school, or church to think of women as second-class citizens, she couldn't get excited about many of the causes so dear to the women's liberation movement. To Dorothy, Christian femininity had many pitfalls. She felt that many women destroyed their cause by majoring on the minors.

She always understood that certain gender terms were generic in meaning and took for granted that she was a "son" of God. Inclusive language seemed clumsy and awkward to her. Perhaps, as a hopeless academic, Dorothy was more concerned for the flow of language than for the feelings of ignored women.

She does not ignore, however, the neglected potential of some Brethren in Christ women. "I realize that in the past, many gifted women were passed by for leadership roles simply because they were women. But I feel I have been given all the responsibility I was prepared to accept. I could do anything I wanted in the church. I have nothing but praise for the respect and honor which I have received from my brothers in Christ. As a woman, I didn't experience any roadblocks to leadership. Rather, I received positive affirmation to do what I was gifted for in the church and to follow the leading of the Holy Spirit."[4] With respect to the role of women in the church, Dorothy had a clear sense of her personhood and calling. She sees herself as one of many talented women who were doing significant things in the denomination. But although she recognizes that singleness has eased her way into the public sphere, she does not undervalue the influence of women who serve as full-time homemakers. "The hand that rocks the cradle rules the world," she concedes, "and some women seem to manage well with a pen in one hand and a dishcloth in the other. For me, either vocation would be full time."

Spreading Her Wings

After 16 years at Niagara Christian Collegiate, Dorothy was earning $100 a month without charge for room and board. But by then she felt a desire to spread her wings and fly into the larger world. "I was feeling out of touch with the real world. I wanted a broader view of life. I needed to move out of this Christian ghetto," she comments.

An advertisement for an English and history teacher at Waterloo–Oxford High School near Baden, Ontario, tweaked Dorothy's interest. She applied and was hired. She began in September 1956, earning a salary of $4,000 a year.

With about 350 students, Waterloo-Oxford was located in a community of small towns and prosperous farms. Many of the farmers were Mennonites; some of the more conservative among them thought that high school was a waste of time. During the summers, Irving McNaughton, the principal, visited every rural family in the area to encourage them to send their children to high school. "I wondered if part of the rationale in hiring me, an educator from a conservative Christian high school, was that I would be a drawing card to the Mennonite community," Dorothy ponders.

Ray Schlegel, a Mennonite and former administrator of the Niphview Mennonite Home near Hamburg, Ontario, was one of Dorothy's students. "Out of my grade eight class," he recalls, "I was the only student who went on to high school. I was so pleased to be assigned to her class because I had heard what a great teacher she was. I remember hearing people comment on how fortunate a small school like Waterloo–Oxford was to get such a highly qualified teacher as Miss Sherk. She was a remarkable person. She used a 'carrot' rather than a 'stick' to motivate us."[5]

Other students of Dorothy have evaluated her in similar terms. Ronald J. Sider, a professor at Eastern Baptist Seminary and president of Evangelicals for Social Action, considers Dorothy "one of the greatest teachers who shaped my life. . . . [She] had high standards and demanded quality work. . . . I admire her wide reading and critical thinking. Over the years, she has continued to encourage me with an occasional note. . . . I consider her as one of God's special gifts in my life."[6]

Robert Sider, for many years a professor at Dickinson College, in Pennsylvania, thinks of Dorothy in terms of a mentor, in part because for the one course that she taught him (grade XIII analytical geometry), he "demonstrated no capacity whatever." As mentor, she encouraged him to attend a Canadian university, one of the first Canadian Brethren in Christ to do so. A few years later, he recalls, "It was as a mentor that Dorothy appeared again to me when I left for Oxford University on a Rhodes Scholarship. Just before I left, I received from her in the mail a large package that contained a complete and beautiful tea set for the English ritual of afternoon tea. I understood this as an affirmation of the direction in which I was moving, an affirmation I most desperately needed, since the course on which I had embarked was filled with many uncertainties, and seemed to me in crucial ways to challenge the values I had inherited. This quiet mentoring—so gracefully saying 'yes' to my future—has been a beacon throughout my life."[7]

Peter Erb, a professor at Wilfrid Laurier University, recalls Dorothy introducing him to great literature in her grade 9 English class. "I no longer have the books [studied in that class] in my library, but the page and the painted words of the opening declaration of *Twelfth Night* come clearly, and exactly, to mind, as do works I studied with her in later years: large sections of *Macbeth*, *Hamlet*, and almost the whole of Milton's *L'Allegro* and *Il Penseroso*, in their soft brown cover, Chesterton's 'Battle of Leponto' (a peculiar piece for a pacifist Amish Mennonite boy to memorize), and to excitement of ideas in an ugly pink and cheaply printed edition of Lester Sinclair's *Socrates*."

Dorothy introduced him to Plato and, "although innocently, she initiated me into one of my worst vices: book buying. Had she not praised the source of Sinclair's words and quietly encouraged me to read the Greek philosopher behind him, I might not have noticed a densely typeset paper edition of Plato's major dialogues for which I paid the outrageous sum of $1.95. The volume has required replacing more than once, but whatever edition falls into my hands—in Greek, English, or Schleirmacher's German—it raises the perennial questions first placed before me in Miss Sherk's grade 11 English class."[8]

Ron Mathies, executive director of Mennonite Central Committee, had Dorothy as a teacher in grades 11 and 12. "The teacher that she replaced was a very strict disciplinarian and grammarian. Dorothy's style was warm and invitational, instilling confidence and eliciting creativity for her students. She had an openness to, and was supportive of, students at all levels of ability. Her stature as a wise teacher gave increased status and profile to the Inter-School Christian Fellowship which she nurtured at the school."[9]

Although Dorothy was hired to teach English and history, the principal also invited her to establish the Guidance Department. Students and teachers alike sought her wisdom and counsel. Her love for learning continued, but counseling stretched her comfort zone.

Leaving the Chrysalis

She had always been an ivory tower sort of person who was happier learning about life from the mirror of her books than from firsthand experience. Although she had many friends, she didn't bare her heart and soul to them or expect them to do the same; it would have seemed indecent, somehow, to tear down all the emotional hedges around herself or someone else. Dorothy expected others to have the same strong sense of personhood that she had. Gradually, she came to see that she was leading a lopsided existence.

Now that she was about to leave the classroom for counseling, Dorothy says she was like a moth struggling to come free of her comfortable chrysalis. "I finally came free and began to fly. While learning was still important to me, I finally admitted what I should have known all along: good relationships are what truly matter to God. Learning does not take place in a vacuum."

While Dorothy had always loved God and cared about people, it wasn't until her final years in education that she began to learn the fine art of relating to others. She saw with new eyes young people who needed to be encouraged, informed, and comforted.

Her own life tragedies—the untimely death of her brother James in World War II; the sudden death of her niece Sue Hasty, killed in an automobile accident five months into her medical practice—enabled her to walk alongside and emphasize with students facing heart-wrenching tragedies. At such times, books offer some help. But the warmth of an understanding friend who listens with compassion makes a very significant difference. "In retrospect," Dorothy reflects, "I can see how God used Mr. McNaughton to prod me into a position of leadership where I had to open up that still-closed part of me."

Ron Mathies describes Dorothy's values as a counselor. "[She] was the first real guidance counselor at the school [Waterloo–Oxford] and gave this function of the curriculum credibility. Because of her deep concern for students, especially for those on the margins, she quickly gained the confidence of the student body. I suspect there were many students who were kept in school long after they and some of their teachers had given up all hope of [school] being a positive experience. In the days when vocational choices seemed rather limited, she was among the first to suggest new options and raise new horizons."

Later, following graduation from university, Mathies became Dorothy's colleague on the high school staff. "Dorothy's ability to change my status from student to colleague was exemplary. Because of her interest in people, she could be a supportive mentor to all [faculty]. She was both a formal and informal leader in the education system. Because of her professionalism and personal integrity, she was deeply respected by her colleagues. She was a gracious presence and an effective reconciler, always open to other perspectives and persuasions. Her office and her home were always open to colleagues and their friends."[10]

Early Retirement and Open Doors

At 58, Dorothy decided to retire. Like many of her choices in life, this was a difficult and prayerful decision. "I was having such a great time at Waterloo–Oxford with the staff and students," she recalls. "I held a position on the Guidance Association in Waterloo County. When I thought about retiring, I wondered why I would leave such a fulfilling career. I wasn't sure, except I knew there were other great opportunities in life to experience while I still had energy. I also knew it was a good thing to quit while everyone wanted you to stay."

Dorothy left Waterloo–Oxford after 16 fruitful years, during which time the school grew from 350 students to 1,200. She retired to a house in the city of Waterloo at full pension, or at "the Lord's provision," as she calls it. "Just another way the Lord blessed and cared for me."

While Dorothy never followed the traditional route of marriage and family, her life has been full of many meaningful and lasting relationships. In many ways, she considers that her singleness has allowed more opportunity for relationships and career opportunities that may not have been available had she married.

Reflecting on later relationships, she observes that her nature and the circumstances of her life were conducive to new relationships and opportunities. "I'm just like a mother hen. And, you know, in all my years of life, I've never lived alone! Can you believe it? I guess coming from a household of 11, I was used to a lot of hustle and bustle. . . . At Niagara Christian Collegiate I was part of the boarding community, surrounded by young people. When I moved to Waterloo, I met the Snider sisters, whom I boarded with and later cared for during my retirement when they were dying. They left me this home, so I've never had the hassle of buying or selling a home. My doors are always open to whoever needs a place to stay."

Dorothy's generous hospitality has been a home for many. When Brethren in Christ pastoral couple Harvey and Gladys Stickley retired, they weren't sure where they would live since they had always lived in a parsonage. "Why don't you live with me? I have plenty of room," offered Dorothy. So the Stickleys lived with Dorothy for eight years before moving to a retirement complex.

Harvey and Gladys were thus in a good position to observe her hospitality and care for many people. Harvey notes that Dorothy's driveway on 174 Vermont Street is large enough for six cars, and that frequently six cars are parked there at one time. "There are times when it seems like Grand Central Station at her house with people coming and going. No problem. Everybody is welcomed with a hug and sometimes a kiss and possibly a meal."[11]

If hospitality came easily to Dorothy, it was because she was reflecting the atmosphere in which she was reared. As she was growing up, her family's door was never locked, literally or figuratively. Her mother never knew how many children had come to sleep over until she went around the bedrooms in the morning to count heads. One Christmas morning, a brother brought a "tramp" home to dinner. Everyone was at ease with the situation except the tramp. There was always unconditional acceptance, and the rather meager Depression meals were served with love and laughter.

Over the years, many Laotian and Vietnamese refugees have stayed in Dorothy's home while establishing themselves in Canada. When Dorothy heard that Mennonite Central Committee was looking for refugee sponsorship, she thought this was a wonderful opportunity to help people in need. She reconnected with Ray Schlegel, then executive director of Mennonite Central Committee. Dorothy filled out the necessary forms and took them to her Westheights Brethren in Christ Church. "Don't worry. I'll look after everything. I just need to have the signature of a sponsoring group," she said with a smile.

While she hasn't kept track of how many refugees she has sponsored, Dorothy recalls them by name and keeps in touch with many of them. They are her children and grandchildren. Their photos grace her coffee tables and walls.

In 1982 Dorothy was asked by the Mennonite Central Committee to sponsor an 18-year-old young man from Vietnam. Jonathan Pham arrived without knowing a word of English. Dorothy expected that he would gravitate toward the Vietnamese community; instead, he remained with Dorothy, who soon found that she had a son, and he found the peace, security, and love that he had never known before. Later, he married in Australia, but the couple soon returned to Waterloo and stayed with Dorothy until John's wife, Susan, could learn Canadian ways.

John comments on Dorothy's contribution to his life. "The tender, loving care that our family has received from Dorothy is beyond words. Before coming to Canada, life was tough for me. I lived in a refugee camp. I faced an uncertain future and a hostile environment. But then I was sponsored by Dorothy in Canada. I was confused and surprised. Where I come from, no one would vouch to help a total stranger like me unless they could benefit from it. But I had nothing to offer Dorothy and the other women living with her who were in their retirement years. But in time I realized that what they did for me was part of their future, their love of God and of people who needed help.

"How can one person reach out and touch so many lives? Using her own money she helped people financially. She does this even though some people have taken advantage of her generosity. I guess the biggest reward for her has been to see people, like me, whom she has helped to become successful, productive citizens."[12]

Dorothy relates that when John Pham was newly married and living in Australia he telephoned to ask, "Mom, when you get too old to do anything at all, do you think that you could come and live with us [in Australia]?"

Dorothy tells of the time he said to her, "Miss Dorothy, Sears have cameras on sale." She replied, "When your government allowance starts coming, you can buy one." But he pointed out that by that time they would no longer be on sale. "I thought it over," Dorothy remembers, "and decided to take a risk. I put the cost of the camera—$125—on my credit card. Before the bill came, he had paid up."[13]

Her hospitality has also extended to international students who are studying at Wilfrid Laurier University and the University of Waterloo. Her name has been added to the temporary housing lists for these universities.

Members of her congregation have been recipients of her generous hospitality as well. Dorothy was instrumental in starting Westheights, a daughter congregation of Rosebank Brethren in Christ Church, through the Bible studies she held with Delores Winger. Soon after Westheights was established, Dorothy was invited to serve as deacon. She was among the first women deacons in the Canadian Conference of the Brethren in Christ Church.

Today, she continues to offer wisdom to many at Westheights who call her daily when they need a listening ear. "There are a lot of people who just need someone to talk to," she relates. "Everyone seems so busy today. It is hard to find someone who will listen to people who are going through a difficult time in life. I spend a lot of time listening to people." Harvey Sider, former bishop of the Canadian Conference, notes that "for over two decades Dorothy has stuck with this church plant, enhancing vitality and outreach, until Westheights has become one of the most significant congregations in the Canadian Conference."[14]

Lee Bryant is among those who have been helped and influenced by Dorothy. The two met in 1957. Lee sees Dorothy as "one of the last links in the chain of Christians who led me from an early life in extreme fundamentalism to an equally extreme art world, a subculture where I'd lived out my desperation as an existentialist alcoholic. I wasn't creating much any more when I met Dorothy. She graciously discussed literature and classical music with me and we listened to a record of Marian Anderson singing Bach arias. Until then, I was convinced I'd have to commit cultural and intellectual suicide if I became a Christian.

Dorothy was the first Christian who knew what existentialism was. . . .

"I borrowed many books from her personal library in the autumn of 1957—books by A.W. Tozer, C. S. Lewis, and the journals of John Wesley. We talked about Christianity versus atheism and nihilism before and after my astonishing turnaround in February of 1958. After my conversion, Dorothy handed over the records of Marian Anderson singing arias from *The Messiah*, and my favorite, *St. John's Passion*, by Bach. 'Here it is,' she smiled. 'You might as well have it—Marian Anderson has played an important part in your conversion.'"[15]

Margaret Dailey is another woman influenced by Dorothy. "I had the good fortune," she comments, "of being part of a Bible study group which met in her home for over 20 years. It was a wonderful oasis of time in which we were nurtured and nourished both intellectually and spiritually as we explored the word of God. . . . We began to grow in the Spirit and became more mature as Christians.

"The studies were always interesting because Dorothy loved what she was teaching and knew the Bible with a keen mind and a passionate heart—and we were all the beneficiaries of these gifts. Dorothy's studies were never hurried. An atmosphere of peacefulness prevailed and there was always time for questions, answers, and discussions. . . . Secure in the confidentiality of the group, very deep needs were expressed in almost every area of life, and as we prayed for each other at the end of the afternoon, we were strengthened as a group and as individuals. We no longer carried our burdens alone.

"Encompassing everything were Dorothy's own particular gifts of the Spirit—love, tolerance, patience, wisdom, understanding, and a constant showing forth of the love of Jesus Christ in her life."

Reflections on the Journey

Dorothy enjoys retirement. "It offers me 'special privileges' like saying no to something because I'm getting too old. At the same time, I don't think old age is a license to fritter away my life. I tried to take up watercolor painting but I was always getting interrupted with other things," she laughs.

As Dorothy reflects upon her life, she sees it as a series of interruptions. "You can make a plan but you can't be rigid in following your plans. I was never much for goal setting," she muses, "because the best made goals are always changed. I think the story of my life is interruptions!" (The telephone rings and interrupts her train of thought. Someone needs a listening ear.) "The most important thing in life is that you follow Christ and use your gifts to serve him," she continues after a compassionate response to the phone call.

And that is what characterizes Dorothy's life. It is truly a remarkable mosaic. Her wit and sense of humor, her love of knowledge and her keen mind, her hospitality and generosity, her wisdom and counsel, her commitment to Christ and contributions to the Brethren in Christ Church, and her care both for biological and "extended" families are rich qualities that accurately portray Dorothy.

While the acquisition of knowledge has been at the core of Dorothy's quest in life, she has never seen learning as an end in itself. "If wisdom does not broaden the awareness of self, the world around us, and the God who made us, it is better to be ignorant," she observes. "Knowledge must heighten our sense of morality. In our brave new world of technology in the twenty-first century, we are beginning to experience what learning without moral and spiritual moorings can do to one's personhood and to society as a whole. Mere training produces robots; education provides an atmosphere for intellectual, emotional, and spiritual growth. Although I have fallen short of my goal, my aim as an educator has been to impart wisdom alongside knowledge."

At age 86, Dorothy continues to practice this philosophy of life. Harvey Sider, one of her students at Niagara Christian Collegiate and later her bishop, captures the essence of Dorothy's life: "For more than half a century, Dorothy has been shaping people's lives, congregations, and the Canadian Brethren in Christ Church. Her modeling of the Christian graces will continue to influence and bless those who witness her selfless service to Christ and humanity." [16]

A Tapestry of Wisdom, Service, and Simplicity

Esther Susan Dourte Spurrier

by Elaine Thuma*

Many people in Brethren in Christ circles see Esther Spurrier as a serious, articulate woman who can stand with confidence before an audience and speak with knowledge on whatever subject she is presenting. Those who sit on committees with her know that she will always bring a different perspective if she feels another side needs to be represented. But Esther's character is much more complex than that. While bold threads from Esther's strong character weave through the tapestry of her life, occasional pale strands of self-doubt and personal unworthiness are also present. Prominent strands of compassion, service, and commitment complete the blend.

If Esther is not giving a presentation or attending a committee meeting, she might be organizing a food pantry, cleaning house for a friend, cutting hair, cooking a meal for a group, or laboring over a missions writing project. Or she might be found overseas in Macha, Zambia, involved in comforting someone who has just lost a loved one, making frequent hospital visits with food for a patient, organizing a get-together to encourage the community, or cycling to a nearby village to visit a friend.

---

*Elaine Thuma first met Esther Spurrier in 1970 at a Messiah College function. Over years, their paths continued to cross—in Philadelphia, where their husbands attended medical school, and in Zambia at Macha Hospital, where both couples lived and worked. At Macha, Elaine and Esther shared many wonderful experiences, mentored each other in a variety of ways, and became beloved friends. Elaine enjoys helping with ministries of her church (New Creation Brethren in Christ, Dillsburg, Pennsylvania) and working with her husband at Macha Hospital as a support person for ongoing malaria research.

Esther's character blend rises from a solid background of faith and weaves its way through experiences and responsibilities with family, community, and the church, both local and worldwide.[1]

Early Ministry Encounters

Esther Susan Dourte was born March 1, 1949, to Ruth and Eber Dourte in Waynesboro, Pennsylvania. From her parents, a pastoral couple for 35 years, Esther learned qualities of sacrifice, commitment, and service. The Dourtes began pastoring in an era when ministers supported themselves: Eber taught school to provide income for the family. In later years, the family began to receive some financial support from the congregation. Esther saw that the amount of time and energy her parents poured into their ministry was not dependent on congregational support. "They just worked with all their hearts to utilize the gifts God had given them," she comments. She admits that she is a strong woman, just as her mother is a strong woman and a "good partner to Daddy." These character traits, whether genetically received or environmentally learned, are some of the strands with which Esther's own weave began.

As a middle child, Esther was more accommodating than older brother Ray and younger sister Faithe. She tried hard to please those around her. Her mother remembers: "Esther never had to be told to do what she was supposed to do. She always performed par excellence both academically and otherwise. I only remember spanking her one time, and that was for something she did in church." Esther's accommodating nature made her feel less loved than Ray, whose less-than-compliant behavior at the time warranted more parental attention.

When younger sister Faithe was born in 1957, Esther was already eight years old. Faithe states, "I didn't really know Esther until I was an adult. She left for college when I was nine. We shared a room, and even a bed, and Esther never complained about that, but our relationship was more parent/child than sister/sister. I remember watching Esther and her cheerleader friends practicing on the front lawn and being so impressed with their uniforms. And I can still picture her rolling her hair in orange juice cans."

In the year of Faithe's birth, the Dourte family moved to Upland, California, to become the pastoral family for the Upland Brethren in Christ Church. Esther recalls her years in California (1957–1966): "Growing up in California was great—lots of opportunity and gracious, generous people." She remembers the kindness of many parishioners who provided meals, shared milk, eggs, and produce, and baby-sat, sewed, and cleaned for the pastoral family. "One parishioner bought season tickets to the local concert series for us, and I was introduced to great music," Esther recalls. "Another couple lent us their camper for yearly family vacations to the mountains or beach. We had only one vacation before that time."

But the difficulties of life as a pastor's daughter also began to surface. One woman from the congregation, for example, was convinced that Esther's high heels were from the devil. Though her parents tried to shield the children from the criticisms and political schemes that are sometimes part of a pastor's life, Esther became aware of conflict within the church during the California years.

Esther attended the local junior high school, receiving an award for being the best student in the eighth grade. She continued to excel during her high school years at Western Christian Academy (an interdenominational school), "where classes were small and teachers were caring." She was a busy youth—involved in basketball, softball, cheerleading, and school and church choirs. Singing and music, in particular, were an important part of Esther's life. Her strong musical heritage led to unique opportunities, such as singing a duet on television at a very young age with older brother Ray.

Spiritual Awakening

In 1966, Esther entered Messiah College in Grantham, Pennsylvania, after her junior year of high school. Her move coincided with her parents' cross-country relocation to a new pastorate in Lancaster, Pennsylvania. She arrived with the sad awareness that she would not be returning in the summer to friends and family on the West Coast.

During her years at Messiah, Esther grappled with spiritual issues. Although she considered herself a theological conservative, she found out much later that other students viewed her as a "liberal California girl" and even wondered why people like her would attend the small, rural school at Grantham. Esther comments, "People decry the rebellious 1960s, but I am thankful that I came of age during that time. I was challenged to examine carefully what I believed and to live it consistently. I also became more aware of the large world beyond our borders, the needs that exist, and our mandate as Christians to do something about those needs."

Two men stand out in Esther's memory as mentors for her during those years. Pete Willms, the college chaplin, helped her to understand that it is good to ask questions and wrestle with your faith. Martin Schrag, her Bible professor, "lived a life of faithfulness and discipleship to Jesus Christ that I could emulate."

In addition to having her spiritual eyes opened while at Messiah College, Esther's eyes also opened to John Spurrier, a star basketball player from northeastern Pennsylvania. Esther and John courted for the remainder of their time at Messiah and wed in June 1970, after her college graduation. They began their life together in Philadelphia, where John, after graduating from Messiah in 1969, was studying in his second year of medical school at Temple University.

The new environment challenged Esther's values and her approach to money and possessions. "I joined the auxiliary [for spouses of medical students], which functioned as both a fund-raising/project-promoting organization for the medical school and a support group for lonely family members adjusting to the demanding working hours of their spouses. During one meeting we got into a discussion about the problems of raising children on a doctor's income without their becoming spoiled brats. Perhaps naïvely, but very sincerely, I suggested that we could just give away a good portion of our income so we wouldn't need to deal with the problems of excessive wealth. The suggestion fell flat, not gaining a response from anyone. Maybe they thought I wasn't being serious."[2]

Since medical school required full-time studying and work for John, Esther was the family breadwinner. Although she obtained her master's degree in elementary education from

Temple, a teaching job seemed out of the question. The city of Philadelphia laid off 500 teachers the year she graduated from Temple, and her experience subbing in an urban setting left her feeling "burned out." Instead, she began teaching courses in mobility and orientation to blind adolescents and adults at the local Residential Center for the Blind.

As the end of medical school approached, Esther and John traveled around the country so John could interview for residency programs. Traveling together for (seemingly) endless hours gave the couple opportunities to learn more about each other, to explore, and to meet family and friends from distant areas. Following John's medical school graduation in 1973, they moved to Hartford, Connecticut, where John began his internship at Hartford Hospital. During that first year, Esther began a new venture—motherhood. Daughter Rebecca Faye was born on February 10, 1974; six weeks later Esther was hospitalized with appendicitis. Those weeks of adjusting to a new and often crying baby, sleepless nights, and surgery were very difficult. John's rigorous schedule left no room for giving much help to Esther, so she traveled to her parents' home in Lancaster to complete her recovery. She welcomed extra hands to help with the new baby. Ruth, Esther's mother, recalls thinking that Esther seemed overwhelmed by the idea of being a mother and dealing with a demanding baby.

Cultural Awakening

When Rebecca was 18 months old, John and Esther pursued work overseas. Their call to missions began as children, both having grown up in homes where missionaries were frequent guests. Coming of age in the 1960s, when young people wanted more from their futures than settling down to the good life, fostered their calling. With the Vietnam War escalating, John also needed an alternative to the military draft. They approached the Board for Missions looking for a short-term opportunity. Working at an under-served area in the United States seemed most desirable and offered John partial forgiveness of his medical school debt, but the Mission Board asked them to consider going to Africa. At first Esther and John hesitated—in part, Esther writes, subscribing to the myth that "travel to, or residence on, this continent is a highly dubious proposition for people from Western countries." But, she continues, "a great deal of fear can often be dispelled by a little knowledge," and they agreed to go following conversations with former missionaries and encouragement from both sets of parents."[3]

In September 1975 the Spurrier family of three arrived in Macha, Zambia, to work at Macha Hospital. After coming from the obvious racial tensions in Philadelphia and Hartford in the 1970s, John and Esther had prepared themselves to be kept at a distance. The warm welcome from the Zambian people and their sincere expression of gratitude for the Spurriers' arrival came as a pleasant surprise.

Esther's worldview, which began to expand in college, was about to be stretched even further. She comments: "A person doesn't really understand his or her culture until exposed to a different one. It was then that I learned all of the values and assumptions I had unconsciously absorbed as being part of my own society, and I started to re-evaluate those in light of scripture and understand that the way I grew up is not the only way, and maybe not even the best way in some circumstances, to live as a Christian."

Learning, in all areas of life, became an important part of Esther's routine. She observed, listened, and asked questions of trusted friends. Her African teacher, Sara Mwaanga, a good friend and mentor, explained the culture, taught her the local language (Tonga), and helped her understand the way a woman in Africa should act. A seasoned missionary and mentor, Erma Jean Bert, helped her adjust to life as a missionary mother. The Zambian women modeled lives of prayer that challenged Esther spiritually: "I don't think I learned how to pray until I went to Zambia and prayed with women who really had no resources other than their trust in God."

And the generosity of the Zambian people, who had very little materially but shared liberally, challenged her concept of hospitality. In an article for the *Evangelical Visitor*, Esther writes: "It is the custom here to give visitors something to eat or drink while they are visiting, then something is also given for the visitors to take home. . . . I come home laden with . . . vegetables, wild honey, milk, or whatever happens to be available. When I see how graciously these people give out of the little they have, I am challenged to give out of my comparative abundance. Worry about tomorrow has long been one of my besetting sins, but I can see God at work in me to change me through my ministry to others."[4]

The unpredictability of life at Macha provided more opportunities to learn. Not having the assurance of adequate water, especially in times of drought, was particularly trying. "I remember the time I had five children under my care and used the last bucket of rather muddy water to bathe them all, wondering where and when we would get the next [bucket of water]. The following day there was rain enough to collect water from the roof. It was very tough—I am a planner, and I like to know I have enough in store."

The challenges of cross-cultural living could also be advantageous. As a Community Resource Person (title given by Brethren in Christ World Missions to the spouses of missionaries on specific assignments as medical doctors, teachers, etc.), Esther filled a variety of roles—one of the things she enjoyed about life in Africa. She reflects, "I have often wondered how John can train for years and then just practice medicine. What if he didn't like practicing medicine?"

Her assortment of roles included a brief stint with John in the Macha Hospital operating room as a scrub nurse. She quickly learned how to thread needles and identify one instrument from another, and even learned how to anticipate what the surgeon needed during various procedures. She recalls being stretched by the experience: "I remember dropping the bone saw on the floor during an amputation—the only bone saw we had. They had to finish the procedure with a bone cutter [a smaller instrument that removes small chunks of bone with each clip]. And I stuck a knife blade into my hand the first time I tried to put it on to the handle. It was also a different dynamic for John having a scrub nurse who could give it right back to him if he got testy during surgery!"

Other responsibilities included supervising the tailors who sewed and repaired linens for the hospital, and communicating with the Missions Sewing Auxiliary in the United States about supplying patient gowns and other necessities. In addition to her practical duties, she held Bible studies in her home and planned evenings of singing with the students from the Nurses Training School.

Although other diverse responsibilities, from tutoring to book keeping, occupied Esther's time and attention, her most rewarding experience was teaching Theological Education by Extension (TEE) courses (an on-site leadership training program). She also tried to facilitate a literacy program—training tutors who could teach other people how to read. Not surprisingly, these rewarding experiences were accompanied by the usual cultural challenges. "Both [of those programs] required me to be out in the villages . . . often traveling by myself and staying overnight. I always would leave very unsure of where I was going, and I hate not knowing where I am going. So I would have to stop and ask how to get here and there because the paths would change how they looked from season to season."

Although travel circumstances could be less than ideal, Esther still valued her interactions with members of the community. She entertained many guests in her home (often daily), participated in women's meetings, attended funerals and weddings (major social events of the culture), and visited in local villages. As neighbors in Zambia, Esther and I shared a favored activity of cycling to villages to visit friends. While visiting I would listen, trying to learn the language, as Esther and our hosts conversed easily. She would interpret for me as needed and model how to receive hospitality in the Zambian culture.

With the constant flow of activity around her, Esther rarely worked alone. People stopped by her house on a regular basis for all kinds of reasons, and sometimes for no reason at all. An introvert by nature, she sometimes felt weary from being a constant hostess. To compensate, she occasionally made arrangements to use the house of another missionary as a place to spend some hours in solitude—a rare, and cherished, luxury. But she learned to enjoy the communal aspect of life in Zambia too, and became more of a "people person" by understanding the value of working together and sharing responsibilities with the local women. As a testament to her mastery of the culture and the language (she eventually became the language tutor for area missionaries), the local Tonga population called her a Tonga as well.

Church leaders began to recognize Esther's gifts. They appointed her to a commission studying polygamy in the African church—a difficult and sensitive issue. Esther remembers arguing that "faithfulness is the issue rather than marital form. Marriage was instituted by God as a demonstration of his faithfulness to his people, and the Western model of serial polygamy misses that mark at least as much, if not more, than the polygamy practiced [in Africa]." Although not always sure of her contribution to the commission, her insight was typical of her different, but wise, perspective.

The missionaries were also recipients of Esther's wisdom and generosity. While I was recovering from a C-section and the birth of my twin sons, I remember Esther coming over to give me a refreshing bath and to wash my hair. She knew how miserable I was—my hair was dirty and the temperatures were hot at that time of year. Typical of her nature, Esther was quick to see the need and fulfill it.

Brother Ray, who visited Macha in 1985, comments, "I observed her role in the community and her language proficiency. I realized that Esther's role in Zambia was just as important to the community as John's role, even though they went [to fulfill the need for a] missionary doctor."

Ray's observations seem to fit Esther's personal philosophy of missions, as stated in a 1982 article she wrote for the *Evangelical Visitor*: "Wherever God has led us—in whatever job we find ourselves—we are commanded to do it heartily as unto God. The mandate for a Christian in a cross-cultural setting is no different from that of Christians who have lived their entire lives in the same community. We are to be God's people, to show his love and spread his message, to support and further his work."[5]

Finding a New Niche

In May of 1987, the Spurriers decided to leave Macha. This was not their first venture away from their African home. They had returned to the United States for a brief period in 1979 so that John could begin a surgical residency program. But after hearing about the continuing need for a physician at Macha, John relinquished the remainder of the program, and the

Spurriers returned to Macha in 1980 to serve two additional terms. Now, after serving a total of 12 years in the country, they left with mixed emotions.

They chose to relocate in Dillsburg, Pennsylvania, close to the homes of their parents and siblings on the side of a mountain. Coming together on "the Dourte/Spurrier mountain," as it is often called, fulfilled a dream of Esther's mother after years of family separation. During the process of building the family houses, several families lived together in Eber and Ruth Dourte's house until the construction could be completed. John and Esther's family shared living space and meals with her parents for four years.

Living in a family community had its relationship challenges. The family discovered that proximity did not necessarily produce intimacy, and they had to make communication and relationship-building an intentional focus of their life on the mountain. For Esther, tensions ran high at times. "I often felt in the middle and more than once wanted out, but when we suggested moving to a house just across the road, our children protested. They loved being in the middle of the family circle, despite its bumps and bruises. I am sure that for my parents it also took a great deal of grace to have all of us in their house with our erratic schedules, food preferences, activities, and traditions. We found that unstated expectations caused the greatest disappointment. But we also cherish the support and encouragement we received from each other in that setting."

By living so close together, they learned to know one another in ways that most families never do. Faithe, for example, says that she really began to know her sister through all the tensions and joys of living together. Many now consider life on the Dourte/Spurrier mountain to be a model of Christian community at work. Ruth, Esther, and Faithe have often been invited to speak to women's groups about family relationship issues.

Building family relationships wasn't the only adjustment Esther made after returning to the United States. John found work in the emergency room at a nearby hospital and the children enrolled in the local public school system, but Esther could not immediately find her niche. Finally in 1988, at the request of Don Zook (then Executive Director of Brethren in Christ World

Missions [BICWM]), she began compiling the two missions publications—*World Christian Intercessor* and *Today*. "Writing for BICWM was sort of a lifesaver for me. I really didn't want to come back to the States from Zambia, but it just seemed like it was the right time for our family to do that. [This position] put me in contact with people all over the world—church leaders and missionaries—and kept me in touch with what was going on. I felt like I was still involved with mission work." Over the next thirteen years Esther continued her involvement in the writing and editing of newsletters and prayer publications for BICWM, including the monthly *Prayer Challenge* in 1997, mostly on a volunteer basis.

Other opportunities kept her active in missions. For several years Esther served as a member of the committee that planned events to celebrate the centennial of Brethren in Christ World Missions in 1998. Her enthusiasm, creativity, and missions experience contributed significantly to centennial programs and activities. The Spurriers also became involved with BICWM as representatives-at-large, traveling to congregations and meetings on behalf of missions. "That has been fulfilling," Esther observes, "even though it seems like a drag sometimes to put together something and take a weekend to drive someplace and speak. It is almost always very rewarding because of the people you meet and the response you get from giving a missions presentation."

John and Esther joined the Grantham Brethren in Christ Church soon after their return. The children thoroughly enjoyed the youth program there, and John and Esther became very involved in the life of the congregation. Esther, in particular, found roles that connected her with missions and outreach. She served as chairperson for the congregational Missions Prayer Fellowship for several years and as a member of the Missions Committee. Esther also helped to launch a monthly women's salad supper, an exciting outreach ministry for the Grantham congregation. She comments: "Our time overseas gave us much more of a passion for outreach when we returned. We realized we had to be more intentional about giving a witness for the Lord, so we got involved in an outreach Bible study, which has brought different people into our lives and into our circle of acquaintance. . . . We tend to get really busy in the church, especially me, so it is good for us to intentionally rub elbows in a significant way with other kinds of people."

Unexpected Setbacks

The bottom seemed to drop out of the Spurriers' life in 1994 when son Matthew, born October 23, 1976, at Macha, was in a serious automobile accident. He sustained several areas of injury to his brain and was in a deep coma for several days. Matt eventually woke from the coma, but his recovery was long and grueling with multiple set-backs over the next 18 months. Due to the nature of his injuries, Matt had somewhat of a personality change during his recovery. It was very hard on Esther and John to have a new child to learn to relate to, not knowing when and if the ordeal would end.

For Esther, this period was a "plodding" time—taking one day at a time and not thinking about tomorrow or the months and years to come. She observes, "I look back on that time and I don't understand how we were not totally devastated. I learned to rely on God day by day in a new way, and also to trust him with the outcome. I knew that God was going to give us the strength to deal with whatever happened."

Faithe comments, "It took so much energy to keep things going and not know when it would end. I never saw Esther fall apart. She buckled down and did what had to be done. She put everything in low gear and kept going. I have always admired the disciplined way she approaches her spiritual life. I guess that helped to prepare her for dealing with this."

Around the world, acquaintances and friends prayed for Matt's recovery. Spurrier friends at Macha, who considered Matt to be a son of their village, joined the prayers. Their prayers were answered—he eventually recovered fully. When his recovery was more assured, someone commented to Esther that God is good. Her immediate response was, "God is good even if the outcome would have been different."

Service in the States

Once the crisis and follow-up concerns with Matt were over, Esther picked up her service involvements in church and community again. In 1997, she became a volunteer staff member at New Hope Ministries (an inter-church social service agency that provides food, emergency help, and ongoing counsel to the poor and disadvantaged). As food pantry coordinator, she checked expiration dates on all donations, kept the stock rotated, valued the donations for record-keeping purposes, prepared for the food drives—especially during the holidays—and found storage space for donations until distribution time. As a self-imposed responsibility, she took all outdated foods and disposed of them at home in her compost heap or burn barrel. For Faithe, this kind of action typifies Esther's commitment to service and simple living: "I have often seen Esther by the compost heap opening and scraping out tins so they can be recycled, and I think, 'Here is a woman who graduated *summa cum laude* from college.' I see her willingness to do anything if it is important to have it taken care of."

After their children graduated from high school, John and Esther joined the Dillsburg Brethren in Christ Church, where John's brother Jim and Esther's sister Faithe are the pastoral couple. Esther and John soon became congregational deacons with a number of families under their care. Faithe sees their deacon work as another example of Esther's service mentality: "Esther has a huge heart. No one knows how many meals she has prepared for people, how many times she has cleaned houses or mowed lawns. She cares that people are cared for and loved in specific and tangible ways. She is very sensitive that way." Older brother Ray agrees: "She is a strong woman who gives selfless service to others and has a capacity for great compassion, yet she does not see herself as worthy. She needs to care more for herself."

The failure to concentrate on personal care brought new issues to light after the children went off to college. Esther and John realized they had become so focused on the children that they rarely did things together as a couple. Esther comments, "We realized that our different styles, interests, and gifts had taken us in two quite different directions. A Mennonite/Brethren Marriage Encounter weekend provided an opportunity to get things out in the open, and we learned to plan for times of communication and activity together on a regular basis. Working on our relationship and learning about it in a new way sounds funny after thirty years of marriage, I guess. It was very affirming when Rebecca returned home, after serving in the Ukraine for three years with a Mennonite service organization, and told us that our relationship was obviously better than it used to be."

Personal Reflections

At this time in Esther's life, she reflects a bit on who she is. "After participating in a Sunday school class on the subject of mother-daughter relationships, I have a new understanding of family heritage and how that has made me who I am. It was helpful for me to understand how my mother came to be the person she is, and how she influenced me to be the person I am."

She ponders the tensions in her life. "I wish I weren't so compulsive. When I am out walking I cannot pass a piece of trash without stopping to pick it up—that is bordering on pathology! I am also very organized and that creates problems in our family because John isn't that way. I wish I were more laid back."

Being a person of opinion also creates tension. Although Esther is a self-described people-pleaser, her tendency to approach issues from a different perspective often keeps her at cross-purposes with pleasing others. She often wonders "if I am doing the right thing—especially if I am involved in a controversy or presenting a differing point of view. It's just not comfortable, and I wonder if I am really doing God's will. I don't enjoy being negative."

This challenge was especially evident when Esther served for several years as a member of the denomination's governing body—the General Conference Board. "I know that I was picked as a representative because I am a woman, and there was some sentiment that we need more women on that board. So do I [serve] to represent the constituency, or to represent women, or am I just my own person? I do think there are some situations where women need to be spoken for. . . . I wish it weren't so. When you sit on a board and you are in the minority, the dynamic changes. The men on that board don't have to speak for men, they just speak for themselves or their constituency. When you are a woman in the minority, you are representing women—how you behave is a reflection on all women."

Although she sometimes struggles to determine her role in the denomination, the Church has been an important part of Esther's heritage and her own life, both in the United States and overseas. She shares some hopes for the future: "I would love to see the church give more of its resources to help others outside the local congregation. I hope our church learns to be more generous all the time with what God has given us—generous beyond our four walls."

Esther's own gift of generosity—offering her life and her resources in service—continues to blend colorfully with intellectual insight and a commitment to simple living in the tapestry of her life.

Finding a Song Through Suffering

Lana Clinton Zahn

by Sandra Spurrell*

As you sit in the Living Room, a Christian coffeehouse, you hear muted conversation and smell freshly brewed coffee; aromas of pastries and fresh breads enhance the delectable fragrance. The room is darkened; on each of the oak tables gleams a candle. Stained glass windows add to the ambiance. On the platform, musicians are preparing for the night's performance. As you move out into the gallery, you note paintings by local artists and a variety of other items that attract your attention. The Living Room is the vision of Lana Zahn of Ransom Creek Community Church (Brethren in Christ), Clarence Center, New York. Her vision is the positive result of many, often difficult, turns in her life.[1]

A Troubled Childhood

Lana was born in Buffalo on December 2, 1948, the third of five children of Edmund and Norma Coffas Clinton, members of the Roman Catholic Church. Norma was a gifted singer who went to New York City at the age of 16 to debut, but her potential career as a professional singer was cut short by the death of her mother. Norma met her husband at the Wurlitzer Company where she worked, and where he was a salesman in the showroom. Lana's father was also a musician who played violin and trumpet and directed a local band.

*Sandra Spurrell is a crisis counselor at a women's shelter in St. Catherines, Ontario. From 1996 to 2001 she was Lana Zahn's co-pastor at the Ransom Creek Brethren in Christ Church, Clarence Center, New York.

Lana was born during an ice storm, which may be seen as a herald of her early life. She was shy, preferring to play alone with her dolls and enjoying the clinic that she set up in her bedroom so she could administer injections and treat imaginary wounds—a portent of her life as a nurse.

She and her parents faithfully attended the Roman Catholic services in the suburbs where they lived. Lana was also a student in the local public school and attended religious education classes once a week.

Although shy, Lana had a mischievous streak. Like other schoolchildren, she liked to tease and mock other children. And, as often happens among children, she sometimes carried such actions too far. A neighbor boy, Bobby Roblins, had trouble talking. Lana and her friends would tease him as he sat on his porch by repeatedly calling him "marble mouth." His mother would come out with a yardstick to do battle for her son, then Lana and her friends would run away. Years later Lana met Bobby, engaged in Christian ministry at an outdoor concert. When they established that they knew each other, Bobby related that for years he had been hurt by the teasing of Lana and her friends. Lana now had an opportunity to receive forgiveness for actions for which she still carries some "baggage."

Another action for which there is a less satisfactory ending was throwing rocks at a young blind girl, a foster child of a neighbor. She and a cousin, who joined her in this activity, did not intend to hit the girl, but the girl would hear the thud of the rocks and become startled and scared. Then Lana and her cousin would roar with glee. "She still haunts my memory," Lana says. "I have never come across her, but I have asked God to forgive me."

The family's fortune changed in 1959 when Lana's father relinquished his position at Wurlitzer's. When he was offered a job in Florida, the family moved there. They now had little money and few possessions. Lana had to wear her winter clothes in May; embarrassed, she pretended that she was cold because she came from the North. When first asked to pay 25 cents for lunch at school, she said that she had lost her money on her way to classes. She told a lie because she did not want anyone to know of the family's poverty.

In the same year, the family moved to another location in Florida, where her father started his own business and Lana attended a Roman Catholic school. But the business failed, so the family returned to western New York.

Back in New York, surviving through the generosity of relatives, Lana felt like a waif. The family was surrounded by people, especially people of Lana's age, who judged a person's worth by where they lived, how old one's parents were, how one dressed, what one ate, and on what the food was served. To make matters worse, Lana's mother was different from other women in the area: she did all the jobs that supposedly were men's jobs, such as mowing the grass and painting the house. The neighbors waited to see what she would do next.

The Clintons definitely were not one of the status families of the neighborhood. According to Lana, they were close to being on the wrong side of the tracks. All of this meant that high school was a very awkward time for Lana, although she did socialize with a group of Catholic girlfriends who still get together once a year for dinner.

Lana and her family through these years remained faithful Catholics. The family attended mass regularly. Her mother always prayed at bedtime, and the children added names of people for her to pray for. Lana too said prayers that she had learned. Although the family did not have a Bible (only a prayer book), she claims that there was never a time when she did not know about Jesus. Later, however, she regretted that she didn't know him in a way that would help her through the difficulties of her life.

The Challenges of Career and Marriage

Lana took nurses training at D'Youville College in Buffalo. Meanwhile, she had married Bill Zahn. They met when she was only fifteen. Their first real date was in 1964 when Bill used $12 saved from his paper route work to take Lana to dinner at Leonardo's in downtown Buffalo and then to a movie.

Five years later they married. Their first years as a couple were "stormy." Lana thinks that this was because she was working full time, and also because she wanted to get married more quickly than Bill did.

The birth of their first child, Jill, nearly four years after their marriage, brought a new dimension to their sometimes troubled marriage. A second child, Cheryl, was born nearly four years later. A son, Justin, completed the family. Lana loved being a mother. Even as a teenager she had enjoyed cleaning the family house. And she had earlier learned how to cook, although she didn't always like that type of work.

A turning point came in Lana's life with the birth of Justin. Over the years she had continued her work as a nurse. She worked intensively, determined to advance in her career. Sometimes she even forgot to eat or drink, which resulted in dehydration. Now she discovered that she was pregnant again, even though she had used a contraceptive. She says, "I didn't know whether the Catholic church was against [that device], and I didn't want to find out."

Six months pregnant, Lana spent a long weekend at home. But for a pregnant woman, the weekend was not wisely spent. She and Bill "rough-housed" on the floor in fun. And she carried one of her daughters home following a bicycle accident in which the child hurt her leg. The result of such action was hospitalization for bleeding, injections to strengthen the unborn baby's lungs, and the premature birth of Justin. The baby remained in the hospital, fed through a tube. Now at home, Lana received a call one night that Justin was bloating. She promised God that if Justin survived she would look after the child for him. The next morning Justin had improved.

At this point, Lana realized that she had failed to live up to her responsibility to the Lord in raising her children. She herself had not been going to church, claiming that she was too busy with her job and motherhood. She immediately enrolled Jill in Catholic education classes as a way of fulfilling her bargain with God. Her children attended Catholic schools. They prayed and sang songs to Jesus' mother, Mary, at night.

But she was driven by her nursing career. "I wanted to stay home," she explains, "but there was this passion inside me to be out there, honing my skills, interacting with people. It was hard to keep from working, and sometimes I overworked. I was an army reserve nurse on weekends for three years. It was hard trying to compromise between my passion to be out there and accomplishing [things in my career] and my desire to be with my family."

By mid-marriage, Lana had experienced many disappointments in her relationship with Bill. Her expectations for perfect harmony were not being fulfilled. "My mind began to imagine what it would be like to be married to another man," she recalls, "or just what it would be like to relive the same excitement of my early relationship with Bill. Daily my mind wandered and found a resting spot in fantasy." While she enjoyed these thoughts, at the same time she suffered from guilt. Although she did not have, as she says, "a personal relationship with Jesus," she prayed about her addiction to fantasy and chose a day when she would relinquish what had for her been "pleasurable thoughts." The next day, at the given hour, she "could not reach into that drawer in my mind. It was as though my thoughts could not go to that depth or even skim the surface."

The family moved to Clarence, 20 miles east of Buffalo. Here, her children stopped attending the Catholic school. Jill met some born-again believers in her class at the local public school. Soon she was going to their youth group and attending activities and services at the Baptist church. One night Jill came home with two gifts in a box—a T-shirt and a Bible with her name in it. Jill tried unsuccessfully to hide them from her mother, undoubtedly because the family was Catholic. Lana questioned her daughter about these items. Jill replied, "Mom, I have some beliefs that you don't have."

These words penetrated Lana's heart. She thought she had lost Jill. She told Jill that she believed in Jesus, but Jill responded by saying, "Mom, there is so much more." Lana felt "so hurt." She recalls, "I felt I had broken the vow I made on my wedding day to raise my family Catholic. I also felt confronted by the implication that all I had believed in and lived for all these years wasn't true. I couldn't handle that thought, especially coming from my daughter. I cried." But a seed had been sown in Lana's heart.

Health Problems

In 1984, Lana started to have unusual physical symptoms. It began as a strange floating sensation on her right side and then progressed to a painful condition involving her nerves and muscles. She would experience incapacitating nerve pain on the right side from her upper back to her arm and ankle. Medical opinions for the cause of the pain ranged from stress, repressed depression, and a cervical bone spur pressing on a nerve. But the doctors did not have the answers she needed. She was exhausted from waking several times a night. She took a variety of painkillers, but they gave her only temporary relief. After seven years of such suffering, she began to wonder whether life was worth living.

She asked Jill's Baptist youth group to pray for her. One week later while in the library, she came across, quite by accident, a book that described a relaxed position called the Corpse Pose, which, when practiced several times a day, reduced blood pressure. Although she did not have blood pressure problems, she began to do this exercise; within two days she felt some easing of the pain. Because the technique meant lying on her back on the floor, she decided to sleep on the floor. After several months of such action, the pain had vanished. Lana was convinced that God moves in mysterious ways.

The Road to Recovery

Lana began to go to the Ransom Community Church (Brethren in Christ) because her younger daughter, Cheryl, attended there, originally attracted by the youth program. At first Lana thought that the pastor, Jeff House, seemed to be speaking directly to her. She could not understand how he seemed to know what was happening in their home. She now considers that this was the Holy Spirit working in her life.

Lana and Bill began to meet in a small group with the pastor. She later realized that this was a discipling-membership class. They arrived at the church for their class during a prayer meeting. "The door opened," Lana recalls, "and all these people would come out of the room real happy and talking to each other. I wondered what was going on in there—a service or something? There seemed to be something mysterious about this, seeing people get together and praying without a priest."

After several meetings of this small group, the pastor said that he thought they were ready for membership. He invited the members of the group to be baptized in a baptismal service at a local pool. As a Roman Catholic, Lana, of course, had been baptized as an infant, but now she felt that another, adult conversion was the right thing to do. She sometimes wishes, however, that she had waited until she had learned more about baptism, until she had a clearer testimony; but she has learned that the Lord has his way of doing things.

Around this time, on one of the busiest days of her career, Lana had an evaluation made of a suspicious growth. A biopsy was ordered. The diagnosis revealed a small cancer. From the options given, Lana chose radical surgery.

Although painful and full of stress, this period became a time of spiritual growth for her. "The days that followed seemed endless," Lana remembers. "I learned that only God could comfort me, even though at times I didn't understand how he could do that. The Holy Spirit would lay scripture on my heart in a variety of ways, or give me an experience through which he spoke clearly to my heart and mind. I realized that any strength—emotional, physical, or spiritual—came from God. I also experienced an overflowing love for people. I was being prepared to serve our Lord."

Extracts from her journal illustrate her feelings during this difficult time. On November 19, 1993, she notes that she has been diagnosed with having colorectal cancer. Other entries follow: "It seems as if I can't recover due to all the perplexities of this situation I'm in. How could such an event cause the upheaval it has? Although I know you [God] have a purpose . . . sometimes I want to die except for my family who needs me and [for] my belief that it is wrong to give up."

In late December 1993, she learned that she was cancer free. She writes about the "euphoria" of being without cancer and thanks God for lifting her up when she needed help. She also remembers with gratitude Christian friends, church members, and family who helped her through this period. Of her family, her journal records: "Thank you Lord for Bill. He truly loves and supports me. Hope I don't drive him crazy. Thank you for our supportive loving children."

The journal makes clear that this period of sickness was valuable because it brought Lana and her husband closer to each other. "The special bond that has developed between Bill and me is something which truly surprises me and amazes me. At one point in our marriage I felt we were put together to challenge each other's ability to love. Now I feel we were put together to achieve perfect or unconditional love. He has managed to tolerate my inability to cope with loss and the paranoia I've experienced. He says things I need to hear at the right time. I'm sure God is guiding him."

Of significant help to her during her trouble was a copy of Mrs. Charles (Lettie B.) Cowman's *Streams in the Desert*, which someone had given her earlier. Lana had placed the book on a shelf, thinking that some day she might have time to read it. During her physical illness and mental stress, she began to read it daily. Later she purchased two additional copies, and always carried one with her to read to help her get through the day. The book became worn and torn from use. When she recovered, she gave these books to others who were struggling and could not understand why God allowed suffering in their lives.

Another entry emphasizes the spiritual growth that has occurred in her. "I've been through many ups and downs. From nausea over things I can't change physically to joy over what has been revealed to me about the spiritual growth that has occurred in our immediate family."

Finally, in her journal, Lana recognizes the invaluable help that the Bible was to her. "During the intense struggling years of 1994–1995," she says, "God used scripture to speak to me through verses which were placed in my mind often during the night or when I awoke in the morning. I was amazed, nourished, and strengthened by these verses."

In addition to her physical problems, Lana had several automobile accidents during these years, all of them her fault. During a rainstorm, she momentarily took her eyes off the road. The car in front of her came abruptly to a stop at a traffic light, and Lana's car slammed into it.

A month later she rear-ended another car as she was about to enter an expressway. Fortunately, the driver of the other car, Rev. Chang of the Buffalo City Mission, knew Clif Phillips, a friend of Lana from her church; the two had been in missionary work together in Jamaica. Clif's words to Lana were that these accidents occurred because the Lord still had something to teach her.

From these experiences—her recovery from cancer, and her accidents—Lana and Bill were led into their coffeehouse ministry. This sense of God's leadership is caught in a journal entry of August 20, 1996: "Victory at last! . . . We are now ready to begin on Your work within and outside our church. The inspiration of the Holy Spirit is obvious in our lives. I am so excited. God has given me an inspiration to do a coffeehouse ministry. Thank you, Father God, for bringing a new ministry to our Church family. Thank you, Father God, for choosing to use me as your instrument in the planning process."

The story of Karen is an illustration of the coffeehouse ministry. Karen is Bill's sister. One day Lana and Bill received a telephone call which reported that Karen was in jail in Kentucky. They traveled to the jail and visited Karen, then returned to write and distribute a prayer card during one of their coffeehouse Musicfests (an all-day event held in a big tent). The card in part reads: "Karen is 35 years of age. Karen has been through many struggles, some self-inflicted. Many wrong decisions have led her into the dark side of life. She has been in and out of jail. . . . She lacks understanding of God's Word and is easily frightened and deceived by Satan."

Shortly after this Musicfest, Lana and Bill heard from Karen again. She was found in the parking lot of a church in Columbus, Ohio, confused after taking Atavan, an anti-anxiety drug. The wife of the former pastor took Karen home and fed her, and the church placed her in a motel room. When Lana and Bill received Karen's call, Lana drove to Columbus, took Karen back to Rome, Georgia, to get her few belongings, and, after informing authorities at the courthouse there, drove back with her to their home in New York State.

On Friday night they brought Karen to the coffeehouse, where, Lana says, "she gave her heart to the Lord in full surrender." Later, Karen wrote a letter thanking Lana and Bill "for being there in that critical time in my life."

Since writing that letter, Karen met a musician and pastor from Canada in the coffeehouse. The two later married and are now living in the southern United States.

Many other good things have happened at the coffeehouse. Lana observes, "So many people—musicians, sound people, artists, young Christians using their gifts for God, seasoned Christians—are spreading salt and light through their music and testimonies, and lives." Some performers are not in God's family, but they too receive exposure to the Christian faith in the coffeehouse. One secular musician wrote to Lana and Bill after a performance in the coffeehouse: "I do believe that someone is knocking on my heart and mind . . . so we'll see if I let him in. Either way, I have become a better person, father, and husband because of the Living Room."

Lana's Christian service does not end with the coffeehouse. She sings in the worship team of her church (she is also a soloist), serves as a trustee of the church, runs a pregnancy center in the old white church next to the building presently used by the congregation, and nurses part time. "Life is not always roses," she says; she continues to struggle with physical and emotional scars. But people are lifted by her smile and encouraging words. Her song is in honor of God.

Carving Out Her Own Identity

Alice Grace Hostetter Zercher

by Laura Fox with Valerie Weaver-Zercher*

Alice Grace Zercher is often known in the Brethren in Christ world more for the people to whom she is related than for her own character and accomplishments. People once knew her as the granddaughter of C. N. Hostetter, Sr., bishop and president of Messiah College, and daughter of Henry Hostetter, local minister and denominational leader. Then she became the wife of John Zercher, editor of the *Evangelical Visitor*, the denomination's periodical. Now, in some circles, she's the mother of Gene Zercher, teacher and coach in Nappanee, Indiana, or the mother of David Weaver-Zercher, a professor at Messiah College. More recently, some know her as the grandmother of Amy Zercher, northern Indiana basketball star.

Alice Grace accepts her relationship to these public figures in a casual, satisfied way, with no desire to distance herself from them. "I think she is, in many ways, a very strong woman," her son David says. "At the same time, I think that she, like many women in her generation, accepted being defined in her role as daughter, wife, mother, and now grandmother."[1] He echoes Alice Grace's own words from a paper she wrote in 1968 while updating her teaching credentials: "The fabric of her [a woman's] life seems to revolve more often around relationships, and these are much more intricate than the hard, factual approach expected of

*Laura Fox presently teaches in an alternative high school setting in Elkhart, Indiana. She has known Alice Grace for six years through Nappanee Brethren in Christ Church, where Laura's husband, Joseph, is the senior pastor. Valerie Weaver-Zercher, a freelance writer living in Harrisburg, Pennsylvania, is married to Alice Grace Zercher's son David.

men. . . . There is no beginning at the bottom and rising to the top, for relationships involve prime consideration of someone else's good; it is best achieved in light regard of herself."

Yet to assume that Alice Grace lived her life demurely in the shadows of her father, husband, and sons would be incorrect. As a teacher, parent, deacon, and mentor to many people throughout the years, Alice Grace carved out a space of her own that remains distinct from all the accomplishments of those around her, as one learns when she recounts the story of her life. And even though her relationships do not define her, Alice Grace's various and overlapping roles as daughter, student, wife, mother, teacher, widow, and local church leader are helpful windows into her identity.

Daughter: Learning the Rhythms of the Church

On October 8, 1925, Alice Grace was born to Henry and Beula (Hess) Hostetter. Beula was the daughter of Conrad and Adda Sue Hess, who lived in Pequea Township of Lancaster County, Pennsylvania. Henry's parents were Christian Newcomer (C.N.), Sr., and Ella Neff Hostetter, who lived in Washington Boro, also in Lancaster County. Both Beula's and Henry's childhoods were steeped in the traditions and routines of turn-of-the-century Brethren in Christ life, and they created a similar faith-centered home for their daughter, Alice Grace.

After marrying on January 19, 1924, Beula and Henry lived in part of a farmhouse while Henry worked for Beula's brother Ziegler. Although Henry and Beula had planned on having more children, Alice Grace remained an only child because health problems didn't permit Beula to go through another pregnancy.

Before marrying at the "older" age of 24, Beula attended business school and worked as a bookkeeper-accountant at the Armstrong Linoleum Company. Her education and employment, both of which were rather unusual for women in that day, forged Alice Grace's own view of women and education and independence. "I remember my mother saying that her sister Anna once said to her, 'You have only one [daughter]. Why don't you keep her at home?'" While her mother was overprotective, Alice Grace says, she did instill an interest in the wider world that has stayed with Alice Grace throughout her life. "My mother had a grasp of life outside that basic farm existence [common to many Brethren in Christ Church members at the time], and I think her education gave her that," she reflects. She passed on this love of learning to Alice Grace, who later went on to advanced education.

When Alice Grace was about six months old, she and her parents moved to the Hostetter homestead in Washington Boro. As an only child, Alice Grace learned to be alone without being bored. She wandered into the meadows to pick big handfuls of violets, and her relatives and friends knew her as the little girl with many dolls. She also spent many hours playing with her cousins, especially those who lived nearby. Alice Grace had responsibilities, too—from mowing the lawn and dusting the house to feeding chickens and helping to prepare for farmers' market.

As the denomination began calling Henry to various roles, he formed a farming partnership with his brother-in-law which enabled him to earn a living while giving much of his time to church ministry. This was not an easy balance to forge during the Depression, when the family's main income came from selling eggs, chickens, and vegetables. Often, Alice Grace remembers, her father worked on the farm up to the last minute before leaving for church responsibilities. Even while farming, however, his passion for ministry and pursuit of God remained constant; Alice Grace recalls walking by one of the farm sheds and hearing her father's voice in fervent prayer.

Sometimes Henry went away for weeks to lead revival meetings; during these times Beula helped manage the farm and, in emergencies, did some of the farm work. "She worked very hard," Alice Grace remembers. "I don't think my father ever realized how hard she worked and what demands were put on her. She would not speak out against these things either, but rather bottled them up inside." Beula was also a perfectionist and excellent cook, and Alice Grace struggled for years with her mother's high standards. "As I became an adult, I felt as though I couldn't measure up to her expectations," she says. "With my mother, there was always a best way of doing something. When I got into education, I discovered that sometimes there are multiple ways to do something well."

The rhythms of church gave form to Alice Grace's early life as they had for her parents' childhoods, and the frequent services meant she not only became acquainted with Scripture and hymns, but also memorized them as well. At the age of five, Alice Grace talked to her mother about inviting Jesus into her heart. At the age of 12, she was baptized in the local Conestoga Creek and joined the church.

Alice Grace became involved in Sunday school, Bible memorization, and youth conferences. Her father was on the denominational board for young people, and believed that youth had a significant place in the church. Alice Grace attended youth activities, including Sunday evening youth meetings and the yearly love feast, a time to interact with cousins and friends.

Alice Grace also fondly remembers the annual youth conference at Messiah College in the summer. Youth from all over Pennsylvania and beyond came together for several days. They lived together in the dorm, attended sessions led by ministers, learned new choruses, explored the campus, and made new friends. One year during this conference she made a deeper commitment to Christ.

Alice Grace's parents did not encourage her to participate in unscheduled teenage activities. She feels that her parents' overprotectiveness led to her frequent feelings of awkwardness around her peers. Rather than spending much time with peers, Alice Grace grew up listening to and watching the adults who visited her parents' home.

Along with church activities, music was an important component of Alice Grace's youth. Beula made sure that Alice Grace took weekly piano lessons, even though that meant squeezing the lessons into an already crowded schedule. From elementary school through high school, she sang in choirs and small groups. The local church offered similar opportunities. Her appreciation for sacred classical music began when a local minister's wife organized a choir to perform Christmas music. She also fondly remembers Christmas caroling, when her father would find an owner of a flat-bed truck, pile on straw and blankets, and at 2:00 a.m. take the young people out caroling. They would stop at houses of older people and begin singing; if a light came on, they knew they had been heard. During college, Alice Grace continued to sing in choirs and learned to appreciate the hymns of other traditions. Her love of a broad range of musical styles, nurtured in her early life, continues to this day. "Music feeds my soul," she says simply.

Student: 'Slow and Deliberate' and Successful

As deemed appropriate by her mother, Alice Grace's education took precedence over all but church involvements. She attended a one-room schoolhouse about one mile from her home, an experience which allowed her to learn at her own pace by listening to the teacher's lessons for older students. When she was in the fifth grade but doing sixth grade work, several area schools consolidated, and Alice Grace went on to seventh grade. She then attended high school in nearby Millersville, and chose college preparatory classes. Alice Grace describes herself as a "slow and deliberate" student who spent her evenings completing homework. When she was 16, she graduated from high school with honors.

After high school, Alice Grace went on to Messiah College. Leaving home and being on her own allowed for more freedom to make friends and participate in social activities. She enjoyed dormitory life and the "sisters" she now had, although she admits that her grades dropped significantly, for she had not learned how to study efficiently.

Realizing that she enjoyed nutrition studies and food chemistry, Alice Grace transferred to Goshen College after two years to pursue a major in dietetics. Her advisor at Goshen was Olive Wyse, chair of the home economics department. Dr. Wyse began teaching when women faculty were few and unrecognized, and Alice Grace remembers her as a dignified model of a Christian woman in higher education.

As Alice Grace completed her course work, she needed an internship in dietetics. She submitted applications to several hospitals but was turned down by the program she most desired. About this time, in 1946, the Academy of Messiah College approached her about teaching and directing the food services. So off she went to consult with Dr. Wyse: should she accept the position that another hospital had offered, or should she accept the invitation to serve within the church? She had had no plans to become a teacher, yet she felt drawn to Christian service. She finally decided to accept Messiah's offer, and after a year of additional study, worked at Messiah College until the summer of 1950. A personnel change soon after she was hired required Alice Grace to focus on food services more than she had planned, and left little energy for teaching.

In 1946, Alice Grace enrolled in classes at Temple University to obtain a master's degree in home economics. She did classroom observations and student teaching in the mornings and took evening courses to begin the master's program. Alice Grace describes her classroom observation experiences as unique, in that they took her to many schools around the city. During this time she wrote stacks of observation notes; someone once suggested that this collection would suffice for a dissertation.

Her Temple degree signaled the end of Alice Grace's formal schooling—for 18 years, that is. In subsequent years, she now turned to bearing five sons, keeping a house, volunteering in the church, and supporting her husband's career.

Wife and Mother: Juggling the Stresses of Church and Family

In the summer of 1948, Alice Grace met John Zercher through her work on a committee of the Alumni Association of Messiah. John was the chair of the eastern Pennsylvania chapter of the Alumni Association while being employed as the business manager of Millersville State Teachers' College. Alice Grace knew him only as an older ex-serviceman whose parents worshiped at the Grantham church. Later she would learn that the characteristics she had come to admire—his passion for reading, his conscientious spirit, and his ability to think deeply—were developed in his childhood.[2]

Joining the military had meant that John, along with numerous Brethren in Christ men, came under the discipline of church leaders who advocated a pacifist stance. Ironically, the bishop who placed John on probation was C. N. Hostetter, Jr., Alice Grace's uncle. This probationary period entailed counseling sessions, the content of which were private and which John never shared with Alice Grace. He shared few details of his inner spiritual journey with anyone; in fact, this reticence to talk about his personal thoughts and feelings characterized John from childhood, Alice Grace says. She does remember a time when, after reading a book he had found on her parents' shelf, he renewed his commitment to Christ and, subsequently, to the Brethren in Christ Church. Although many in the church were curious about John's journey from a captain in the military to a voice for peace among the Brethren in Christ, he remained silent about it. And while many people have said that John's relationship with Alice Grace was the catalyst that brought him back to the Brethren in Christ, Alice Grace, in her usual self-effacing manner, believes she's been given too much credit for this.

At the time that Alice Grace learned to know John, "he had his eye on several young women" (as he confessed to her later), and decided to put her on a committee of the Messiah Alumni Association to get to know her better. This committee work required that they attend a meeting in Lebanon, so John, Alice Grace, and her aunt, Pauline Hess, rode together. Not long after that meeting, cousins invited John to a steak fry and asked him to bring a guest. He, in turn, asked Alice Grace, who "felt honored since he was older, more experienced, awesome," she reflects. After that initial date, John continued to ask Alice Grace out, and they enjoyed summer evenings and weekends in the out-of-doors. John shared with her his enjoyment of unique restaurants. After the summer, Alice Grace went back to Messiah to teach. Ironically, John's parents lived within a mile of the campus, and John lived within five miles of *her* parents.

With his continuing love of learning and a portion of his G.I. Bill still remaining, John resigned his position at Millersville and began studies at Princeton Theological Seminary. He frequently returned to central Pennsylvania on weekends, and Alice Grace visited him at Princeton and met some of his friends. They announced their engagement on Valentine's Day and were married on a hot summer day in 1950, in the then-small Manor Brethren in Christ Church.

After a wedding trip to Lake George, New York, Alice Grace and John moved to Allentown, New Jersey, where she obtained a teaching position, and John continued his studies at Princeton. In the summer of 1951, their first son, Gene, was born, and Alice Grace stopped teaching. "At that time," she says, "I thought I would never go back to teaching again." She wasn't disappointed to give up her career, she says; in fact, she hadn't found much satisfaction in teaching up to that point.

When John graduated in 1952, he began to pastor the Pequea congregation in addition to working full time at Millersville State Teachers' College. He would work five and one-half days a week at Millersville, and then fit three church services, visitations, and administrative duties into evenings and weekends. Adding to the hectic pace of life were the arrivals of two more sons, Dick in the summer of 1953 and Daryl in the summer of 1955.

As in her childhood, Alice Grace's life again centered around the patterns of life in a rural congregation. "John felt a pastor should identify with his people as much as possible," she reflects now. "They gardened and preserved food; we should do likewise. They began work early in the day; so should the pastor. They knew little about vacations; neither did we." In fact, John identified so much with his congregation that when he wanted the church to have a punch bowl for serving refreshments, he bought one as an anniversary gift for Alice Grace. "It matched glassware we received for a wedding gift, and was rather expensive, yet it went to church frequently," Alice Grace remembers.

Eventually the church employed John half time, and he cut back to half time at Millersville. The denomination called John to board and committee responsibilities, which meant his vacation days were used for General Conference and board meetings. "Neither of us knew how to relax or take a vacation," Alice Grace reflects now, adding that they also had little time for a social life. She remembers feeling isolated during these years, yet says that it was tolerable "because we felt that we shared ministry together."

John and Alice Grace determined their roles as leader and helpmate, respectively. In many ways, she remembers, John wanted his world to be like Alice Grace's mother's—organized, with no clutter, and with good food. Yet even as John maintained a high public profile as decisive and controlling, the home was different. "I don't remember the family life being dominated in any sense by my father," says David, the youngest son. "I sensed that they shared decision-making; I think they talked through things with us as equal parents in this role." John would sometimes consult Alice Grace for her opinion on church matters as well. One time, when a parishioner complained about a younger member who had stopped wearing her covering, John wondered aloud whether he should ask the younger person to withdraw from a church assignment. "I strongly advised against it," says Alice Grace now, and John took her advice.

In 1958, John was offered a position at Evangel Press, the denominational publishing house, in Nappanee, Indiana. He was enjoying his pastorate, and at first declined. When the denomination's Board for Publications asked him to reconsider, however, John turned to several church leaders for guidance, called home to discuss it with Alice Grace, and finally accepted. In October they moved to Indiana and lived in a parsonage for 16 months. Chuck was born in 1959, and soon afterwards Alice Grace and John built a small house on the edge of town. During their first ten years of marriage, the Zerchers had lived in eight different places; it was finally time to burn their moving boxes.

Their last child, David, was born in 1960, after they had moved to their new house. "The house was sometimes too small, but comfortable," she remembers. Alice Grace still lives in this house today, and likes to remember how the boys used various parts of the house and property for play: the basement for roller-skating, the backyard for ballgames, the fireplace beside which to eat apples and popcorn on Sunday evenings.

Alice Grace says now that her younger children probably have better memories of home life than the older children. "We didn't add TV to our household until the Kennedy assassination, and, following our own upbringing, we evaded professional sports on Sundays," she recounts. "When we realized our children preferred to visit their friends for this reason, we declared there was a higher goal for us—to make home more acceptable for our children. We learned that the fewer no's, the better."

Chuck remembers the home of his childhood as comfortable and contented, and says his mother played a big part in creating that atmosphere. "I felt that Dad was the disciplinarian, and she was much more likely to listen and hear us out," says her second-oldest son, Dick: "She was consistent, but she wasn't rigid."

Alice Grace thinks her sons probably considered her a "fussy worrier." For example, after purchasing his first car, Gene discovered that the engine was supercharged. Rather than give Alice Grace one more thing to worry about, John told Gene, "Let's not tell your mother."

Those early years in Nappanee continued at the busy pace which had marked the Zerchers' lives in Pennsylvania. "It seemed that with the chores of housekeeping, there were hour-by-hour interruptions for about ten years," she says. Feeding a family of seven on a church worker's salary meant scrimping and saving wherever possible, so summers involved a constant stream of fruits and vegetables from John's garden into the kitchen for her to preserve.

John continued his fast-paced and high-energy church work. "He thrived on a challenge to accomplish, and moved logically and forthrightly through assignments," Alice Grace recalls. When the house was somewhat settled for the evening, John would retreat to his desk, open his briefcase, and continue working. Alice Grace seldom traveled with him: "He said that these were our God-given children, and it was our responsibility to care for them; and besides, we were not able financially to hire child care," she recounts.

When she and the children did accompany him on business trips to Pennsylvania, John would count the two days of driving as vacation time. "I can't say that a 600-mile car trip with four or five children is a mother's idea of vacation," says Alice Grace. "These were the days before disposable diapers, and when fast-food restaurants were limited." The family traveled across the country twice and took several other vacations; even during these times, however, "John usually let me know that his idea of a real vacation was to spend time in a quiet place reading books."

While at home during John's absences, Alice Grace coped with managing the household of five boys as best she could. "There were times when I felt absolutely inadequate," she reflects. "My resource was to retreat to the bedroom, where I asked the Lord in his wisdom to make up to my children what I was lacking."

Alice Grace's son Dick says he remembers the quiet way his mother dealt with his father's many involvements. "I know [my father's schedule] put a great burden on her, but she never voiced that," he reflects. "I think she also felt strongly about the work he did, that it was important work, and so there was a balance to the extra work that she took on."

One time Alice Grace's mother overheard her mentioning John's overload to another church leader. "[My mother] very definitely told me that I was out of order," Alice Grace remembers. "A wife was expected to stand by her husband and his call to service." John said no to a few assignments, partly due to her urging, but, she adds, "another way to handle this was simply not to tell me about his obligations." She does remember him bringing her and the children gifts from his travels—unusual items for the boys, a cookbook for her, and, one time, a turquoise and silver necklace.

Tragedy struck the Zercher household on April 12, 1962. A car hit and killed Daryl when he ran onto the road to catch the school bus. Alice Grace recollects that she did not shed many tears "but had a big lingering ache down inside." After Daryl's death, she says, "John and I had a difficult time remembering how many plates to set for a meal, and I found myself listening for his feet coming down the hall."

Surrounded by the prayers and support of the church, the community, and the school, Alice Grace felt God's presence through the care of others. She remembered the death of a neighbor's child as she was growing up, and that the parents made the child into a hero whom they held up as a standard for their other children. Alice Grace was determined not to do this to her family; in fact, she admits that perhaps she did the opposite. They did not talk much about Daryl, the middle child who tried so hard to keep up with his older brothers. "They grieved quietly," says Eva Martin, Alice Grace's cousin, who was with them immediately after Daryl's death. "They would talk about it sometimes, but didn't lay it out in front of everybody. I think they felt they needed to get on with life for the sake of the other boys."

As the remaining sons grew older, they became increasingly involved in their own worlds, from sports, drama, and band to youth group, paper routes, and student government. Alice Grace enjoyed having her sons participate in extracurricular activities, especially because she hadn't been able to join in such events as a child. Chuck remembers his mother encouraging all these involvements but not pushing her children into any of them. "She did not live her life vicariously through us," he reflects. "She enjoyed seeing what we were doing, but I don't think she took any sense of personal pride through our activities." His wife, Laura, agrees. "She has an ability to get into people's worlds without being invasive." Laura's impression is that Alice Grace supported the boys in what they were interested in, not what she wanted them to be interested in.

To relieve the pressure so many stay-at-home parents face, Alice Grace typed genealogies for Evangel Press, the denominational printer. She describes this as a fun way to take herself outside her four walls. In addition, John Hostetter, an uncle and editor of the *Evangelical Visitor*, assigned Alice Grace to compile the news from church bulletins for the magazine while he was away in Africa, a task she continued until his retirement. She served as secretary of the building committee of the Nappanee congregation and taught a youth Sunday school class. To this day, she feels connected to these youth, who are now middle-aged. Alice Grace's responsibilities at the church served as a precursor to her return to teaching, which came in 1969.

Teacher: The Journey from Dread to Satisfaction

With the shuffling of the monthly bills, the need for replacing well-worn furniture, the entrance of David into first grade, and approaching college bills for the older sons, Alice Grace and John decided that she should return to work. "It was with hesitancy that I went back to teaching," Alice Grace admits, "because it would mean giving up free time that was becoming more available. I remember telling Gene that I felt like I was giving my life away."

After taking classes to update her teaching credentials, she secured a position in home economics at a junior high school in Goshen. Employment for Alice Grace meant more home involvement for John, who was now editor of the *Evangelical Visitor*. "I could tell a significant change in the dynamics of the house," says Chuck. His father changed his schedule so that he wouldn't leave the house until the children were preparing for the day, and Dick became the breakfast cook for his younger brothers. When the younger children were ill, John would bring work home so that Alice Grace could still get to her job. Rather quickly, their income more than doubled. Even considering costs for a second car, better clothing, and more store-bought food, the extra income relieved some of the pressures of daily living that they had faced earlier in their marriage.

As with her studies in her younger years, Alice Grace found herself working very hard in her field: "I had to catch up with that gap of 17 years." Determined to make the suggested curriculum appealing to early teens, Alice Grace found herself constantly writing new material and planning new projects. She strove to make her classes practical, hands-on, and geared to middle-schoolers' experiences. "All the while the scene was changing," Alice Grace says. Courses were shortened to nine weeks, then six weeks, and classes became coeducational. In addition, out in the world, the skills needed for family living were those of a consumer, not a producer. Yet the basic goals of instruction remained the same: reading and interpreting directions, using math applications, working within groups, following a schedule, and taking personal responsibility.

For the first number of years, with every evening devoted to planning for the next day, Alice Grace wished she could be an aide rather than a teacher, "so that at 3:30, I could have walked out and been free." Slowly but surely, however, as she gained confidence in the classroom, Alice Grace found more satisfaction in teaching: "It was my thing. I loved it." Later still, after John died, Alice Grace was relieved that she had returned to her teaching career. "I've thought back with a great deal of gratitude that my parents helped out with my education," she reflects now. "When I needed employment, I was prepared."

According to Helen Fretz, who taught with Alice Grace for 11 years in Goshen, Alice Grace was "a smiling type of teacher. She was never loud, but she still had good control over her classroom. She was friendly to people in general; she wasn't aloof." She was impressed with the challenges that Alice Grace took on in the classroom; for example, she taught the ninth-graders to make pastry, hardly an easy process.

At the time of John's death, Alice Grace was in the process of transferring to the Nappanee school district, where she taught until her retirement in 1992.

Widow: Moving from Grief to Normalcy

In 1973, Alice Grace and John traveled to Africa to take part in the 75th anniversary of Brethren in Christ missions on that continent. Before this trip, Alice Grace had seldom traveled with him. The trip to Africa was special; as a child, she had read the names of missionaries and mission stations in mission manuals and the *Evangelical Visitor*. Now she actually saw these places. She and John also observed their 25th anniversary in a celebration planned jointly by their oldest son, Gene, his wife, Paula, and their congregation.

John was increasingly busy during the 1970s. He served as denominational treasurer, became editor of church publications, and helped to establish the Jacob Engle Foundation, a financial entity of the denomination (now called the Brethren in Christ Foundation). John was also a Messiah College board member, and as a member of the denomination's Board for Schools and Colleges, he promoted seminary training for pastors. Alice Grace recalls accompanying John to summer retreats for seminary students and denominational conferences.

She often reminded John of his frantic pace and, especially as the sons got older, urged him to slow down and spend more time relating to them. By August 1979 John was "exhausted but not willing to admit it," she reports. Editorial responsibilities were weighing heavily on his shoulders. Earlier in the summer, Alice Grace had received the invitation to teach in Nappanee, which meant that she and John would be working just blocks from each other, thereby reducing some stress. Their youngest son was leaving for college in two weeks, and on the eve of John's death, they talked of simplifying their lives.

On August 24, 1979, John suffered a heart attack and died while attending Foundation Series Christian education curriculum meetings held at the Nappanee church. Alice Grace was attending a training session for new teachers in the school system, but no one at the church knew where she was. Gene, who was coaching on the football field adjacent to the church, was summoned, and then several of Gene's colleagues discovered where Alice Grace was and took her to the church.

In the following hours, days, and weeks many decisions and arrangements would need attention, such as phone calls, funeral planning, and Social Security benefits. Alice Grace's experience with Daryl's death somewhat prepared her for the finality of her life with John. And as with the loss of a son, her husband's death brought daily reminders of his absence. "After a few days,

I realized that I was subconsciously listening for him to enter the front door," Alice Grace remembers. "But most of all, I wanted to tell John what was happening," she recalls. Invitations to dinner, notes, and phone calls from family and friends relieved those early lonely moments.

Her son Chuck offered to drop out of college for a year so she did not need to live alone. "I appreciated his thoughtfulness, but I couldn't think of him delaying his education," she says. She recalls feeling that same lingering ache inside her that she felt after Daryl's death; this time the tears came most easily when she tried to sing hymns on Sunday morning. But now, to best honor John's memory, she says, "I needed to be courageous and carry on my life with the strength I had observed in him." One cathartic experience was assembling information about John's life for *Lantern in the Dawn*, the collection of his editorials published by Evangel Press in 1980.

As her children returned to their lives and her parents returned home, Alice Grace felt fortunate to have her job. Ten days after John's death, she was back in the classroom: "It became time to move on as a single professional," she recalls. Earlier, Alice Grace had told John how much she was in awe of her new job. "I was sure his abilities and my sons' successes in the local school had gotten me this new job," she recalls. "Only later did I learn they had given me the job because they thought of me as a stable married person in contrast to hiring a widow who had applied. And now I was a widow!"

The transition from married to widowed life was not an easy one. "One needs to learn how to be a middle-aged widow in a small community," Alice Grace reflects. "It seemed I was lumped with a group of older people, but as a wage-earner with no responsibility for children at home, I had a desire for activity common to younger persons." In addition, she had to learn basics about car and house maintenance. Gene assisted her with repair projects, and the other sons, home from college for the summer, were "drafted into 'Mom needs help' projects," she says.

Alice Grace didn't talk much about her grief in the wake of John's death, remembers her son Chuck. Sometimes on the phone she would allude to feelings of loneliness, he recalls. "But

I think she really tried to avoid burdening people with what she was feeling."

In addition to Alice Grace's adjustment to widowhood during this era, her role as daughter became more salient as her parents aged. To make it easier for her following John's death, they moved 50 miles from their local community to Messiah Village. Most of her vacationing time was spent with them. After her mother's death, she continued to care for her father; sometimes she would take him with her to Nappanee, and often returned to Pennsylvania to assist him until his death in 1998.

Within a year after John's death, Alice Grace began taking classes for continuing education credit. Every eight hours of study meant a salary increase, and she set a goal for herself to earn the four available increments. Six years later she reached her goal. While most of her previous goals had been the intangible ones of family life, this one was clear-cut: "In the summer of 1986, I was driving on Interstate 70 between Terre Haute and Indianapolis when I was swept up in the knowledge that I had reached my goal."

Local Church Leader: Serving in Formal and Informal Ways

Since John's death, Alice Grace has taken on several active roles in the church, denomination, and community. She has served on the local church board, and currently serves as a deacon in the Nappanee congregation and also as an advocate in the congregation for Mennonite Mutual Aid, a stewardship agency.

Much of Alice Grace's work these days is centered around older adult ministries. As a member of the Mennonite Association for Retired Persons, she has come into contact with older adult ministries and volunteers who serve nationwide. She also serves on the Central Conference Task Force for Service and Discipleship, through which she has helped to initiate a ministry to seniors and puts together a quarterly newsletter for older adults. Alice Grace is passionate about working to help older adults feel connected to and valued by the church: "If people like me who are entering older adulthood don't support or give attention to them, our fast-paced society will pass them by."

Alice Grace's desire to learn and her ability to lead have aided her in several other church roles. She has served on a committee charged with planning for a Brethren in Christ encyclopedia, as well as on the denomination's Bishops Nominating Committee. She also remains connected to the community by serving as a volunteer for the local library and school system.

Leadership comes naturally for Alice Grace in this era of her life. "She does it in a low-key sort of way," says her son Dick. "I think she's very dependable, steady; the same things we [her children] saw in her as we grew up, she brings to bear in her leadership roles."

In addition to these more formal roles, Alice Grace has served as a mentor to many people, often opening up her home for extended periods of time to folks who need a place to stay. She speaks matter-of-factly about this ministry of hospitality: "What justification could I make for having a home this size to myself unless I was willing to share it with others?" she asks.

While juggling these volunteer responsibilities, Alice Grace also makes time to visit her sons and their families, who are spread out between California, Indiana, Pennsylvania, and New Hampshire. Even while on these trips, however, Alice Grace doesn't leave her servant stance at home. "Whenever she's here, she asks, 'What can I do next?'" says her son Chuck. "She's always wanting to serve; that's just what she does."

Chuck's wife, Laura, attributes this service mindset to the way that Alice Grace has coped with the tragedies in her life. "She's experienced a lot of grief during her lifetime, but she doesn't live there. She's moved out of that spot," Laura reflects. "I think she's coped very gracefully, mostly by helping others. . . . Whenever we call, she's always just been visiting someone or helping someone. And I never hear bitter things coming out of her mouth; it's just not part of her character."

"Some people wonder why I get myself into so much volunteer ministry," Alice Grace says. She attributes her commitment to service, in part, to her background and the influence of her grandparents, parents, and husband. "They were sincere, authentic—though not perfect—people who incorporated Christ's model of self-giving in the way they lived. Each generation expresses it differently, but the principle remains the same."

While moving between her various roles, Alice Grace Zercher has been influenced significantly by her more public relatives. At the same time, she has preserved a distinct identity. "She maintained her own personhood," says her son Dick. "In fact, I think she is a lot stronger than we even realized."

NOTES

Harriet Alice Sider Bicksler

1. Unless otherwise noted, information for this biography is taken from interviews with Harriet Bicksler, January 2001–January 2002.
2. Harriet Bicksler, "Celebrating 100 Years of Brethren in Christ Missions," *Shalom!: A Journal for the Practice of Reconciliation*, Summer 1998, p. 1.
3. Ibid.
4. Ibid.
5. Lewis B. Sider, *Missionary Reminiscences: An Autobiography* (Grantham, Pa.: Messiah College Reprographic Services, 1989), p. 106.
6. Bicksler, "Celebrating 100 Years," p. 1.
7. Ibid.
8. Harriet Bicksler, "Blessed are the Peacemakers," *Evangelical Visitor*, June 25, 1978, p. 6.
9. Harriet Bicksler, "Turning Swords Into Plowshares: The World Peace Tax Fund," ibid., December 25, 1980, p. 11.
10. A complete bibliography of Harriet's writings is available in the Brethren in Christ Historical Library and Archives (hereafter referred to as BICHLA), Grantham, Pennsylvania.
11. Titus Peachey, e-mail to the author, December 31, 2001.
12. Sider, *Missionary Reminiscences*, p. 4.
13. Harriet Bicksler, "Phoebe's Journal," *Evangelical Visitor*, November 1989, p. 30.
14. Harriet Bicksler, ed., *Perspectives on Social Issues* (Nappanee, Ind.: Evangel Press, 1992), author's preface, n.p.
15. Harriet Sider Bicksler, "Review of The American City and the Evangelical Church: A Historical Overview," *Brethren in Christ History and Life* (April 1995), 148.
16. Harriet Bicksler, "The Brethren in Christ Experience," *Shalom!*, Summer 1996, p. 1.
17. Jane (Light) Raser, e-mail to the author, December 30, 2001.

Katie Sheets Bollinger

1. In researching this biography, the author conducted interviews or corresponded with the following persons: J. Bert Carlson, Louis Cober, Rebecca Ebersole, Chris Frey, Archie and Naomi Heer, Alvin and Naomi Hoover, Kenneth Hoover, and Ruth Kitner.
2. Paul and Laura Carlson papers, in the possession of the Carlsons.
3. For details, see Helen Dingle, *Past and Present Towns of Dickinson County, Kansas*, p. 97, and *Portrait and Biographical Background Record, Dickinson, Salina, McPherson and Marion Counties, Kansas* (Chapman Bros., 1893).

4. Notes from Avas Carlson interview, August 4, 1979, BICHLA.
5. Katie Bollinger Papers in BICHLA.
6. "My Experience," Katie Bollinger Papers in BICHLA.
7. Ibid.
8. Ibid.
9. Ibid.
10. Paul and Laura Carlson papers.
11. Notes from Avas Carlson interview.
12. Letter provided by Paul and Laura Carlson.
13. Ibid.
14. Katie Bollinger Papers in BICHLA.
15. Ibid.
16. Ibid.
17. *Evangelical Visitor*, September 26, 1903.
18. Bollinger, "My Call," Katie Bollinger Papers in BICHLA; "Being Sure of Your Call," *Mt. Carmel Tidings*, March 15, 1915.
19. For the history of the Mt. Carmel Home, see Wilma J. Musser, "Big House on a Little Hill," *Brethren in Christ History and Life* (August 1999), 234–272.
20. For descriptions of Mt. Carmel Home life, see Bollinger, "My Call."
21. *The Daily Gazette* (Sterling–Rockfalls, Ill.), April 12 and 13, 1961.
22. *Mt. Carmel Tidings* (April–June 1963); *Evangelical Visitor*, June 26, 1961, p. 12.
23. For the events surrounding her illness and death, see *Mt. Carmel Tidings*, October–December 1964 and October–December 1966. Also see her obituary in the *Evangelical Visitor*, January 16, 1967, p. 22.

Ernestine Begay Chavez

1. In researching this biography, the author conducted interviews with the following persons: Anna Jean Charley, Ernestine Chavez, Ernie and Faye Francisco, Jana Harris, Janet Harris, Janice Harris, Wilmer and Velma Heisey, Nancy Larvingo, and James and Jenny Simpson.
2. A family camp is the home place of the oldest woman in the family—adult children live close by in tents or "hogans."

Dorcas Mildred Slagenweit Climenhaga

1. Dorcas Climenhaga, "Women's Page," *Central Conference Star*, May 1979, n.p.
2. In researching this biography, the author conducted interviews and corresponded with the following persons: David and Laona Brubaker, Eva G. Brubaker, Ruth Byers, Arthur Climenhaga, Daryl Climenhaga, David Climenhaga, Esther Ebersole, Harold H. Engle,

Anna Graybill, Frances Harmon, Mabel Hensel, Martha Lady, Fannie McBeth, Ruth Slagenweit, and Donna (Climenhaga) Wenger.

3. Dorcas's personal diary from 1938–1940 provided most of the information about her early life prior to marriage.
4. Interview with David Climenhaga, February 6, 2001.
5. Interview with Ruth F. Slagenweit, February 5, 2001.
6. David Climenhaga, "From Model Ts to Modems: The Memories of David E. Climenhaga," (hereafter referred to as "Memories"), p. 95. Unpublished copy in the BICHLA.
7. Ibid.
8. Ibid.
9. Ibid.
10. Climenhaga interview.
11. "Memories," p. 125.
12. David and Dorcas Climenhaga, "The Fabric of Marriage," *Evangelical Visitor*, February 1984, p. 6.
13. Dorcas Climenhaga letter to Mother Climenhaga, February 19, 1945.
14. David Climenhaga letter to Father Climenhaga, February 13, 1946.
15. "Memories," p. 155.
16. David Climenhaga letter to Father and Mother Climenhaga, February 4, 1946.
17. Ibid., May 11, 1946.
18. Ibid., December 15, 1946.
19. Ibid., December 28, 1946.
20. Dorcas Climenhaga letter to Mother and Father Climenhaga, April 12, 1947.
21. Interview with Anna Graybill, March 28, 2001.
22. Dorcas Climenhaga, "Lesson in Biscuit Making," *Evangelical Visitor*, October 29, 1951, p. 11.
23. Conversation with Donna Wenger.
24. Climenhaga interview.
25. Ibid.
26. Interview with David and Laona Brubaker, April 2, 2001.
27. "Memories," pp. 213–214.
28. Climenhaga interview.
29. Dorcas Climenhaga, "Ladies of the Great Commission," August 10, 1966. On tape in BICHLA.
30. "Women's Page," *Central Conference Star*, January 19, 1981, n.p.
31. Ibid., February 1981, n.p.
32. Ibid., January 1982, n.p.
33. Climenhaga interview.
34. Daryl Climenhaga, e-mail to the author, November 6, 2001.
35. *Central Conference Star*, November 1980.
36. Conversation with Eva G. Brubaker.

Eloise Dawn Smith DuBose

1. Charles Burkett, e-mail to the author, November 28, 2001.
2. In researching this biography, the author conducted interviews and corresponded with the following persons: Charles Burkett, Dawn DuBose, Delaine Niesley, Virginia Proctor, and Russell Smith.
3. Burkett, response questionnaire, October 31, 2001.
4. Russell Smith, response questionnaire, October 29, 2001.
5. Carolyn Kimmel, "Her First Love: Missions," *Yes!*, Fall 2001, p. 8.
6. Burkett, response questionnaire.
7. Ibid.
8. Ibid.
9. Ibid.
10. Virginia Proctor, response questionnaire.
11. Delaine Niesley, phone interview with the author.
12. Smith, response questionnaire.
13. Proctor, response questionnaire.
14. Burkett, response questionnaire.

Anna Miller Espenshade Forry

1. One of the girls listening that night later became Anna's sister-in-law. Sixty years later she clearly recalls that first memory of Anna. Interview with Ellen Gantz Espenshade, January 5, 2001.
2. In researching this biography, the author conducted interviews and corresponded with the following persons: Arlene (Neff) Adair, Ellen (Gantz) Espenshade, Anna (Espenshade) Forry, B. Musser Forry, Anna Ruth (Sherk) Kibler, Mary (Wolgemuth) Kuhns, Dorothy Jean (Espenshade) Rutt, and Vivian Shank. Other sources include: Adam Forry interview with B. Musser and Anna Forry (located in BICHLA), scrapbook of 50th anniversary tributes for B. Musser and Anna Forry, scrapbook of Anna Fishburn, *The David and Anna Miller Story*, 1979, Scottdale, Pa.
3. Dorothy Jean Rutt, "My Sister Anna," written January 2001.
4. Anna Ruth (Sherk) Kibler, "Memories of Anna Forry," February 2001.
5. Scrapbook of Anna Fishburn.
6. Darlene Keller, letter to Anna Forry, November 29, 1978.
7. Betsy Wolgemuth, letter to Anna Forry.
8. Dorothy Jean Rutt, "My Sister Anna."
9. Interview with Vivian Shank, February 5, 2001.

Beth Laverna Winger Frey

1. Beth Frey, *Evangelical Visitor*, December 25, 1971, p. 4.
2. Beth Winger (who was in South Africa on holiday) letter to Glenn Frey (who was at Mtshabezi Mission), August 12, 1952.

3. This quotation (and all other quotations of Beth not otherwise attributed) is from Beth Frey's personal statement upon her nomination for Messiah College's Distinguished Service Alumnus Award in 1991.
4. Enclosed in Beth's letter to Glenn, August 5, 1952.
5. *Evangelical Visitor*, June 5, 1967, pp. 7–12.
6. Interview with Bekitemba Dube at a reception held in his honor at Messiah Village, July 1, 2001.
7. Form letter from Youngways Guest House to friends and family, January 1988.
8. Letter to Beth and Glenn from Owen and Ardis Alderfer, May 10, 1988, after a visit to Zimbabwe.

Dorothy Jean Gish

1. In researching this biography, the author conducted interviews with the following persons: Mary Jane Davis, Dorothy Gish, Ken Hoke, Mary Holland, Fellistus Munakombwe, and Karen Sellers.
2. Dorothy's articles about singleness include: "Ministry—Single File," *The Asbury Seminarian* (Fall–Winter 1984), pp. 14–29; "Singleness 'Acceptance,'" *The Encyclopedia for Today's Christian Woman*, Fleming Nevell Co., Old Tappan, New Jersey, 1984, pp. 416–419; "Single, Sane and Satisfied," *Today's Christian Woman*, Spring 1982, pp. 102–105; "Singleness & Relationships: From Rebellion to Celebration," *Single Voices*, Bruce Yoder and Imo Jeanne Yoder (eds.), Herald Press, Scottsdale, Pennsylvania, 1982, pp. 3–10.

Elsie Detweiler Underkoffler Hahn

1. From a letter to her son and daughter-in-law, Willard and Violet Underkoffler, June 6, 1937, written the day she learned of the sudden death of their baby boy.
2. Fred later was excommunicated because of his charismatic teaching. He became the founder of his own evangelistic movement. Another brother, John, served as mayor of Kindersley. He later moved to California with his family. Some of his sons and grandsons are prominent in the political life of the state.
3. Enid Hahn Holloway, "Henry Hahn's Second Family," *Kindersley Memories* (Kindersley History Book Committee, 1985), p. 111.
4. In 1920 it became part of the Alberta Conference of the Church of the Brethren.
5. Hazel married Stan Clemence, another Kindersley area pioneer.
6. Letter of May 9, 1931.
7. The government paid a bounty for gopher tails, since they were pests for the farmers.
8. A story my father, Ross Nigh, heard from his father, Ed Nigh, who served on the Board of Benevolence.

9. Holloway, *Kindersley Memories*, p. 111.
10. A reminiscence of Shirley Clemence Bradley, a granddaughter.
11. Letter to Roxena Hahn Nigh, January 1947. She is referring to Roxy Carmichael, who remained her next-door neighbor and close friend until her death.
12. Letter to Doreen Hahn Crider, January 1947.
13. Letter to Roxena, 1947.
14. Letter to Willard and Violet, May 1931.
15. Letter to Doreen, January 1947.
16. Undated letter to Roxena.
17. Ibid.
18. Letter to Roxena, February 1959.
19. Ibid., December 1945.
20. Undated letter to Roxena.
21. Letter to Roxena, January 1947.
22. Ibid., June 1954.
23. Undated letter to Jackie Underkoffler Mohr.

Nancy Ruth Heisey

1. In researching this biography, the author conducted interviews and corresponded with the following persons: Ray Brubacher, Christopher Friesen, Mary Jane Heisey, Nancy Heisey, Wilmer and Velma Heisey, Cara Longacre Hurst, Paul Longacre, Urbane Peachey, Morris Sider, and Marta van Zanten.
2. Nancy Heisey, "Thoughts on Symbols," *Evangelical Visitor*, November 10, 1972, p. 13.
3. Nancy Heisey, "In Zaire Questions and Friendships Grow," *Evangelical Visitor*, October 10, 1976, pp. 9–10.
4. Nancy Heisey, "Of Two Minds: Ambivalence in the Language of Brethren in Christ Missionaries. Part 1," *Brethren in Christ History and Life* (April 1988), 10–43.
5. Nancy Heisey, "Response to Chester Wingert and Harvey Sider," *Brethren in Christ History and Life* (August 1988), 155.
6. Valerie Weaver-Zercher, "Nancy Heisey's Vision for World Mission," *Christian Living*, October–November 2001, pp. 4–6.

Clara Engle Hoffman and Mary Engle Hoffman

1. The author thanks Esther Ebersole, Lela Hostetler, and Dori Steckbeck of the BICHLA for providing research assistance, and the interviewees. In researching this biography, the author conducted interviews and corresponded with the following persons: Elsie Bechtel, Earl Brechbill, Sara Herr, John Hess, Kenneth Hoover, D. Ray Hostetter, S. Lane Hostetter, Gladys (Kraybill) Kaltreider, Homer Kraybill, Mary (Wolgemuth) Kuhns, Grace (Stoner) Lady, Ethel (Fetrow) Lenhert, Anna (Brechbill) Martin, Clarence Musser, and

Ralph Snyder, Notes from interviews and correspondence with the above individuals are filed with the Wilma I. (Wenger) Musser Papers, BICHLA.

2. Much of the information about their early years was taken from the "Librarian" and "Professor of English," *Clarion*, May 1935, p. 2. "Librarian" duplicates a handwritten manuscript by M. V. Long entitled "The Life of Sr. Clara E. Hoffman," Clara E. and Mary E. Hoffman Papers, BICHLA.
3. Clara's conversion (in September 1903) and church membership (on October 25, 1903) is shown in the record book of church members of the Mount Joy Church of God. See copy of records sent by the church secretary to the author in Wilma I. (Wenger) Musser Papers, BICHLA.
4. Clara Hoffman, "Reminiscences," 1945, unpublished manuscript in the Clara E. and Mary E. Hoffman Papers, BICHLA.
5. Ray M. Zercher interview with Virgie Kraybill, March 19, 1991, BICHLA.
6. Since the size of the school contributed to family-like interactions, the informal use of "sister" and "brother" with the given name was the approved title for faculty members. See November 23, Faculty Minutes, BICHLA.
7. Ray M. Zercher, *To Have a Home: The Centennial History of Messiah Village* (Mechanicsburg, Pa.: Messiah Village, 1995), p. 77.
8. *Columbia Star*, June 2, 1911, n.p.: BICHLA. The Star was the paper of Messiah's Americana Literary Society.
9. E. Morris Sider, *Messiah College: A History* (Nappanee, Ind.: Evangel Press, 1984), p. 134.
10. See the faculty tribute to Clara at her funeral in the folder "Clara Hoffman's Funeral, " C. N. Hostetter, Jr. Papers, BICHLA.
11. Ray M. Zercher interview with Vergie Kraybill.
12. See Clara E. and Mary E. Hoffman Papers in the BICHLA for their contracts.
13. "Campus Sketches," *Clarion*, December 1935, p. 4.
14. Sara E. Herr letter to the author, August 6, 2001.
15. Sider, *Messiah College*, p. 135.
16. "A Word With Our Librarian," *Clarion*, December 1940, p. 8.
17. For nature writings, see for example, "The Resurrection of Nature," *Clarion*, April 1928, p. 152. See also Clara Hoffman, "Reminiscences."
18. Sider, *Messiah College*, p. 108.
19. "Editorial," *Clarion Periodical*, February 4, 1947, p. 2.
20. The wheelchair is now in the BICHLA.
21. Homer Kraybill interview, November 15, 2000.
22. Faculty tribute to Clara at her funeral, C. N. Hostetter, Jr. Papers, BICHLA.
23. Faculty tribute to Mary at her funeral, ibid.

R. Virginia Kauffman

1. Author interviews with Virginia Kauffman, February 7, 2001. Other interviews were conducted on February 12, 2001, and March 15, 2001.
2. E. Morris Sider, ed., *My Story, My Song* (Mount Joy, Pa.: Board for World Missions, 1989), p. 283.
3. For this arrangement, see *Handbook of Missions* (1955), p. 7.
4. Ardys Thuma letter to the author, March 4, 2001.
5. David Climenhaga letter to the author, February 8, 2001.
6. Virginia Kauffman letter to family.
7. Ibid., March 1, 1975.
8. Ibid., Febuary 26, 1976.
9. Ibid., August 7, 1975.
10. Ibid.
11. *Evangelical Visitor*, January 17, 1955, p. 8.
12. Ibid., September 8, 1969, pp. 6-7.
13. Kauffman letter to family, December 21, 1974.
14. Ibid., September 11, 1975.
15. Ibid., August 7, 1975.
16. Ibid., September 26, 1975.
17. Ibid.
18. Jake Shenk letter to the author, February 26, 2001.
19. Lois Kipe letter to the author, February 25, 2001.
20. Kauffman letter to family, March 27, 1971.
21. Ibid., May 8, 1971.
22. Ibid., February 3, 1973.
23. Shenk letter.
24. *Evangelical Visitor*, September 10, 1972, p. 9.
25. Ibid., January 17, 1955.
26. Ibid., September 8, 1969, p. 6.
27. Kauffman letter to family, November 27, 1969.
28. Shenk letter.
29. *Evangelical Visitor*, March 13, 1967, p. 7.
30. Ibid., April 25, 1972, p. 8.
31. Kauffman letter to family, November 21, 1970.

Virgie Felker Lehman Garman Kraybill

1. In researching this biography, the author conducted interviews and corresponded with the following persons: Esther Ebersole, Ruth Garman, Lela Hostetler, Homer Kraybill, Morris and Leone Sider, and Mary Helen (Kraybill) Solomon. The author also relied on transcripts of Virgie Kraybill interviews with Morris Sider, Carlton Wittlinger, and Ray Zercher, and a Homer Kraybill interview with Morris Sider. Transcripts of these interviews are available in the BICHLA.

2. Obituary of Amanda (Felker) Lehman, *Evangelical Visitor*, September 8, 1941, p. 8.
3. Information about Virgie's early life was primarily gathered from an interview with her conducted by Karen Ives, November 1978. A summary of the interview is located in the BICHLA.
4. "The Power of the Medical Missionary," *Evangelical Visitor*, January 10, 1916, p. 8.
5. E. Morris Sider, *Nine Portraits: Brethren in Christ Biographical Sketches* (Nappanee, Ind.: Evangel Press, 1978), p. 130. A more detailed account of this story is given in a Virgie Kraybill interview with Morris Sider, BICHLA.
6. For more information, see Minutes of Special Council, February 9, 1928 and February 10, 1928, Grantham Church Collection, BICHLA.
7. The following accounts are told in E. Morris Sider, "Virgie Kraybill," *The Body Builder*, July/August 1992. Located in the Grantham Church Collection, BICHLA.
8. Ruth Winger Smith interview with Isaiah and Doris Harley for the Grantham church history, E. Morris Sider Papers, BICHLA.

Kathleen Ruth Shaver Leadley

1. In researching this biography, the author conducted interviews and corresponded with the following persons: Robert (Bob) Leadley, Jessica (Leadley) Purdy, Rachel Leadley, Rob Leadley, Irene Leadley, Leonard Chester, Don and Pat Cornell, John Gibbins, Gordon Gooderham, Stan and Melva Kizul, Jill Sauer, Dale Shaw, Harvey Sider, John Sider, and Darrell Winger.
2. "Viewpoint," *St. Catharines Standard*, Saturday, October 21, 2000, p. A15.
3. Ibid.
4. Ibid., Wednesday, May 10, 2000, p. A11.
5. Ibid., Wednesday, August 30, 2000, p. A9.
6. Kathleen Leadley résumé.
7. Kathleen Leadley, "Women in Ministry/Leadership," *Brethren in Christ History and Life* (August 1993), 210.
8. Pastor's report to bishop, March 1, 1996.
9. Pastoral Midterm Review, May 8, 1997.
10. Kathleen Leadley, "Pluralism: A Response," *Brethren in Christ History and Life* (April 1993), 109.
11. 105th Annual Conference Minutes, April 27, 1996, p. 64.
12. Kathleen Leadley letter in "Readers Respond," *Evangelical Visitor*, April 1993, p. 28.
13. Nell Maxwell, former Women Alive executive director, e-mail to the author, February 17, 2001.
14. *St. Catharines Standard*, Wednesday, December 20, 2000, p. A9.

15. Women in Leadership group session, Women Alive annual conference, April 2000, Waterloo, Ontario.
16. Unpublished article written for *St. Catharines Standard.*

Lillian Frey Lehman

1. In researching this biography, the author conducted interviews with the following persons: Charles and Ann Frey, Emerson Frey, George Kibler, Gregg and Marilyn Lehman, Jeffrey Lehman, Roger and Brenda Lehman, Todd and Marian Lehman, Lois Jean Peterman, Eunice (Frey) Steinbrecher, and Marlin and Doris Thomas.
2. Peggy Schmidt, *Lancaster Sunday News*, May 10, 1981.
3. David Osterhout, *Lancaster New Era*, July 5, 1980.

Janet Marie Witmer Peifer

1. In researching this biography, the author conducted interviews with the following persons: Josie Esbin, Rev. Donald Good, Lori (Peifer) Harris, Elvin Peifer, Scott Peifer, and Ruth Zercher. Information in this biography comes in part from various interviews and correspondence with Janet Peifer and selections from her private journals, school papers, published articles, master's thesis, and doctoral dissertation.
2. The first women to be ordained in the Brethren in Christ Church were Anna Kraybill Engle (1921); Lynda Kelly (1987); Martha Lady (1990); Mary Jane Davis, Martha Lockwood, and Janet Peifer (1992).

Sara Cabrera de Peraza

1. Habana is the Spanish spelling for Havana, Cuba.
2. In researching this biography, the author conducted interviews with the following persons: Daniel (Samuel Peraza's brother-in-law), Maria Júlia Delanoval, José Peraza, Samuel Peraza, Sara Peraza, Sarai Peraza, and Zabdi Peraza.

Dorothy Evelyn Sherk

1. Ronald J. Sider letter of August 1, 2001.
2. Dorothy Sherk interview, February, 2001, the basis for Dorothy Sherk's comments in the text.
3. Shirley Bitner interview, March 2001.
4. Dorothy Sherk interview with E. Morris Sider, 1988, on the role of women in the church, BICHLA. Videotape produced by Messiah College.
5. Ray Schlegel interview, March 2001.
6. Ronald J. Sider letter of August 1, 2001.
7. Robert R. Sider letter of August 17, 2001.
8. Peter Erb letter of September 5, 2001.

9. Ronald Mathies letter of August 28, 2001.
10. Ibid.
11. Harvey Stickley letter of August 2001.
12. Jonathan Pham letter of October 16, 2001.
13. Dorothy Sherk letter of August 31, 2001.
14. Harvey Sider letter of September 9, 2001.
15. Account written by Lee Bryant, 2001.
16. Harvey Sider letter.

Esther Susan Dourte Spurrier

1. In researching this biography, the author conducted interviews and corresponded with the following persons: Eber and Ruth Dourte, Faithe (Dourte) Spurrier, Ray Dourte, Esther Spurrier, and John Spurrier.
2. Terry L. Brensinger, ed., *Focusing Our Faith: Brethren in Christ Core Values* (Nappanee, Ind.: Evangel Publishing House, 2000), pp. 150-151.
3. "Raising our Family in Zambia," *Evangelical Visitor*, April 10, 1981, p. 8.
4. "Hospitality Plus!" ibid., June 1985, p. 3.
5. "To Institute or Not to Institute," ibid., March 25, 1982, p. 7.

Lana Clinton Zahn

1. Research for this biography was taken from interviews with Lana Zahn and information from Lana's journals.

Alice Grace Hostetter Zercher

1. In researching this biography, the authors conducted interviews and corresponded with the following persons: Helen Fretz, Eva Martin, David Weaver-Zercher, Alice Grace Zercher, Chuck and Laura Zercher, and Dick Zercher.
2. For more information about John's childhood and youth, see "Biography of John E. Zercher," in *Lantern in the Dawn*, E. Morris Sider and Paul Hostetler, eds. (Nappanee, Ind.: Evangel Press, 1980).

RECOGNITION OF CONTRIBUTORS

The editors are grateful to the following people who contributed financial support for the publication of this book.

Anonymous (3)
Daniel and Edith Asbury
Ronald E. and Grace Z. Barnick
Dwight and Fay Bert
Eldon and Harriet Bert
Kathryn Boyer
William and Esther Boyer
JoAnne Brubaker
Kenneth and Audrey Brubaker
Ronald and Barbara Burwell
Ruth H. Byers
D. Wayne and Ruth Cassel
Daniel and Joyce Chamberlain
David and Verna Mae Climenhaga
Steven and Shelly Crider
Mary Jane Davis
Eber and Ruth Dourte
Jesse and Wilma Dourte
Nevin and Doneen Dourte
Daniel Ebersole
Marilyn Ebersole
Wayne and Alma Ebersole
Earl and Esther Engle
Harold and Mary Elizabeth Engle
J. Harold and Ruth Engle
Lareta Finger
Charles and Anna Frey
Don and Shirley Frymire
Ruth Garman
Kenneth and June Gibble
Dorothy Gish
Lester and Marjorie Haines
Isaiah and Doris Harley
Maxine Heise
D. Ray and Susanne Heisey
Nancy Heisey
Wilmer and Velma Heisey
Earl and Joann Henry
Sara Herr
Lloyd and Lorna Hogg
Luke and Doris Horst
Paul and Lela Hostetler
Lane and June Hostetter
Mary Kuhns
Martha Lady
Edith Lehman
Martha Long
John and Anna Martin
Kenneth and Yvonne Martin
Rachel W. Martin
Jay and Wanda McDermond
Harold and Lucille Mellinger
Ronald and Joyce Miller
Arthur and Janet Niesley
Marjorie Niesley
Elvin and Janet Peifer
David (Kelly) and Kim Phipps
Kathleen Quimby
Royce and Phyllis Saltzman
Rodney and Lorna Sawatsky
Martin and Dorothy Schrag
Harvey and Erma Sider
Ross and Thelma Sider
Robert and Marilyn Smith
Ruth Smith
Clyde and Dorothy Jean Sollenberger
John and Esther Spurrier
Arlene Steckbeck
Mick and Fern Steckbeck
Kenneth and Lois Stern
Ronald and Lenora Stern
Richard and Pauline Stevick
Dwight and Carolyn Thomas
Mildred Tyson
Richard and Elaine Ucci
David and Valerie Weaver-Zercher
Woodrow and Susan Wendling
Miriam Wenger
John and Marilyn Wolgemuth
Linda Worman
Robert and Winifred Worman
John and Anna Yeatts
David and Velma Yoder
Alice Grace Zercher
Wendell and Faithe Zercher
Avery and Eunice Zook